Mandatory Eight Count

Also by Andrew Fisher

Smoke Ring Day

MANDATORY EIGHT COUNT

Andrew Fisher

International Psychoanalytic Books (IPBooks)
New York • IPBooks.net

Published by IPBooks, Queens, NY
Online at: www.IPBooks.net

978-1-956864-57-1

Contents

Acknowledgments

For Lyndy: My personal person, life companion, editor supreme and fellow Buckeye, whose help and devotion made this book possible.

Disclaimer

Some of the characters depicted in this book are real but the situations are fictitious.

Some of the situations depicted in this book are real but the characters are fictitious.

Some of the characters depicted in this book are fictitious and the situations are fictitious.

Some of the characters depicted in this book are real and the situations depicted are real, and you can guess which is which.

PART ONE

Mandatory Eight Count

The mandatory eight count, also called a compulsory eight count, is a rule in boxing and kickboxing requiring the referee to give any fighter a count of eight seconds once they have been knocked down by their opponent, and before the fight is allowed to resume. Even if the fighter gets up before the count reaches eight, the referee is required to count to eight before checking if the fighter is able to continue unless they make a judgment call that the fighter cannot continue.

The mandatory eight count is part of the United Rules of Boxing as adopted by the Association of Boxing Commissions.

CHAPTER 1

Sodom and Gomorrah
1969–1973

"WELCOME TO COLUMBUS AND DISCOVER AMERICA," a huge sign barks at me through the window of the cab on my ride from the airport. I find the links between the explorer and the town and some idea that I'm commanded to discover the real America slightly amusing and somewhat perplexing, hailing from the capital of Irony, the New York area. In a state of confusion laced with some excitement, I'm dropped off in a secluded part of this enormous campus.

And here I am in the apparent "real" America, on a colder-than-a-witch's-tit-on-Halloween, Saturday morning, at Ohio State University in early January. Frozen solid, the barren, brown ground with wisps of snow only serves to magnify the cold conditions. I grab my two bags and head straight up to my new home, a room on the 8th floor of Lincoln Tower. The region of OSU I find myself in is called West Campus, more reminiscent of my idea of Siberia with the wind sweeping ice and snow across the flat terrain. It's the newest part of the school with two gigantic towers, Lincoln and Morrill, monolithic twins standing over the flat lands. Lincoln and Morrill are the most recently built freshmen dorms to accommodate the large incoming classes of freshmen baby boomers. New. And they are coed. Guys on one floor. Girls on another. Each tower has 16 floors, each floor holds 5 suites of 4 rooms, 4 people to a medium sized room, 16 people to a suite. I do the math. More like a way to house termites than students, but given I'm entering OSU winter quarter, I guess I've become a termite, given that I have no other options.

The din is piercing with this many people, all at large, spread out, on this floor above and below, all at once. Way too chaotic for what I have been used to after my long, pathetically quiet year being ripped from my existence as a fairly typical teen with an edge. In all, glad to be here. Glad to be anywhere. I didn't find out til later that the locals and the college staff had already dubbed the towers "Sodom and Gomorrah." Cohabiting co-eds.. Engaging in premarital sin. Making my way up on the elevator to the eighth floor of this modern, oddly-shaped pentagonal structure, I'm greeted by an assorted mix of lightly southern accents, dotted by maybe a couple of east coast accents. My suitemates. Friendly, agreeable, down-to-earth, some already mildly intoxicated.

"Hey man," one yelled at me after I unpacked and stowed my clothes. "We're headin' ta the Sugar Shack tonight. It's a cool dance club. All the local chicks go there. Wanna come?"

Without a second's thought—I'm in. I am in the mix. Shit. Not too bad. I mean, a month and change earlier I had just gotten out of the looney bin, pronounced sane by the powers that be, and sent home with my Thorazine, an antipsychotic, in hand. Then dropped back into the house where I'd grown up in New Rochelle, where I spent most of my youth, right up to the point when I flipped out that fateful week almost exactly a year ago, January of '68. The shrink's line was if I stayed on the medication and hooked up with a local shrink, all would be well: this is what I was told. "Fuck them," I thought. Took my meds that made my head feel like a zombie for about two weeks after getting out of the hospital. And then, back in New Rochelle, spent the next three weeks partying and hanging out with friends, girlfriends, and would-be girlfriends. It was, I must say, a blast... and I didn't hold back.

I even went to the horse track once, my "go to" place, a couple of nights before leaving for college. Glad I did, too. Being there, at the track, brought back how depressing a place Yonkers Raceway could be. It drove home the reality of it. My romance with harness racing – which is to say, gambling – was finished. Over and out. Onward and upwards.

So off to The Sugar Shack we go in a hopeful state of possibly meeting some girls. The group of guys I'm going with, about eight in all, take off in two cars. I'm with three guys from Ohio, all from small towns it turns out, guys who brag about their drinking, OSU football and how popular they are with the ladies, like they're trying to impress each other. It fits a stereotype I have of frat boys, a scene I told myself I'd avoid. Not exactly my first choice but at least an opportunity.

The place, like so many others we pass on the way, stinks of beer, sweat, and damp sawdust. Big dance floor for the band, featuring Wayne Cochran and the C. C. Riders, a local garage band with a large following who play blue-eyed soul and blues. They play decently, not too loudly and the place is pretty full.

The Sugar Shack has this horseshoe-shaped bar with cheap and sticky laminated wood on its edges and two large rooms for dancing. Lots of girls, each with a 3.2 beer in hand. Me, as usual, I'm a little daunted and shy at first. I hang back for a while with my brand-new roomies, who also are surveying the scene, not dancing. I'm trying to get my land legs. I have myself a 3.2 beer, Stroh's. Synthetic courage. So, I make my move, get out there toward the dance floor and ask a girl to dance. She's kinda nice-looking, about my age with brown hair, not long and not short, and a pleasant smile. And she doesn't say anything. She just nods and we walk together onto the dance floor, and right off we're fruging and boogalooing to "Knock on Wood," C. C. Rider style. Debby, that's her name, asks me, if I'm an OSU student and isn't surprised by my answer, just nods in response. "You ain't from around here," she says confidently.

"How do you know?"

"I can tell by your accent." Hers is vaguely southern, but she calls herself a local yokel, born and raised in Columbus. A townie. This is brand new to me that people from Ohio could have southern accents at all. I really didn't know what to expect. Anyway, this Debby tells me she lives with her parents, works the register at Kroger's, just out of high school and working on saving enough money to get her own place. That is, her own place with friends Joannie and Judy, who, she informs me meaningfully and not very mysteriously, she is with tonight, foreshadowing a plan developing in her head. Her best friends all the way back to junior high. Debby seems nice. Simple, genuine and direct which is a refreshing break from the New York girls I am used to, so often stuck up or standoffish. We keep talking, drinking our 3.2's, and dancing – slow and fast. Some sweat is passed between us, cheeks and hands, despite the arctic temps outside.

She drinks more than I do and gets more looped. Pretty soon we're making out on the dance floor, which is pretty dazzling given that we just met and around 11:30 or so. We get into her car."Wanna come with me?" she says in a tipsy tone.

"Where we goin'?" I ask in a louder voice than usual because of the noise of the place and my excitement.

"Back to Joanie and Judy's place. Joanie's stayin' with her boyfriend tonight."

"Cool," I think then say, figuring I'm gonna get some action, as I get in her car.

Back at the pad, we immediately start going at it, albeit somewhat drunkenly. First making out and then onto Joanie's bed which was available. Then swiftly we tear our clothes off leaving them in a trail on our way to horizontal. We go at it hot and heavy, carried away in our lust.

Next thing I know it's 10 a.m. Sunday. Now sober, but slightly hung over. I feel kind of loopy, vaguely disoriented. Deb plies me with coffee as we sit at her friends' living room table, a wooden round-shaped industrial spool popular with young people especially those without a lot of money. It's a gray, cloudy, gloomy kind of day out, which goes well with my hangover.

"You want anything to eat?" she asks sweetly with a hopeful look on her face.

"No thanks," I reply, thinking to myself, "Where the fuck am I?"

Deb is really nice. But I have nothing to say to this person. I have a sense that I am in another world. After hi, hello, how are you, it gets pretty old. I attempt a little activity to feel more normal so I check out the local paper, the *Columbus Citizen Journal*. Not a lot in it. There's no news compared to the *New York Times*. It felt good to get laid but I was having that "after cum" sensation or to be more technical, post coital depression. Either way, I am out of here. Poor Deb, what if she likes me? Because if she does, it will be awkward. Again it was nice to sleep with her but besides the sexual attraction, it doesn't feel like there's anything there.

Oh no, I can't think about that now because I got other fish to fry back at campus.

Deb drives me back to the dorm and as we say goodbye, I mouth with minimal to no sincerity, "See you soon," knowing full well that I won't. I'm just trying to get some numbers on the scoreboard. I immediately break eye contact, look away with a sigh of relief and slight touch of sadness, maybe guilt, knowing that I will never see this woman again and I may have given her some false hope. I look out at the austere dorm in the middle of fallow, hard, flat ground with a sense of doom and think to myself, "What have I gotten myself in for?" Then slamming the door of her car, without hesitation, I run out into the five degree weather with moisture freezing in my nostrils and leaving a parcel of frozen, steamy breath in my wake. Then into my dorm to the elevator, which takes me up to the eighth floor, activities already in progress.

The scene in the suite is chaotic, loud and filled with people. Lots of horse play, very much like the locker room shenanigans I recall in junior high P.E. I'm not impressed. Been there, done that I say to myself but feign amusement in order to smooth the social waves. I try to pretend to go along with the inane banter but after a few minutes, I feel ridiculous and out of place. I feel as though I'm in a time warp. I'm too hip for this shit, I hear myself say, aware that my attitude about these proceedings might come across as smug or superior, which they are.

Nevertheless, I push out of the common space and head for my room, then bunk bed. Lying down, I pick up a paperback copy of *Growing up Absurd*, a book by Paul Goodman, a scathing critique of mass society. I feel a little like a thirsty guy at an oasis. It was recommended to me by one of my high school friends home for Christmas break, Jeff Miller, a guy who I suspect made out with my girlfriend,

Marla, while I was in the nut house but for which I have no proof. My suspicion is based on the fact that Jeff had gone steady with two of my girlfriends in seventh and eighth grade right after we broke up. He has a hankering for the girls I like, the asshole. Nevertheless, and despite his possible betrayal, he is an old friend going back to grade school and visited me while I was in Hartford in the nuthouse, so I retain a modicum of respect for him and gratitude, making the book recommendation more potent for me.

So the author, Goodman, seems to be on my wavelength. I feel relieved. Here is a book I can sink my teeth into and a comforting foil for what feels like the mediocrity and silliness around me. It describes what my generation is going through. Goodman's book describes who we are with historical analysis and a description of how my generation feels, or at least the hippie-type friends in New York who I stepped out with to the Village and political demonstrations. My fellow inmates at the IOL, the Institute of Living in Hartford, Connecticut nut house I just resided in for nine months, were my more recent

hippie, anti-war and politico flame outs. A similar ilk cultur-ally and politically as my friends from NY who somehow stayed on course, unlike myself and our happy band of nutcases. We were self proclaimed "mutes," short for mutates. Goodman's book feels like a friendly, more eloquent conversation that flowed with my mutate and non mutate buddies. Reading Goodman makes me feel less alone.

People like Deb, or the new bunch of roommates I just met, don't feel that way. They seem much more plugged into the bullshit "American Dream" propaganda we were all raised with: study, work hard, get ahead, kill! Yeah, that's what this band of youth is buying into. Not me. I am done with that shit. For good.

Of course, I don't know that Goodman is gay because if I did, it would have freaked me out and I probably wouldn't have continued reading him. My sexual identity and sexual self confidence is clearly not a sure thing, even though my attractions are unabashedly hetero. I am too inexperienced and insufficiently acquainted with my inner life to know who I REALLY am. So, the thought of my being gay is too frightening to even think about and too confusing. These are things I do not let myself think about or entertain for very long. But this is supposed to be what people my age are discovering: who we are. So, in a way, being confused is supposed to be alright. Not fun but alright. At least that's what experts like Erik Erikson, the best selling psychoanalyst, are saying we are supposed to be doing. It is amazing to me how I go so in and out of clarity. One minute I feel clear about my values, what is important, what my inner life is about, and the next minute I also want all the rewards of the American Dream, recognition, fame, money. But for now I'm deep into seeing myself as part of the burgeoning youth counterculture with its rebellion against the powers that be. It seems right, is right. If anything, those nine months locked away taught me, it's that what my parents' generation bought into was a sham. Well, I feel this way most of the time and when I don't, I'm not about to let on to anyone that I sometimes share the "straight values" of my parents generation. It doesn't occur to me that I'm in good company with a lot of my cohorts.

I spend the morning reading Goodman, then off to the cafeteria for lunch with my suitemates, my plastic smile firmly in place. Finally, downstairs to the basement after dinner where I watch football highlights hyping next week's Super Bowl game between the Colts and my Jets, seventeen point underdogs. Next day will be opening day of winter quarter, so I've got to try to get a good night's sleep and prepare for the eight a.m. Calculus class and the bitter cold. You see, part of me is a "good boy" and I really want to try making a go of it, I guess. So fucking confusing to know what I believe. What I want. But on Monday morning, my early morning preparation encounters the Midwestern winter.

"Nice work if you can get it," to coin one of my old man's phrases from the Great Depression. It is fucking freezing at seven a.m. as I bundle up with a sweater, ski jacket, leather gloves and woolen Scotty hat in preparing to head into the wind with snow, as I watch the steamy exhalation of my breath. As prepared as I can be. I light up a Viceroy, make the trek, grimacing, walking backwards, shielding myself from the howling wind but somehow undaunted, arrive at the math building in plenty of time. The prof, a reedy, goofy-looking grad student type, is one of these dorky guys who makes no eye contact, speaks in a monotone, cracks no jokes and stares at the blackboard for fifty minutes, writing formulas. Grim shit. I do my best to follow what he is talking about. A little rusty after a year away from having taken any math, not that it is my strong suit any way, I manage to concentrate for most of the class. I feel good that I'm able to focus despite these obstacles. Most of the other students look half awake as well, but maybe they're better at math. Hard to tell about the other half-awake freshmen, but I wonder. Next, Western Civ (the ancient world to 1500) at ten and English 101 at eleven. Ah. Slightly disillusioning. These classes are boring. Teachers not very turned on or inspired, and that's important for my level of interest and engagement.

Back at the dorm in the afternoon, I put on the radio and listen to Top 40 AM music. My stereo is not set up as I am too lazy to do so, as is my wont. It's a hassle to negotiate space with the other three guys in the room so I settle for AM radio. "Crimson and Clover" by

Tommy James and the Shondelles gets repeat playing. It's number one in the nation, followed by even more repetitive commercials for used cars at Jack Madsden Chevrolet, and the insipid jingle, "Jack Madsden what a great, great guy, Jack Madsden...." A slow and familiar sheen of depression settles over me.

I am unhappy, alone, lonely. That desolate feeling is described perfectly when Glen Campbell's "Wichita Lineman" comes on the airways, but then 3 minutes later, I'm gone. Stuck with Jack Madsden. This is not going to work out. So about a week into this I give up on the idea of taking the Thorazine I brought, prescribed as a precautionary measure. I decided and promised to try it the first couple of weeks, but think that that's my "good boy" talking. It's not helping me adjust to this new situation. It is not helping me to not be so depressed. I'm right. Thorazine is a major antipsychotic tranquilizer downer. Without it, some of my energy comes back immediately, enough to keep going through the motions of taking classes and trying to fit into this bizarre social situation.

The scene at Lincoln Towers is like some weird Army war movie from the 50's. It's like being in the barracks. All these characters want to do is drink in their off hours, which is frequent. It's not that I'm into getting stoned either. I'm not. I retired from pot smoking about a year ago, right after the ping pong pot incident in New Rochelle, my senior year, when my friends and I got observed by a cop patrolling my suburban neighborhood. He was suspicious that only one light was on in my parents' house. He was right to be suspicious, but it was also kind of ridiculous because it was only my friends and me toking up under the ping pong table in our base-ment. Instead of catching real criminals, the cop notified my father of these goings on. My punishment was the usual hot air from my old man and another in the long line of serious lectures about the legal and medical consequences of such "stupid" behavior. Feeling ashamed and busted, I somehow bought into my old man's trip, so I swore off pot for about a year.

But clearly, I am still much more attracted to the type of people who smoke pot, hippies and such. There is a clear cut division, at least in my mind, between people who drink (frat rats and yahoos) and freaks. Never thinking, of course, that some people did both or neither. But for "fast food" takes on people without getting too deep, it seems simple and less confusing to divide the world of undergrads and others my age into straights and freaks. I'm not the only one doing it either. It seems to be a mass phenomenon, not only at OSU, but in the world in general.

Anyway, to get back to Lincoln Tower, there doesn't seem to be very many freaks or whatever you might call them, here or anywhere else on campus for that matter. Most people look kind of clean cut, hair not too long and not too hip. Straight. Despite my "fast food" categorizing of the Lincoln Tower scene as being very straight, occasionally my simple typology is shaken up.

One Friday afternoon after classes as I'm hanging out in the lobby waiting to go up to my 8th floor suite, a long-haired guy appears and I can see he is approaching a lot of people briefly. Then, he approaches me with a quick question.

"Hey, man. Got your acid for the weekend?" This both flabbergasts me and cracks me up. Apparently, the drug dealer knows of a drug taking scene in Lincoln Tower that I was not familiar with. Things are never as simple as I would like them to be in my quick stereotyping view of the world. Still, it only makes a little dent in my straight/ freak categorizations. And I'm still quite alienated and alone.

"Oh well. Fuck it. I'll get a four point and transfer to Harvard," where my old friend and tennis rival Ricky attends, I think to myself.

There's nothing grandiose about me! I actually believe it. God, I could be so full of shit and a lot of times I don't even know it. This is definitely one of those times and I believe it. All I lack is follow through, and man, I've heard that thousands of times from teachers and parents. Passionate intention in the moment in spades without follow through when the passion fades. In other words, the kid has no discipline and will never succeed until or if he develops some.

It's now February, a month of this routine and I am struggling. I'm trying to do my work, maintain a semblance of contact with roommates, not really meeting any people I connect with and feeling vaguely homesick. I talk on the phone to my parents and Marla, my high school girlfriend, about once a week. I am my usual minimally disclosing self with my parents, having learned that any hint of problems I express to them provokes worry which would only come back to haunt me. They're walking on eggshells enough already around me. Fuck that. So I keep my distance. With Marla, I feel her concern, but she doesn't really get what I'm going through or get me, period, past a certain point. She is still in high school for one and never connects with my deeper feelings of alienation, for two. She's a happy-go-lucky sort, always looking for the positive and so does her best to try to help me see the bright side. I've put her through the ringer with my hospitalization while we were going out last year, but despite what she witnessed, she still retains that bubbly "good girl" patina. But it's also true that I'm not that easy to get to know. If you don't somehow get me right away, well I kind of shut down and give up trying to be understood. I'm impatient that way. Easily frustrated and when I'm down, won't or can't see the bright side. So the phone calls, while comforting from the standpoint of familiar voices of people who care, really don't offer me much in the way of deep connection or understanding. Either I am unavailable or they just don't get me. Of course, I believe it is the latter. With Dad, it's all about achieving, but with Marla I don't know what it is about with her. Maybe she just wants to be loved and appreciated. There's nothing wrong with that. But fortunately or unfortunately, I'm not that simple. Either way and once again, I think, I'm on my own and let out a big series of sighs that don't seem to help either.

Even though Marla and my parents don't get me and I resent that, when I hear about my older brother Dave's engagement party back in New York, I feel relief and excitement to get back on familiar turf, if only for a few days. The trip home to New Rochelle in mid February for the party might actually be fun for me because I'll see Marla, my family and the familiar cast of characters. Though I don't hold out any hope for my cousins, aunts and uncles to understand me either, they at least are people who actually get my quick wit and sarcasm. I didn't realize how much I needed that.

It's how male New Yorkers express affection, with put downs. You have to pick up on the tone, and if you do, you get into a groove. In Ohio, everyone is kind of sincere. They genuinely like you or don't. No tone to decipher, just straightforward. Yeah, it'll be really nice being on familiar ground. I start to realize how much I rely on sarcasm and banter to express love and hostility.

I get on a plane and fly back. During my jaunt to New York, it does feel good to be more clicked into the faster pace and familiarity of home. "Well, look who's here. It's the bucking Buckeye," I hear my cousin Jerry greet me at Dave's party, his tone dripping with sarcasm intended to garner a laugh, which he gets from me.

That familiar edge. Jocular, hostile all in one serving. I didn't know how much I missed that kind of exchange. Feels so familiar and strangely complicated. Homey. Funny. The only thing I don't like about being back at home is that my dad keeps asking me if everything is alright. Possibly Dad is more perceptive than I give him credit for or my acting that things are fine isn't completely working with him. Since my breakdown, my parents seem hyper tuned in to how I'm doing psychologically and attentive to any possible shifts in my mood. I know they care, but I still don't like it. Like I'm some freak in a freak show.

But whatever it is, when I get back to Columbus, Dad calls to tell me he's coming out to Columbus to check out the school, but I'm thinking that's just a ruse. Not thrilled with this idea but I don't offer up a lot of resistance. When my father decides to do something, I know from long experience, it's futile to try to dissuade him. He's like a Sherman tank. Stubborn but persistent. He rarely, if ever, listens to my objections against something he wants to do regarding me or anybody or anything else for that matter. Here's a taste of how it goes.

After hi how are ya', Dad jumps right in, "I'm gonna check out the school and Columbus in early March to see what it's like. I know you won't mind."

And I say, "And if I do?"

"Well, brother, I just want to make sure things are going smoothly. I'm curious about the place."

"Well, I don't like the idea. It feels like you're spying on me."

"That's not it at all. I'm just interested in you and your life. I'll take you out to dinner, go to classes. It'll be nice."

"For who?"

"You'll see. Besides, I want to see what my nickel is paying for." And that's how that conversation went, Sherman tank riding over whatever is in his sights.

So, in early March, around week nine of the quarter, Dad flies out and I allow him (as if I had a choice) to make the rounds with me to my classes. On the way over to English 101 from Western Civ, Dad peppers me with questions: "Am I keeping up with my studies? Am I making friends? How am I feeling? Am I taking my medicine? Maybe I need to see a shrink."

He's all over me like a bad smell. I'm not comfortable with the badgering. Never have and never will. It's all to assuage his anxiety. Don't really feel the caring. It's all about his ego. I don't let him in. I do have control over that. Like always, it doesn't feel safe to open up, and I'm right, like always.

In English class, brazen as ever, as if to prove his superiority, he chats up a moderately attractive freshman blondie. I am embarrassed, annoyed and humiliated but there is no stopping the Sherman tank. Jennifer is quite friendly in return, and Dad asks her to come to lunch with us. She consents. That prick is out here one day, stepping all over my territory and he's making time. I'm in week nine and I don't think I've had a conversation with a woman that has any potential of going anywhere and here he is squeezing in.

The three of us make our way to a local, fancy Chinese restaurant. Dad is paying, of course, and in retrospect pimping me to Jennifer. I'm humiliated but not completely closed to the deal. Jennifer is buying what he's selling because after Dad leaves town Jennifer and I start seeing each other. It feels like she's into me. She's bright but kind of pushy and practically asks me out, which I'm ambivalent about since my pushy dad has set us up. But I'm clearly not opposed to making out, which we do after our first date at an OSU basketball game where OSU wins over Purdue 82-66.

We make out a few times. It's hard to find places to go given that both of us are freshmen, living in the dorms and don't really know people who live in apartments. It's like high school. So a couple of times Jennifer arranges for her roommates to be away, and we use her dorm room, putting a "Do Not Disturb" sign on her door that is strangely honored by the other girls on the floor. This danger element adds a dimension to the sexual excitement. Kissing, hugging feels urgent, yet I don't feel any push to go further after tentative moves to feel her breasts. These are rebuffed, possibly because Jennifer fears being walked in on. I'm turned on but not that turned on to warrant being more aggressive in my moves. I find her sort of physically attractive but her personality is way too clingy and needy. For some reason, it affects my desire for her. She wants too much from me after too little time and gives me more power in the relationship than I want. After these rather clumsy make out scenes, she calls me a lot on my dorm phone, pushing to get together more frequently than I'm comfortable with. I guess she thinks that because we've made out that that makes us boyfriend and girlfriend. I don't. I guess she's smart enough, although the clingy shit interferes with my liking her too much. I can tell she wants more involvement right away. This seems to be the problem a lot for me. Women who want me I generally have no use for and vice versa. A dilemma. I am primarily interested in her body, but not even that interested. But nevertheless, maybe because she's just there and it takes no effort on my part, we will date for about a month after spring break. Obviously, we don't schtup. I'm sure she doesn't want to and I'm not sure I want to either. It's not a conversation we have. More of a vibe thing, but I feel turned off to her, maybe a little embarrassed that I needed my old man's pimping to meet her, but it's mostly the clingy, needy shit that's a turnoff.

Classes continue to be a problem. My attention wavers as the quarter proceeds. I can't seem to mobilize much discipline regarding the courses I don't like, math and freshman English. When I have to put my attention on them, my mind wanders and I rush through readings and assignments as fast as possible just to be done, not caring about the quality of my work. Basic half ass shit. I put energy into music and history because I like these subjects and am naturally drawn to them. These are courses I'd pursue on my own even if I weren't taking them as classes. When all is said and done, my grades for winter quarter are lackluster at best. Two B's and two D's. B's in Music Appreciation and Western Civ and D's in Calculus and English 101. I have no excuses except for my usual half assed efforts, distracted energy, mild homesickness, ongoing low level alienation, boredom and lack of focus, but now that I think of it, that's quite a lot. I guess school is not gonna be my bailiwick. Once again. My plans for Harvard, shot out the window.

Jeez. That didn't take long.

Spring Quarter '69

I head back to New Rochelle for spring break and promptly borrow my mother's Pontiac Tempest and motor directly up to Cambridge, Mass. where my friend Ricky Sidelman from high school is going to Harvard. I stay with him in his dorm, Hurlburt Hall. There I meet a lot of, I must say, cool and unpretentious people, even though a lot of them have the last names of dead Presidents. But they don't act like the hoity toity people they are. Smart, too, but not in an arrogant way. Also, they're interested in the same stuff I am, at least the people who are friends of Rick's. I meet a guy who knows as much about 50's rock, r&b and blues as I do. People into the movies at the same ridiculous, fanatical, esoteric, trivial level as I am, as well as your basic sports fanatic types, which I also am. Although as far as that goes, those sports fanatic kind of people are much more the coin of the realm and could be found more frequently any place, on or off any college campus. There I read "Franny and Zooey" by Salinger, a deeply psychological novel about the brilliance, intensity and insanity of siblings which of course I could relate to, except for the brilliance part.

I'm having a blast in Cambridge with Ricky and his friends and have this recurring thought that this is where I should be. I feel completely at home here. The people are fun, smart and surprisingly unpretentious. If only I had studied harder, been more focused, I could have ended up here. I am always having these regretful, rueful thoughts about what could have been, what should have been. Always putting myself down for being an underachiever, not to mention, constantly having been told that I was not working up to my potential as a high school kid. And it wasn't just in school either.

I frequently find myself obsessing about the woulda coulda shoulda stuff around my underperformance in baseball, where my attitude towards authority got me into plenty of trouble. I immediately think of the time I was sunbathing during a JV game, sophomore year in high school, when I wasn't starting. My coach seemed to take offense at my lack of team spirit and gave me the old heave ho. Fucking prick. The asshole coaches, which they were, don't get me wrong, became my excuse for not focusing, working hard, practicing what have you with the end result being that either I quit, in the case of basketball, or got kicked off the team in the case of JV baseball.

Separate from the breakdown, or maybe connected to the reason for the breakdown, is this deep seated inferiority complex rationalized by a hatred for authority in the form of my father, teachers, coaches. I give a half assed effort to succeed, maybe unconsciously to prove that I truly am a loser or as a way to protect myself from finding out I am a loser. After all, I'd find the answer to that question if I put in the effort or didn't provoke authority figures to hassle me. I feel this very intensely and am very self blaming during my visit with Ricky, who in my mind, is not better than I am ability wise, but always has had more discipline, determination and less hatred for authority. Or if he does harbor those feelings, he doesn't let it get in the way of pursuing his goals which have always been many. Tennis, rock 'n roll band, student government and academics. He succeeded at all four. But I don't take it out on him for his success. He earned it. I take it out on myself, especially this time in Cambridge. I try to tell myself finally, that Ricky is Ricky, and I'm me. I have to make the most of me, whoever the hell that is. I try to take that attitude with me on my return back home.

Back in New Rochelle, I hook up with Marla for a night or two and an old girlfriend, Jean, as well. They don't know about each other. Lots of the usual making out ensues, a la high school. Nothing beyond. Still not doing much schtupping beyond my initial foray at the IOL (the old nut house) and that first night at OSU with Deb, the local townie. I guess you could say I was a "fucking" novice. It bugs me a lot. It's another part of my ongoing "complex" but I don't link it to my inadequate feelings with my academic underperforming or creative/athletic underachievement. I see these problems as separate. And I compensate for these shortcomings in my mind, often by reminding myself that I am a good person with good values and good friends, all of which I believe to be true, which are some of my best qualities. It helps to quiet down my inner tormentor, sometimes.

CHAPTER 2

Comfort Zone

Columbus in spring quarter. I transfer to a new dorm and start making some friends right away, my first real friends since having arrived on campus. I can't hack Lincoln Tower, too crowded, impersonal and with kids not to my liking. I hear Steeb Hall on south campus is a cool place to be. So to south campus I go. Eighth floor again, but very different from the tower. It has that old dusty musty smell. More rundown, the chair upholstery is faded brown with occasional holes, unlike the plastic fumes emitted from the slick and sticky chairs at the towers.

Here I meet Michael Diamo, an Italian kid from Jersey, a grad student in computer programming, who hates it and is in the process of switching into a Ph.D. program in philosophy, much more to his liking. This guy, Mike, seems down to earth, kind of like a more accepting big brother figure. He was once a student at West Point but quit because he became so disgusted with military life that he became radicalized and was instrumental in starting SDS after transferring to Rutgers for his sophomore year. I am impressed. Also on the eighth floor is Joe, a Polish working class guy from Parma near Cleveland.

He's also a down to earth, working class guy from a union family, a Democrat who loves TV, movies, sports and fucking around. Cares about politics, too. So we have stuff in common. Finally, there's Marquis Jones, another Jersey guy from Weequahic, a section of Newark, New Jersey. A Black guy, funny, angry, good basketball player although not as good as he thinks he is, who mumbles a lot about White people under his breath. We take a liking to each other. Maybe it's because I'm not afraid of him or something. We hang out and talk a lot about politics, race, b-ball, music.

He's a burgeoning Black Panther, a group that's starting to become wildly popular in the Black community, particularly on the heels of the King assassination. The Panthers fill a void for the disaffected activists disillusioned with non violence, with a large following especially among the working class and young, poor urban Blacks who never much took to King in the first place as they do to the speeches of Malcolm X. The thing I like about the Panthers is that they are not anti-white, per se. They have a Marxist tinge to their thinking and see issues of class and race as linked in American society. Mark and I have lots of conversations, "raps," as they are known and read *Ramparts*, *These Choking Times* and *Rolling Stone*. Mark turns me on to the Last Poets, particularly their songs "Niggers are Scared of Revolution" and "The Revolution Will Not Be Televised."

Spring is shaping up socially a lot better than the previous quarter and I'm enjoying classes more as well. I'm taking Western Civ 102, Music Appreciation 102, English 102 and for P.E., basketball. OSU definitely wants their students to take P.E. OSU wants their students to take a lot of requirements, it seems like. Two quarters of math, three quarters of science, a foreign language, english comp, western civ, social sciences, all of this before you even get to the classes that might interest you. Sometimes, I think I might as well have gone to community college for all the choices I have in the matter. It's a topic of much grousing and complaining among us students, particularly us freshmen and sophomores, the people I spend the most time with and the people who are dealing with it directly. So, I figure out that this is the situation: if you want to survive at this place academically, you have to just put your head down and plow through it. Well, I'm not the "plowing through it" kind, at least not on a consistent basis. I'm just too damn impatient, easily frustrated, angry and willful to put up with it past a certain point. Maybe it's my rebellious streak, but I've had a hard time buckling down with the courses I don't like, but have to take. But at this point in the spring of '69, my second quarter, I am still up for making good, going with the program, that kind of thing to completely say, "Fuck it!" just yet. Part of me wants to succeed on society's terms and another part, often, says "Fuck it." It's an ongoing battle. So I try to make the best of it with my great, or at least improved attitude, and do a lot better this term than I did in winter. Grades are improving. Even get an A in western civ, almost a 3 point. So by the end, I feel better about myself and my parents are also relieved. I'm partly glad too, because it gets the parents off my back temporarily while an even smaller part wants them to be proud of me, although I am loath to admit that. I feel like I am selling out when I acknowledge this to myself, let alone others. But academics, it turns out, are only a small part of school.

I expend about thirty per cent of my energy on academics, the rest of my time is devoted to hanging out with my new friends from the dorms, Mark, Joe and Mike and an even greater proportion of time of course, trying to meet girls or thinking about meeting girls. Mostly, besides Jennifer, I make timid attempts at chatting up cheerleader type blondes in my history class and getting polite brush offs. The same occurs in the cafeteria, which requires even more balls as you have to go over to their tables to meet them. That's hard to do. When I do encounter these girls, they up to now, all seem kind of sweet, gentle, polite and somewhat dull.

Around April, just back from spring break, Jennifer from winter english class, the one my father solicited for me, is right now the only show in town, as we get together about three or four times for make out sessions. It isn't advancing beyond that, as it's almost impossible to find a private spot. Also, she's a little reticent and I'm not the pushy type when it comes to sex. If the girl rebuffs me, I respect their no, not that I don't try low level sneaky, surreptitious stuff, but basically I respect their wishes. Anyway, it's becoming apparent after the three or four trysts between us that Jennifer is growing an attachment to me. I'm really not that into her. Way too clingy, not that interesting and not attractive enough to compensate for the other stuff. But I have nothing else going on. The thing is, Jennifer starts calling me when I don't call and I'm at a loss as to what to do. I don't like her that much but she's what I've got and I haven't learned the art of letting someone down gently.

Luckily, my friend Joe, the Polak from Cleveland knows my situation and comes to my aid. We have developed enough rapport that he calls me a Yid and worse, so I return the favor and call him a Polak. He's a crack up who loves practical jokes. So when Jennifer calls one evening on the dorm phone, we arrange it so that he'd be on the receiving end when she's speaking, and when it's my turn to talk, he whispers in my ear what to say. It's all designed to keep her on a string. We both know that she's more into me than I am into her, so I am in the hard to get role. Sick shit and I know it. But I'm not thinking about Jennifer's feelings, or about how cruel it is. It's more that the two of us are getting off on the practical joke. Joe and I, hysterical with paroxysms of laughter both during the conversation and after we get off the phone, albeit at her expense, signals the end for Jennifer and me, not that there was much there to begin with. It leads me back on the hunt, more heavily, not that I ever stopped. My guilt about this prank we pull is clearly overshadowed by the laughs it produces in Joe and me. As my mother once said about me when I said or did something particularly brutal or insensitive, "You have a mean streak a mile wide." Maybe she was right.

Marquis Jones, the Black dude from Jersey and I start to hit the streets together on weekend nights, making the rounds on High Street, the main campus drag. It seems like every other storefront is a bar, and we make the rounds to most of them at least once every weekend. Mark is incredibly artful in his approaches, particularly with the White women. Trafficking in the manipulation of White women, utilizing guilt and bravado, he is able to score with some degree of success and proves somewhat handy as a comrade in arms. He and I are majorly full of shit but we have a good time hanging out trying to score. That's really half the fun anyway. We walk and talk about Eldridge Cleaver, non-violence, Malcolm X, Dick Gregory, Stokely Carmichael, the Panthers, the Muslims, Whitey, music. It's great. Sometimes we play a little one on one. Mark prides himself on his basketball prowess which is overrated despite his five inch height advantage. I hold my own with him. He's too flashy and loses the ball too often in his efforts to "style out." Not that I played the Catholic school White boy brand of basketball myself. But I try to utilize my strengths, which in basketball as in most sports, are my quickness, agility and speed. My laziness on defense and recurring asthma limits my effectiveness in that department. It's a good place to put our respective aggressiveness and we never come to blows. Nasty verbally, yes, but blows no.

Diamo and I have more of an intellectual connection. He's four years older, engaged to be married, more mature, solid. Has read a lot and turns me onto some interesting books that I might not have found on my own, certainly not through this fucking school. He likes Updike and recommends *Rabbit Run* and his new one *Couples* about the sexual revolution in the 'burbs. Wife swapping and shit. I find Updike pretty erotic, racy and erudite. I eagerly inhale them and subsequently, Diamo and I along with some of the other kids on the floor have interesting discussions, particularly about values, ethics, conduct and what is important in this life. Diamo has an expression that he uses incessantly. He says whenever the opportunity presents itself, "I can say 'so what' about anything except love." I think by that he means that love of his fiancé, friends, family is the most important thing and after that no issue or problem is really worth getting uptight or upset about. The thing about love, he keeps pretty vague, but the idea of "so what" catches on and it helps me and my dormmates keep things in perspective when things get to us. "So what, sew (so) buttons," becomes the Steeb Hall eighth floor mantra for most potentially upsetting situations or problems. It also becomes a quick and dirty way to cut through complaining, whining or kvetching on the dorm floor for which there are plenty of opportunities. "So what" becomes another way of saying, "I don't want to hear about it." Here in this all male dorm, stoicism, keeping a stiff upper lip, is the expectation for guys. A strict code. And "so what" is one more tool for enforcement of the buttoned up code of male conduct. And enforced it is.

I personally didn't mind this code so much. I knew because of my experience at the IOL that I am sort of a different kind of guy anyway. I can access my feelings. I've had no choice. My feelings overwhelmed me during my breakdown, so by necessity, I am in touch with them. But on the other hand, the "macho" stiff upper lip thing provides a nice corrective, keeping things in balance. Maybe that's why I like it even though I can't articulate why.

CHAPTER 3

The Oval People: A Tribe May, 1969

Walking to classes from OSU south campus Steeb Hall involves trekking through two paths of greenery. First are the Hollow and Mirror Lake, a tiny little pond, part of a reedy wooded area. Really quaint. The other, the Oval, is a huge expanse of lawn, sidewalks, oak and buckeye trees that physically unifies the schools west, north and south campuses. In the spring, particularly from noon to five in the afternoon, the place is teeming with kids, just sitting on the grass often in impromptu circles, many sitting lotus style. It is here that I meet some soul mates.

As I walk by this hippie-esque crowd one day in early May, I can see that this group is circulating pamphlets regarding the Ohio 34, a group of Black students who were banned from campus for taking over the Administration Building on February 21, 1968 in commemoration of the day Malcolm X was killed. They were suspended from school for making non-negotiable demands on the administration regarding the Black Student Union, Black Studies, etc. Some of the Black students were radicals, most were liberals who believed in working within the system. They were arrested on Feb 21,1968, suspended from school, put on probation and were awaiting hearings. Their demands had not really been taken seriously by the administration.

These White students on the Oval are passing out homemade pamphlets and imploring students to come to a campus demonstration regarding the plight of the banned students. I talk with their leaders Hal and Jed, both White students, one a Jewish guy from Cleveland, the other a bonafide pacifist, a minister's son, Jed from West Virginia. Both very mellow, almost self consciously gentle. It's what feminists would later describe as the "sensitive male." I find these guys very appealing, likable and a striking departure from the macho posturing characters of New Rochelle and the East Coast. Plus, there are girls, too. Hippie types, long straight hair, braless, friendly, sweet and easily affectionate. Hugging is the bill of fare upon meeting, greeting and farewell. I have nothing against that, particularly given my tendencies towards reticence. The ritualized hugging thing makes it easier to overcome my shyness. Of course, there are unofficial rules to hugging. It's waist up. No hip hugging. Waist down, is reserved for the dance floor like at the Sugar Shack, with 3.2 beer in one's system. But these folks, about 10 of them in all, Hal, Jed, Linda, Rachel, Barbara, Ellen, Jerry, Barry and Cal, are all very cool. All politically conscious, socially aware, hip to underground music, intellectualish, interested in fun and generally alienated from the dominant OSU, jock, frat, rah rah football culture that dominates the campus scene.

We hang out. Surprisingly, this group is not a big dope smoking crowd. Of course, they've all tried it. Not much drinking either, and mostly see themselves as high on life. They're into vegetarianism, organic gardening, some early feminist consciousness, but the unifying thread is a kind of gentle, non violent, pacifist mode of being both with each other and other people as well. Jed, the minister's son from West Virginia and Linda, a small town girl from Chillicothe, Ohio both exemplify this vibe. Both are really soft, kind, accepting and pure. Jed models himself on Jesus, Gandhi and Martin Luther King as the way to be in life. Linda, as beautiful as she is soft, reminds me of the Amy Semple McPherson character as portrayed by Jean Simmons in the movie "Elmer Gantry." Radiant, virginal, pure of heart, kind of untouchable. I fall head over heels in love with her for the next month and a half. This is emotional infatuation, not just the libidinal kind. This feels different. Almost spiritual. I fall under her spell and long to be around her.

Barbara, Rachel and Ellen, are three Jewish girls, all of whom I like, but they are very familiar to me in outlook, humor and ways of expressing themselves. Down to earth, practical, and sort of skeptical about everything. Kind of on the same wavelength. Likable, but definitely familiar. They would become and remain good friends while I was at OSU. I don't feel as though they are attracted to me which is fine because I only see them as friends.

But Linda, she is something else. Kind of like the opposite of down to earth. Ethereal. Otherworldly. Pure. It's not just a physical attraction of which there is some. She's very pretty. But a kind of innocence, virginal. I put her on a pedestal. It's like she's untouchable in her pureness. Everything she says or does I experience along with some of the other guys, as her desire to live a morally exemplary life. To be good. I am enthralled, yet mostly see her as beyond, uncatchable. Like a butterfly. Linda takes this Jesus stuff seriously. Everything she does is an attempt to be like him. I've never met anyone like her. I am smitten. The flame I feel for Linda, will burn hot, but burn once. Linda, after all, is a real Christian girl, the likes of which I have never seen. Not Irish, Italian. No. Not Catholic. No. I knew Christian girls from New Rochelle but those New Rochelle girls had a much homier familiar feel to them. I almost didn't see them as Christian. The Irish, Italian, Black and Puerto Ricans who I grew up with, I related more to their unique ethnicities and racial aspects. But Linda, by God, she's a bona fide Christian. American. Fucking exotic. I swear to God. This is new for me. The sincerity, the genuineness, the lack of sarcasm. I kind of like it. Definitely exotic. I am in a state as if in the presence of something sacred when I'm around her. A hint of a real positive difference between Ohio and New York. And for the first time, I'm glad to be away from New York.

From that day and every day for two months, the Thirty-four committee and I hang out on the vast sylvan Oval. We are, for the most part, inseparable. I see one or all of them every day. There are never plans to get together. It's more like at around 3 everyday during the week, some or all of the members show up at the same spot in the middle of the Oval. We sit together in a circle, each of us in the lotus position, a self created spiritual family. I develop relationships with all of them one on one, but most intensely with Hal. Hal and I share a savant-like love of rock 'n roll and singing a cappella. Hal is Jewish, from a Cleveland suburb, but like all things Midwestern, softer, more sincere, self consciously gentle. He's the political ringleader of the Thirty-four coalition. He and I immediately form a singing duo, doing our impressions of Don and Juan, "What's your name?" and James and Bobby Purify, "I'm your Puppet." Hal and I are certain that these two duos are really the same guys. They sound so alike.

Also prominent to me is Jed, the pacifist soul of the group, and Rachel, the wisecracking, humorous, vivacious Long Island girl and of course my virginal beauty Linda, my Joan of Arc. What we do mostly is "frolic," our word for hanging out, which consists of low level drinking, mostly talking, listening to music in our daily meetings on the campus Oval. Hal, Jed and Rachel do most of the talking and not just about politics. But mostly. Nothing sexual. Nothing sexual at any level between any of the members. We are pristine. It isn't like we are anti sexual. It isn't like it is part of any religious or political ideology that we are trying to live out. It's just how it is. Maybe it was our political purpose. Not sure why. It is a relief from the sexual hunting that had been so much a part of my activities with women up until then. Clearly, there are attractions between members, but there's a superordinate emphasis on the platonic, brother –sister component that overrides all of the erotic consider- ations and provides the glue, the fun and the ongoing connection. We glory in each others' presence this spring of renaissance. Being a part of a small local, basically liberal non violent, social-political group gives us cohesion. From time to time, the collective energy of the group congeals and we come together to plan actions or write communiqués to the larger student populace about the status of the Thirty-four and/or the counter actions of the OSU administration as each side prepares to meet to resolve the suspensions and arrests. We are united in anger at the injustice done to the Black students but just as much united in a nonviolent approach to addressing problems. In a way, we are a sort of hokey OSU Peter Paul and Mary, Joan Baez, Donovan, Smothers Brothers, Simon and Garfunkel kind of crew. But we don't see ourselves as hokey, no one ever does. We are an idealistic though not humorless bunch, unlike some of the more radical groups I would encounter later.

The crescendo event for our social/political scene is the last night of the spring quarter when eight of us, following our last final, get together at Mike's Pizza on High Street, the only place where "it" is really "happening." We hit Larry's Bar, the hippie drinking spot, for some beer. At midnight or so, the eight of us are tipsy, loose and directionless except in our desire to get off the streets and make our way onto the campus Oval. There for the next four hours, we take turns singing solo or in tandem, seven of our favorite Broadway shows, from *South Pacific* to *West Side Story, Oklahoma, The Sound of Music, My Fair Lady* to *Fiddler on the Roof* to *Hair*. Electric energy. We are ecstatic. No drugs. I am probably a little manic on the heels of finals week, staying up late into the night but I feel it's from the experience itself. I have found my people. I, by far, know the most show tune lyrics, so often lead the crew in the singing, but all of us have half decent voices which adds to the fun. We're carousing, frolicking, singing, and joking. As we're the only ones on the Oval in the middle of the night, we feel uninhibited and at times some of the girls and guys pretend they are Julie Andrews singing from a meadow in the Alps, a la *Sound of Music*. As much fun as it is, I'm slightly preoccupied. I've got some unfinished business to attend to. And it's not here. It's back home. In New Rochelle.

The next morning without having slept, I am wired from the night's reveries but get on a plane and head back to New York where I plan to work and spend the summer. I have fashioned this idea of reestablishing my relationship with Marla which has been rather haphazardly maintained by me and her, but mostly by me, since leaving for school in January. The lackadaisicalness really dates back to the previous January of '68 when I had my breakdown. Our connection, while strong, intense and deep has not been tended to by me with any consistency, but regardless, I miss her with much ardor and conviction. I look forward to seeing her again. I admit to myself that I especially feel this way since I have not succeeded in developing a serious relationship thus far at OSU. But that isn't the only reason. I truly miss her and think we can make something happen again now that we are a little older and hopefully more mature. I have confidence about this, having discussed it fairly intensively with my female Oval mates. Not Linda, because the fantasy of being with her precludes my "formally" acknowledging that we are just friends. But the other females, Rachel and Barbara, both Jewish, are encouraging me to go for it if it's Marla I truly love. Maybe the fact that Marla is also Jewish has something to do with their encouraging me. I assume that that's it but don't bother to check it out with them. I mean Rachel and Barbara are not particularly religious, but I clearly like the fact that they're Jews, kind of like me. Plus, they like the sound of Marla from what I've told them, so it's not purely a Jewish thing, I don't think.

As I arrive home that Saturday morning in mid June, I am pretty high and wired from sleeplessness. Happy to be home, feeling good about my accomplishments of the previous quarter and my guess that I have pulled up my grades. I'm joyous when I turn out to be right and I earn a 3.0, a real improvement over my previous 2.0. I'm also happy about the two pronged social scene I have managed to construct, first on my dorm floor and now most recently through my Oval friends. I'm not drunk or stoned either. Just sleepless, elated, hyped up, and manic? When I am in the first flurry of this state, I feel ecstatic along with a sense of tremendous self confidence. Like I can do anything. The sky's the limit. During these periods, I'm often quite productive, doing my best reading, studying or paper writing and being my most extroverted socially with the guys or women. An intoxicating sense of well being. And this is where I find myself as I arrive back home in New Rochelle.

The first couple of hours I spend with my parents, Milt and Barbara. They are both glad to see me and I glad to see them but they

37

are preoccupied with the upcoming wedding of my older brother, Dave, to his fiancé, Cherise, a woman he has been dating since he was in junior in high school. Their preoccupation means they will be less focused on me, which suits me just fine. Dave and Cherise seem well matched and I feel close to her, almost like a sister I wish I had. We have very good conversations about family, books and movies. She's also pretty and feels very accessible. The only thing about the two of them that concerns me, although I don't verbalize it, is they both seem kind of young to be getting married, twenty-three and twenty-two, respectively. Dave just spent a year teaching in the Brooklyn public schools as a way to get a draft deferment and Cherise just graduated from Beaver college in Philadelphia. The two of them plan to go to Madison (University of Wisconsin) for grad. school, Cherise in English and Dave in French History.

Lew, who is also home, just having finished junior high, seems to be doing all right. He and I still share lots of stuff in common like sports, tv show favorites and rock music. I think we express our closeness through our mutual love of the Mets, Knicks and Jets, not Giants or Yanks. We go for the underdog teams. The whole family has rooted for the underdog since I've been around, maybe because we started out as Brooklyn Dodger fans, who had Jackie Robinson, the first Black ball player in the majors, later extending to our heavy adoration of Muhammad Ali, a hero to our generation. Whatever it was, it was there, heavy. And I recall our bond and fervor when years back, Lew helped me make my list of the top 40 songs of all time. He gave his input on his favorites and I took it somewhat seriously. Our relationship feels easy and fun, relatively conflict free. At least, that's how I see it.

The entire family, along with Cherise, gather at *Tung Hoy* in Larchmont, our favorite mainstay Chinese restaurant that the

Brucher family has been going to for years, since the 50's. It's been like our home away from home every Sunday. Jimmy, the greeter or owner, nobody is sure which, is always there to find us a table, and we always see people we know when we get there. We know all the waiters. They know us by our first names and know our favorite dishes by heart.

Besides all that, it's an opportunity to get away from my mother's monotonous cooking routine. Dry baked chicken on Monday (bears no further description), lamb chops on Tuesday (which I have never cared for), rolled fish on Wednesday (Mom trying to be fancy but it's tasteless), spaghetti on Thursday (now we're getting somewhere) and brisket on Friday (now we're talking). Week in. Week out. Always. The Same. On Saturdays, Mom and Dad went out so we kids were on our own with Chef Boyardee spaghetti and meatballs from the can. Lew loved the stuff. I couldn't eat that crap so I opted instead to eat Corn Flakes for dinner.

At our food oasis, *Tung Hoy*, while eating our usual orders of (humongous) egg rolls, wonton soup and shrimp with lobster sauce (more predictability), my father brings up the topic of summer jobs. His thought is that I will work for my Uncle Bill in Manhattan as I had done two previous summers ago. Sounds good to me. This time it's my hope that I will work in the office, not on the hot, non-air conditioned floor where I worked in 1967, picking orders. Bill's place of business is a wholesale book warehouse. It's homey and familiar, smelling like a combination of sawdust and sweat. Despite the general good vibe, there's the fact that Uncle Bill can be grumpy and disgruntled on a good day and pays minimum wage, $1.50 an hour. In a phone call to Bill later that night at home, he agrees to hire me for office help and I casually ask for a pay increase from the minimum wage I had gotten two years earlier. He replies in his typical grumpy tone,"That is even more than you are worth!" In other words, "NO." Nice guy! What can I say?

Back at the kitchen table, there is talk of plans for the wedding happening later in the month, politics (Nixon and his bullshit lies about "winning the peace," all the while keeping the war going, big time) family stuff, how my dad's brother is doing in his new business and of course, sports. Tonight, the tone is playful, jocular, even festive. It feels great to be home. Everything right now feels great. The next day, I plan to see Marla. I am excited and eager to see her again.

CHAPTER 4

Mandatory 8 Count – Numero uno

I wake up from a really good night's sleep around 10 a.m. and smell the familiar and beloved aroma of bacon, eggs, rye toast and coffee being made for me by Zora Lee Hill, our housekeeper. I have a vague sense of how lucky and privileged I am but mostly I take it for granted, because it's what I know. When I really think about this, which isn't often, I feel uncomfortably guilty. But now full, sated, cigarette in tow, I get into my mom's gold Pontiac '67 Tempest for the four block ride over to Marla's house. Really looking forward to seeing her, I think to myself. It might be fun to surprise her so I don't call in advance, as is my habit with her. She's never seemed to mind or I've never noticed. Either way, she's never said anything about it.

Bouncing from the Tempest and knocking on her front door, I'm greeted by Marla's mother, Alicia, the southern Jewess from Georgia and in asking for Marla, I am shocked… stunned to see Marla stepping in front of her mother, opening the door and walking out of the house. Looking as though she has lost about ten pounds, she has this tense, tight, disgruntled look on her face that clearly I have never seen.

"Hi," I say as I make a move to give her a hug and kiss, only to be greeted by a visible cringe in response.

Then she says, "I've been meaning to call you but I figured you would be home from college soon so I just waited."

"What's up? "I ask with a curious tone.

"This is up," she replies. "You suck. You're the worst fucking boyfriend a girl could ever have. You never call me. You flirt with all of my girl friends. Who knows what else you're up to and I am just sick and tired of it. Plus, I don't think you know what an ordeal you put me through with your going to that fucking hospital. The worry, the loneliness, seeing you like that, you don't have a fucking clue. Really sucks."

Then starting to cry as I attempt to hold and comfort her, she recoils, shouting, "Don't come near me you fucking asshole. I hate you, Arnie. I fucking hate you. Why don't you just go back to that fucking nut house where you belong! Leave me the fuck alone!"

Stunned and incredulous, I can't think of one thing to say. Blown away, I just stumble to my car and quickly as I can, gun the accelerator and make my way back home. I'm flabbergasted. Ringing the doorbell, my mom opens the door and immediately sees that something is wrong. Before she can ask, I simply bark, "I don't want to talk about it now," and bolt up to my room, leaving my mom with her mouth open after stifling her question. I try lying down to relax. I put on the radio and attempt to regain my bearings. After five minutes of lying on the bed and constantly switching radio stations, I'm up and agitated. I'm beside myself. I feel myself simultaneously unraveling on one hand and desperately trying to withstand the unraveling on the other. Clearly, the emotional power of the wound to my psyche is winning. I am staggered by the emotional blow and make the physical movement of trying to clear my head, shaking it rapidly from side to side like a boxer, only it is my heart that is in tatters. I light up Viceroy after Viceroy trying to regroup. It's no good. Fuck, thirty minutes before, I'm feeling about as good as I have ever felt in my life, ebullient at the thought of seeing Marla and with the comfort of family support and being home again. Now the bottom has fallen out. "I don't know what to do. I don't know what to do," I hear myself saying out loud, that acute combo of hysteria, panic and anger all converging in moment to moment emotion like little Molotov cocktails exploding my soul. The ego deflation is deafening as I feel myself shrink and start to feel like I'm disintegrating.

I'm up and down from the bed several more times, I finally decide, fuck it. I know what I'll do. I'll call Jean O'Bannion and go see her. I don't need Marla. Not really thinking, just reacting blindly, instinctively like a wild animal under attack. And so I do. I set up a visit with Jean for that night thinking this will make that bad feeling, that blow to my ego, go away.

A major mistake as it turns out. For, not only does Marla have a piece of her mind to dish out to me but it turns out that Jean does, too. Basically about the same thing. For being an asshole. Meaning, a shitty boyfriend, for not calling and two timing her. I knew that Jean liked me, maybe really liked me, but we were never really a couple, so I didn't really think that much about her feelings. I liked her, found her really attractive, but when I wasn't around her, I really didn't give her much thought. Kind of one of those out of sight, out of mind deals. I can see now how she thought of me as an insensitive asshole. But, I'm too wrapped up in my own feelings to think about how she could see me as an inconsiderate jerk. She, too, reads me the riot act but with cutting sarcasm and doesn't let me near her. Boy, I got her so wrong. Because her parents used to let her smoke and drink in the house, I thought they were the coolest parents ever. And here I'm thinking because of this and how Jean acted in the past that she would be cool with anything. Well, she isn't. She, too, lets me have it like a second after I come through her front door, spewing bile.

"You fucking low life piece of shit. You take advantage of me for two years, never realizing how much I care about you, acting like I don't exist except when it suits you. Get the fuck away from me. Get out and don't come back." Again, I can't get a word in edgewise. The verbal assassination is harsh as shit. The most I can muster to get in through the fuselage of rage is a few "buts" and a couple of "justs." No complete sentences.

This visit lasts less than ten minutes and now I'm really fucking reeling. A double knock down from two women in one day. How could this be happening to me? No doubt I deserve this, but there's no way I am gonna let myself feel THAT fully. Yes, my guilt is a recognition that I have fucked up but Jesus Christ, give me a break, I don't need this shit. Maybe deserve but definitely don't need. Heading home on "queer street," I stagger back to the house, dazed, confused and agitated.

Well, it doesn't get any better from there. I continue to unravel in the next few days just like January '68 when I had my first break. But clearly I now have some experience with the struggle to stay on my feet. I'm no stranger to guilt or fear or that sense of spiraling down and losing my bearings, so I'm less frightened and freaked out this time. But I'm not in good shape by any stretch of the imagination. I am fucked up. I can't hide it and after about three days of this reeling and not really sleeping, my parents make an appointment for me to see a shrink psychologist in NYC. My parents are less freaked out than worried and disappointed. They were hoping I was "all better," so they're bummed by the sudden change of affairs.

The psychologist dude I see specializes in late adolescents with drug problems. He's cool. Seems to know what's happening with my generation, speaks the lingo. I like him and immediately feel comfortable. I see him alone and then at the end of the session with my dad. He informs me and my dad that he doesn't think I have taken any psychedelics or pot or heroin or coke. He instead thinks that I'm in a manicky state and suggests that I not live at home for the summer but try to go back to Ohio State, go to summer school and hook up with a shrink. He thinks the home situation is a set up for things to escalate. Given my history with my dad and my parents' tendency to walk on eggshells around me, he advises me to go back to OSU. He thinks it's the best of two bad options given my lack of stability, but definitely preferable.

CHAPTER 5

The Other Half of It (Marla)

That asshole just left with the usual burning rubber when he's pissed. I'm just so upset. Alicia, my mom, can see by the look on my face that something's wrong. Besides, she's not deaf, she could hear the screeching of the tires on the street. She tried to talk with me about what just happened. My father, he's there, too, about three feet away in the hallway. But I'm not having it. They're the last people I want to talk to right now. So I do what I always do, I call Nancy, my best friend and leave my parents in the lurch with befuddled looks on their faces. I'm not ready to talk to them, yet. I race up to my room and grab my pink princess phone and dial.

The phone rings. Nancy picks up.

"Hello?"

"Guess who I saw today?"

"You're kidding."

"Yup. That prick came over like nothing had happened."

"Jesus. What did you say?"

"I gave him a piece of my mind. I told him what a shitty boyfriend he is. How he never calls, how he treats me like shit, how he flirts with my girl friends. And then he did his usual trying to comfort me when he saw me so angry. But I wouldn't let him touch me. Not this time, the fucker."

"Sounds like a break up."

"Yeah, that prick. He put me through hell with his breakdown. He has no clue what the last year and a half has been like for me. Has no idea how loyal I've been. I got really pissed. Told him he should go back to the nuthouse 'cause that's where he really belongs."

"Jesus, Marla."

"Yeah, maybe I shouldn't have said that. That was mean but he really hurt me and I was so angry. I really loved him and he treated me like shit. Put me through hell."

"So, now what?"

"We're done. Besides I leave for North Carolina and camp in a few days. I'm just gonna try to forget him. I mean, you know how much he hurt me and how much I cried over him and worried about him. I just don't need that shit anymore."

"Wow."

"Yeah. It's fucked up but you know what? I deserve better."

"You know what we should do Marla? We should go out and get you good and drunk and stoned. How about I pick you up around 9 with Lisa and we'll go to Albo's and tie one on. It'll help you forget and take some of the sting away."

"Ok," I said reluctantly, with a sigh. "Maybe that's what I should do."

And so that's what I did. Nancy picked me up in her mother's Continental and we hit Albos. She had one 7 and 7 and I had three. Buzzed. We talked. Mostly I continued cursing out Arnie, occasionally tearing up with sadness, but mostly still pissed. We had to shoo away the advances of some Eastchester guys who approached our table. Guys were the last thing I was interested in. I needed to spew. And Nancy, like always, was there for me. Lisa, too.

Later that night, still a bit drunk, after Nancy drove me home. Glad she wasn't looped. I pulled out my diary, already almost completely filled with Arnie stories and began to write, trying to put a bow around what I'd been feeling the last almost 3 years. I write the following:

I am through. He rarely called me. I loved him deeply, unlike anybody before. He's the first guy I really fell for and hard. But he treated me like shit.Then that fucking hospitalization in January '68. Then nine months of his being away and when I saw him there, he was a zombie from those horrible psych drugs. It was too much. It still is. I was only sixteen, seventeen years old then. Not fair. That fucker. My friends tried to get me to see other people and I tried but my heart wasn't in it. But Arnie's crappy behavior has just gotten to be too much so by the time I saw him today when he came home from college, and "dropped by" I was more than done. I gave so much and I got so little. I loved him, but I am way beyond being willing to put up with his bull shit anymore. So I let him have it. He deserved it. Maybe I was a bit brutal. I don't know, I was just so done and angry. And god dammit, I still am. He hurt me badly. I know now that I need something different. Maybe better. I'm glad I'm leaving New Rochelle in a few weeks for camp. Even though I love this place and my friends, I need a change of pace. A change of scenery.

So, I can't wait to go to camp in North Carolina, Camp Blue Star, where I'm gonna be a counselor. Fucking Arnie. Why does he have to be such an asshole? Sure he was funny. Sure he could be fun, even nice when he wanted to. I'm sorry I was so brutal, but I'm beyond angry. I've never felt this angry in my whole life. But he hurt me and it's weird that he doesn't even know how much. And I loved him so much. Probably still do but I need better. I'm just so miserable. But I think things just have to get better for me.

CHAPTER 6

The Best Laid Plans

Fucking defeated. Just so fucking defeated. I come home to New Rochelle in triumph, thinking I'm gonna spend the summer here, reclaim Marla and have a great time. I'm off from school and Columbus, but it's just as bad as last summer when I was in the IOL. Only in a way worse, because this time I know I'm partly responsible when I have the presence of mind to admit that to myself. I treated Marla like shit, yes, but Jesus, this tag team with Jean hit me where I live. I can't think straight. I can feel my confidence going in the dumpster. Just down to my back burner instincts. OSU feels like my only choice now. Goddamn it.

So I do go back, but it's too little too late as a strategy. The damage has been done. About a week after moving into my summer school dorm that I secure at the last minute, I register for classes. My strategy, if you can call it that, is to try to pick up as many chicks as I can, no doubt as a way of compensating to shore up my damaged ego. I continue to feel agitated, unhinged and obsessively try to understand myself with all the half assed psychological theories that I've picked up along the way. Half-baked Freud mostly. All the while,

I'm not realizing that the incessant self analysis is not helping, if anything, it's making me even more agitated. My head is filled with desperately trying to figure out the source of my problems. Am I a bad person? Is it my fucked up family, society? I'm not sleeping, not really able to focus on the two classes I have, just spiraling and really miserable, really unsettled. So, now I'm desperate and not knowing what else to do, I call up the psychiatrist in Columbus referred by the New York shrink and I make an appointment.

I take a bus to his office which is about three miles away from campus. It's in Worthington, the next town over. There I see a dark brown, two story brick building that seems impersonal and ordinary at the same time. I'm sweating profusely and wipe my forehead with my tee shirt, look up at the windows and sigh. It's one of those impossibly hot 90 degree humid summer days. I open the door to the doctor's air conditioned waiting room and feel momentarily better. Small comfort to be out of the Ohio summer sweat box.

A middle aged man with a goatee and a determined stride, which later in my angrier moments I would refer to as a goose step, appears in brown checked pants and short sleeve white shirt and green tie, a Dr. Heinrich Leuchter. I notice a slight but unmistakably foreign accent. In his office, I immediately, with no hesitation, without even sitting and barely making eye contact, go into my diatribe. I announce to him the discovery of the root of my problem on which I have been frantically ruminating to uncover all day and all night. My theory is succinct and simple. I say, "You see, doc. I finally figured out the cause of all my troubles…. I want to fuck my mother and kill my father…" I'm pacing and speaking rapidly, with bizarre but unmistakable assurance.

The shrink, who doesn't know me from Adam, is alarmed but still calm. The only thing he knows about me is who referred me to him. Without much of a pause he says, "Hmm. You sound manicky, and I think you need to be in a hospital, right away." He easily convinces me to check into Upham Hall, the University Psych. unit. I'm just so exhausted and beyond my tether to mount an objection. Not exactly willing, more resigned. He calls me a cab and off I go, thinking to myself, I'm a fucking failure, a fucking fuckup. Really down on myself.

Dr. Leuchter consulting with his colleague, Dr. Jacob Jacobsen, Upham Hall's Chief Psychiatrist

"This Arnie, who I saw for the first time this week, is a pretty mixed up kid. Tangential as hell, pretty incoherent, manicky with delusions of grandeur. And that stuff about thinking he had decided he had figured out his problem with that ridiculous Freudian nonsense about screwing his mother and wanting to kill his father said with such certainty, all mixed in at the same time. Pretty damn disturbed."

"I tell you Jake, I've seen my share of these young kids with their half-baked anti-establishment, anti-authority attitudes, who have no clue how to control their emotions. Look, it's not that I'm not sympathetic to a lot of what they have to say. There are a lot of inequities in our society. After all, I grew up in Hitler's Germany. Served in his army as a foot soldier. No, I didn't believe in Hitler, but I wanted to survive, so I did what I had to do. It was either go in the army and fight, or go to jail, or be shot. The whole thing was a horrendous, grotesque monstrosity. So, believe me, I know what it's like to live under a fascist regime. I'm sympathetic to the impulses of these American youths, but their way of going about change is self destructive. Bound to get the establishment powers to repress them in any way they can. Besides, these American kids don't know how good they have it."

"Well, anyway, Jake, this Arnie kid is about as acutely disturbed as anyone I've seen and he needed to go to the hospital for his own good before he hurt somebody or hurt himself. Besides, when I suggested it, strangely, he didn't fight it, as if he secretly knew that's what he needed. A bright kid, but so mixed up. So disturbed."

"Heinie, I concur with you. His manic agitation is really a facet of his schizophrenia. So I think the phenothiazines, Mellaril or Stelazine, will help to bring down the psychotic behavior and restabilize him. And yes, I agree with you. This kid's gonna have a long road to hoe to get back to any stable functioning, not to mention a productive life. We just gotta do the best we can for these kids. So misguided.

Arnie

After the typical rigamarole, medical model bullshit intake, I am immediately put back on Stelazine, an old antipsychotic that I used to take at the IOL along with a new antipsychotic, Mellaril, just to add to the mind numbing fun... But Lithium, which has just come out on the market about a year earlier to treat manic depression, is not under the doc's consideration as he is operating under the assumption that I am a paranoid schizophrenic, basically just following the diagnosis I was given at the illustrious and well honored IOL. No attempt to rethink it or even to observe in a fresh way what was in front of him. Me, manicky. The shrinks think anyone who is psychotic is a paranoid schitzo. They have the drugs for that and they work, after a fashion. In retrospect, it will be not a small whatever.

But this is now, the summer of '69, and that is the rule of thumb. So Stelazine and Mellaril it is.

My stay at Upham lasts two weeks until I come back to earth, thoughts clearing, agitation lessening and sleeping more regularly. My time there is spent playing ping pong with the psych residents and schmoozing with the other patients who I feel an instant, but transient connection with. So, I'm released, feeling betterish. I return to my dorm. Glad to be out, sort of, I attempt to make up for lost time in my classes which include English Composition and History of Cinema. Quickly, I make some friends in the new dorm, this time on North Campus, which feels strangely more impersonal with the buildings more concrete ish, newer than South Campus. Not at all like the south campus vibe with its ivy covered walls, the relaxed comfort of creaking floorboards, the strange melodies and crescendos of its ancient plumbing and of course, the proximity to the Oval.

While at the north campus cafeteria, soon after my release, I sit next to and befriend a guy named Tom, from Kettering and his Dutch roommate, Peter, both of whom are into esoteric psychedelic music and psychedelics. Of course, I'm also on the lookout trying to find women to schtup, all the while trying not to think about the doubly inflicted wound dispensed by Jean and Marla earlier this summer. It does not work well. Leuchter, the shrink, who I'm now seeing, is not about feelings but about taking responsibility. I see the importance of taking responsibility, but I have a shitload of feelings to process, not to mention that I kind of see the shrink as an authority figure, not that much different from my old man. As far as being able to use friends to work through feelings as I've always done in the past through jocular interactions, I don't have that luxury now. I like them well enough, but unfortunately don't really know these new guys well enough to talk about my grief for the lost relationships which are still sticking in my craw. So, after a couple of weeks of this hyperactive behavior of meeting, talking to and even making out with some new chicks, as is part of my half-assed strategy, I slip into depression. I become mopey, down and find it hard, if not impossible, to focus on classes.

New friends, Tom and Peter, plus old ones like Joe and Michael from Steeb Hall, are a bit of a help just by their presence. But I am a fucking mess and they're in over their heads with me. The things they say are momentarily, at best sort of soothing, but they don't really stick. I'm still battered, and these new friends have their own problems and needs. And I'm acutely aware of not wanting to burden them, or anyone for that matter.

Dr. Leuchter, the shrink, who has me on meds, is trying a combination of techniques in office visits. Reality Therapy, emphasizing responsibility, is mostly his approach and goes like this: "Yes. You say you're going to schedule time to study, but you have not und ven vill you do that?" In point of fact, the man is a former Nazi. For real, he is a German who fought in the Nazi Army. A Catholic. I "Sieg Heil" him in one of my angry outbursts when I don't like what he's telling me, like not following through on my plans to study, for example. I don't think the guy is all that empathetic or understanding of what a guy my age is going through, after all, he was a youth when Hitler came to power in the atmosphere of fascist authoritarianism. He catches a piece of what I need, but he misses a lot. I don't feel particularly connected to him and worse, I'm on guard a lot, again seeing him as an authority figure. Not that I don't already have other major league authority issues of my own I already bring to the table. But his Reality Therapy approach, stressing the need for the patient to take responsibility for all aspects of their life, no excuses, doesn't work on me. Not even close. I'm too rebellious and angry at all authority to even begin to take that shit in. So six weeks later, after hospitalization number one that summer at OSU, and following a last ditch visit by my mother to prevent a similar fate, Leuchter, once again thinks it's time to be back in the looney bin.

Yet, now, I'm super depressed, not agitated. The decision to hospitalize is made following a session with Leuchter where I am barely verbal, barely making eye contact, just completely low. No energy and not knowing what to do, Leuchter suggests strongly that I need to go back in. I have zero will to refuse, so once again I go along with it.

I'm in for another two week stint. I withdraw from all my classes, luckily in time preventing failing, taking incompletes. I don't have the energy or focus to do it myself, but luckily, the hospital social worker takes care of it for me, which I'm not proud of, but it's the best I can do. The whole time I'm there, I spend the bulk of it either in my room sleeping, or out in the day room smoking my Raleighs. I interact minimally with the patients or anybody really, mostly wanting to be left alone. I feel like shit. Finally, with the depression lifting a little, not a lot, it is time for discharge and then back to New Rochelle. After the two weeks in the hospital, I'm still pretty depressed. Grim shit.

So loaded on Mellaril and Stelazine, I'm released from Upham Hall and it's back to New Rochelle for the month's break before fall quarter in late September. Not in good shape at all. But Dad's not having my psychological state at all. Fearful of my tendency towards what he refers to as "indolence," he is hellbent on my using the month productively. Indolence, sloth, lackadaisicalness, torpor, laziness, lassitude, these are just some of the "old man's" adjectives to describe my attitude towards work and study. He has as many words for my sloth as the Eskimos have for snow. Productivity is his answer for everything and so he gets me a volunteer job in the Bronx doing clerical work at a hospital he's affiliated with. There, I function as a clerk, filing alongside an OSU Oval buddy mate of mine from Cleveland, Hal. Dad gets us both jobs doing the clerical work, and being with Hal makes it all a bit more tolerable.

Hal graduated last spring with a degree in social work and is in transit, on his way to NYC to become a conscientious objector in order to avoid being drafted and having to go to Viet Nam. Hal's willing to do almost anything to escape that fate and so, gets hired to do some kind of social work at Rikers Island Prison. Meanwhile, Hal stays with my family and me for a week before his job starts, after which time I stop going to the job. Hal takes off and my old man loses interest in making me go. The usual pattern that I count on. The old man has a hard time maintaining consistency of focus in making and maintaining demands on me. I know this after nineteen years on the planet that all I have to do is comply with his demands in the moment, and then he will forget after a short while, so I can continue on with my "torporous" ways. I don't really know how much of a part my mother has in this decision, as my father is the one who metes out the discipline. My mother seems to go along with it, as she's mostly a passive participant in this latest disciplinary extravaganza. My go-along-to-get-along-then-forget-it method worked my junior year in high school during the Spanish regents exam study debacle. Dad got me up at 5:00 am to study with him because he was panicking that I would fail Spanish, need to go to summer school, and hence fuck up his summer vacation. Back then, in '67, he woke me up for a week at this ungodly hour, only to seemingly forget about it rather quickly. I then took matters into my own hands by cheating on the Spanish regents to avoid summer school which I accomplished through pure serendipity by luckily getting to sit next to a smart student with a Spanish last name. This imposition by the fates succeeded in getting me the 85 I needed, good enough to avoid summer school. And as I predicted, it works again with the clerical job. Dad forgets, as expected, and I spend the last three weeks before fall quarter lounging around the house or going into Manhattan, hanging out on my own, going to movies by myself or looking for pussy in my usual "lackadaisical," and dare I say, ineffectual manner.

CHAPTER 7

R and R
Late September, 1969

Approaching my, once again, south campus, 8th floor dorm room at the end of the hallway, on this Saturday before fall quarter is to begin, I hear the familiar and altogether pleasing sounds of the Jefferson Airplane coming out of the speakers in the adjacent room next to mine. It's incoming freshmen, Jamie Olian and Curt Robinson, and they're blasting the Airplane's new album *Volunteers*. "We Can Be Together," a rousing song features lead guitarist Jorma Kaukonen's psychedelic raga sound along with the trifecta of the Airplane vocalists, Grace Slick, Marty Balin and Paul Kantner.

Immediately, walking through their open doorway, I yell, "Right On."

Curt and Jamie give big smiles with Curt raising his right arm in a fist and before even introducing himself and says,"Yeah. Jamie and I just saw them at Woodstock. They were tremendous. Almost as good as Hendrix and The Who."

I say,"Wow. Woodstock. I gotta hear about this. I was in the nuthouse at the time, couldn't go. Oh, and by the way, I'm Arnie, your next door neighbor."

"I'm Curt and this is Jamie," Curt says motioning with his hand in the direction of Jamie. "Yeah, we had a great time at Woodstock. We'll have to tell you about it."

This was my intro to my new hall mates, for all intents and purposes, roommates. For, almost from the jump, we go in and out of each other's rooms at will. Jamie and Curt are from Plainfield, New Jersey while my new roomate, Mike DuBrul, he's from Cincinnati. Right from the start, we all get along really well. And like I said, we are at the end of the hall, which suits me fine. More privacy and less oversight by the dorm RA. My new roomies are all mellow and simpatico, which I need desperately. As in no hassles.

I'm enrolled in Biology, Poli Sci, English Composition and Art History. But I'm still quite depressed, withdrawn and not really interested in going to classes. I will be sleeping a lot this quarter, as in 12 hours a day, and as a result, skipping a bunch of classes. I'm escaping and avoiding big time. My daily schedule consists of staying up until 2 am, either getting stoned, listening to music, or both, and then sleeping until 2 the next afternoon. Curt, my blonde haired, goofy smiling next door neighbor, refers to it jocularly as "Arnie getting his 12," a somewhat sardonic joke, not necessarily viewing what I'm doing as a form of depression, which it is, but more a lifestyle choice. To top it off, which doesn't help my motivation, BIO 100 doesn't even have a professor. It's taught via a huge tv screen in a huge lecture hall three times a week. I only do well in school when I have passionate teachers and I love the subject matter. Doing well for me then was a cinch, like when in my senior year in high school, I nearly got straight A's. But now, the situation is reversed and I rarely go to class, don't do the reading, and basically get an F for my efforts. I am too lethargic to drop this class. The school is so immense (45,000 students), so impersonal (they don't really know I exist), that if you don't put out the energy, you're fucked (the school doesn't give a shit). I'm too fucked up to put the effort in to drop the course before it's too late. That's how fucked up and disorganized I am. And I have no social worker like I did in the hospital to help me. Art History is not much different, although my attendance there is a little better, but not much.

One day, at 8am, I walk into Art History, not having been there for four weeks, and ask the student immediately to my left when the midterm will be. She replies, " In five minutes." A scene right out of your basic anxiety dream, except that I have set this up for myself in real life. With no study or preparation, I get a 60 on the mid-term, a D- for the exam. I berate myself for my indolence, telling myself that if only I would have attended and put in the time studying, given that I find art history moderately interesting, I think it's fair to say I might have at least gotten a B. Too fucking bad for me, I think to myself. I sort of give a shit, but I'm too unmotivated, read depressed, to mobilize myself to study classes I even mildly like. This is how I am rolling this semester: Poli Sci, which is another area of ongoing interest, where I do get it together to attend class, I get a C. Pitiful. English Comp, an F. This for not writing or handing in the requisite assignments. In short, once again, academically speaking, I am in deep doo doo. My GPA for fall quarter is 0.6, placing me fairly deep in probation land following my first quarter GPA of 1.9 and second quarter 3.0, leaving me with a composite GPA of 1.65. I can hear the sounds of my dad's rage and beratement in my head as he hears of my grades but luckily I'm in Columbus when he does. He will read me the riot act. I can count on it.

Socially and emotionally, I am also a mess for much of the quarter. I'm not very social, in bed a lot. My roommates, sensing I'm bummed out or something, seem to be accepting and they don't pry into what's going on, just leave me be, mostly. I go with them to the cafeteria to eat dinner, but don't contribute a lot to the conversations. I'm not so depressed that I can't speak or do anything, it's just that my motivation for school is gone. I am going through the motions, at best.

I do retain some interest in reading. It's mostly not the reading that's been assigned. I'm too depressed to do any reading unless I'm interested in the subject. I am pretty inside myself and find myself reading books such as *Siddhartha, Demian,* Herman Hesse's version of eastern religion. That sort of book. It's another angle on my trying to figure myself out, again, and I think that maybe Hesse's interest in eastern mysticism will hold some answers. But mostly I find myself listening to a lot of Bob Dylan, really for the first time, because up to now, I could kind of take or leave him. But now in my depressed, passive yet seething state, he hooks me. I get obsessed with Dylan and often put seven of his early albums on the turntable back to back. And I often listen to them in chronological order. *Freewheeling, Times They Are A Changin', Another Side of Bob Dylan, Bringing It All Back Home, Highway 61 Revisited, Blonde on Blonde,* and *John Wesley Harding.* I do this to understand all the changes he has gone through and to maybe, through him, figure out my own changes. Dylan's albums take me through his folk, political period, surrealistic, psychological period and finally his country, "contented," married man period. Even though I'm not organized or disciplined about school, when it comes to things I care about, like Bob Dylan for instance, I can be quite systematic in my learning.

In my avoiding classes and studying, I substitute traditional academic pursuits by putting Bob on my turntable listening for hours on end. I try to listen when my roommate is away studying at the library which is often, but sometimes when Mike is around. He's generally taken by Dylan too, but sometimes he's had enough and asks me nicely but firmly to take it off the turntable. He's a decent guy and mostly diplomatic, being a midwesterner and all. But after a while, Dylan's grating voice can be too much for anybody and he needs a break and lets me know it. He either needs to go to sleep or just some quiet or something a little more melodic. I comply, but often not without sarcasm. "What do you wanna listen to now Mike?" I will say after a few hours of Bob. "It must be Bobby Goldsboro time." Goldsboro, for me, in case you haven't figured it out by now, was the king of insipid music. I laid it on thick, but Mike took it all mostly in good humor. For me, Dylan represented a lifeline of commiseration, connectedness and identification in my sea of loneliness, isolation and anger. Mike gets it, particularly the anger part, as he is frequently frustrated with school, studying, and the hugeness and impersonal nature of the place, so when I put on songs like *It's Alright Ma-I'm only Bleeding*, or "Desolation Row," he's right there with me. He can relate to Dylan's rage at the system. We all feel it. It's real. He just needs a change of pace more than I do. He's not depressed. Ol' Bob knows about these things, that's for sure. He is a master at articulating these angry, bitter, alienated feelings for us baby boomers. Bob is easily my best friend this quarter. Luckily, I've discovered him just now because he's getting me through this quarter emotionally. I've got him to lean on. Thank you, Bob. Your music is my way to cope. Somebody else besides me feels this way. Somebody else understands. Searching. Searching. The shrinks here at OSU and back home at the famous IOL, diagnosed me as paranoid schizophrenic, including

Leuchter. He tells me that since I had a psychotic episode, thought I was Christ, was delusional, that the origin of my problems are genetic/biochemical in nature, therefore I need anti-psychotic meds. I, however, am still not convinced and operate under the assumption that my problems are psychological, not physiological or chemical in origin. Searching for answers, I read what I can in psychoanalysis, transactional analysis (*Games People Play*) and Erich Fromm's (*The Art of Loving*). Once again, I continue searching for the "ultimate and underlying cause" trying to reduce my problem to some root cause like in that inane, simplistic way I did when I first met Leuchter back in June. I figure it has something to do with my father and my issues around authority and success. But just as often, I'm sold on the cultural ideas circulating around, particularly R.D. Laing's and Wilhelm Reich's writings critiquing the crazy, sick, capitalist society we all have to endure and its impact on families and individuals. I go back and forth between blaming myself, blaming my father, and blaming the capitalist system. The psychological books with their analyses help a little. But I get greater solace from the stirring rock music as it grabs me more on an emotional level and again, makes me feel like I'm not alone. The medical doctors with their way of diagnosing, make me feel like a specimen, and not a person. More alienating shit that I don't need. It reminds me too much of how my father acted when I flipped out, and afterwards as well. Searching for the cause, rather than just relating to me as a person. Ironically, in my relentless search for the cause of my problems, maybe I was unwittingly doing the same thing to myself.

Music is meaningful for me now in my time of isolation and frequent, painful introspection. Besides Bob Dylan, and the afore-mentioned albums, *Volunteers* by Jefferson Airplane, has just hit the stores. It's an album that taps into my anger and generational identification with rebellion. *Days of Future Past*, by the Moody Blues, filled with cosmic fantasizing, psychedelic vibe, is a euphoric escape. Other musical companions are *Salty Dog*, by Procol Harum, again a combo of the psychedelic and old English story telling, and *Let it Bleed* by the Stones. Down to earth, raunchy, sexy, gut level political. *Abbey Road*, the Beatles, pure genius, which functions to ground and center me particularly if I get out of whack when I'm smoking dope, which I can do from time to time now that I'm back into smoking dope this quarter after an almost two year hiatus. Part of my "fuck it" mode attitude, I guess. Other albums I'm into include *Bridge over Troubled Water* by Simon and Garfunkel, which I like less, probably because their occasional lapses into sentimentality, which when I listen, makes me feel embarrassed about my plight, like I'm as insipid as they are. But I especially like Neil Young, whose first album strangely seems to hit the bullseye in my soul at the pain of being rejected. And God, Joni Mitchell's transcendent *Clouds*, provides me with much needed tutelage on the female psyche, which of course I lack big time, partly due to having grown up with brothers. Crosby, Stills and Nash also hit the emotional nail on the head, with their great harmonies and dash of political commentary. Santana, just grooving on Carlos's serene and unique Latin guitar sound. *Green River*, Creedence Clearwater's "big muddy," quasi New Orleans rock n roll sound and finally even Led Zeppelin II, with Robert Plant's voice of hell, which I like very little, but put up with because Jamie and Curt like that shit. Nevertheless, all these records are part of a very fertile period in rock history, and luckily for me, are around and keeping me entertained, stimulated and more grounded. One way my new roommates, Jamie and Curt and I groove is that they are as heavily into this music as I am. We spend hours listening and talking about this stuff. And of course, as Woodstock veterans, they are especially partial to the groups who were there. No argument from me.

So, this is my fall quarter when I am awake. I'm in very good company with my dorm mates, particularly because being around people in general is too uncomfortable or worse, too painful. And in this continuing depression, I have nothing to say. Can't summon up the words. What little small talk skills I possessed to begin with, have simply fallen away. In short, a mostly terrible quarter, but not completely fruitless as I decide to try one new, some might say, crazy thing late in the quarter, and that is to drop acid for the first time. A couple of nights before the drop, Tom, Curt, Jamie and I discuss and make our decision.

"It'll be fine. After all, I've done psychedelics about 10 times. I know the ropes. I'll monitor. Nothing bad will happen to any of you," says Tom.

"It's scary, the idea of dropping, but you're only young once," Jaimie says trying to reassure me.

"Exactly. I'm psyched. Not worried a bit," says Curt.

"Actually, compared to what I've been through with my psychotic stuff, how scary could it be?" says I.

So, in unison, Jamie and Curt say, "Let's do it. Right, Arnie?"

"Yep. I'm on board, totally," I say.

Tom, without hesitation says, "That's the spirit guys. It'll be a gas."

That was our collective thinking. I'm thinking to myself, it'll be a snap. Like I said with regard to craziness, been there and done that. Strangely, I was less afraid to take acid than to smoke pot. My experience with being psychotic gave me weird confidence to face the strange and freaky. But pot felt like playing Russian roulette with my psyche more than acid. With pot, I knew there were a greater range of mental states I could enter and feared I could freak out because they could be unfamiliar and uncomfortable. I either obsessed the entire time or got a bit paranoid. Occasionally when high, I had fun either listening to music or watching old black and white movies. I usually, but not always, backed away from getting stoned unless I was in a really good mood, which these days was rare. But with acid, you knew ahead of time what you're gonna be in for. You were going to be psychotic for eight hours. Scary for some. Familiar to me. I thought that it's gotta be easier to prepare for and I was strangely eager to try it.

Tom, my new Kettering friend and dorm mate, was a relative veteran of "dropping" (10 trips), so he organized and volunteered to be our acid trip guide and monitor our trip. It basically meant that he would pay attention if any of the three of us started to freak out or make sure our acid addled thoughts and impulses didn't propel us into making stupid decisions like jumping off of buildings in case we got the urge to fly. Jamie and Curt, my adjacent room mates, and I are pretty tight; the two of them are to be my co-travelers. As previously stated: our maiden voyage.

So in early December, we "drop" up in Curt and Jamie's room at seven that night, a Thursday. "Purple Barrel," I believe the acid is called. First hour, not much happening. Into the second, a buzz. And then at about an hour and a half... there's take off. Disorientation (the distorted perception of what's real and not knowing how much of what's being perceived is due to the drug), fragmentation (thoughts lack cohesiveness and logical sense), weird feelings (the familiar sense of who I am comes and goes rapidly). Vague discomfort, things not feeling real (the room alternates between looking spongy and looking normal), followed by sharp visual hallucinations

(Curt has flames coming out of his mouth, Jamie has serpents moving through his hair). The three of us communicate mostly nonverbally, as if we know what the other is thinking merely by looking at each other. No question. We DO know what we all are thinking. All at the same time. Maybe we are playing Russian roulette with our psyches, but the music we're listening to, being together with close trusted friends, and Tom's monitoring helps. Just knowing Tom, a tripping veteran, is around makes us feel more secure. He's not doing much yet. So far so good.

But at around 10 pm, three hours into it, by now tripping our brains out, a piercing buzzing sound goes off. The three of us trippers look at each other and simultaneously think it's the end of the world. Curt says it out loud and Jamie and I nod in quick agreement. Without a shadow of a doubt, I should add. The non tripping reality is that it's only an "accidental" fire alarm causing the entire dorm to clear out for fifteen minutes, but the three of us are terrified. We bounce off of and increase each other's panic. Tom, playing his monitor part to a tee, is trying to reassure and calm us when he's not laughing at our idiocy at thinking the world is coming to an end. Tom, still laughing hysterically, commandeers us outside until the drill ends, letting us know that everything is alright between his shrieks of hilarity. Back on the eighth floor after the fake fire alarm, tripping resumes at full force in the bathroom.

Standing in the community bathroom, and looking at myself in the mirror is shocking. I'm watching my face shift, change and vibrate. It's disconcerting and exciting all at once. Taking a piss is frightening. Monumental. It feels and looks like blood is coming out of my penis, not urine. I'm not really making color distinctions right now. But the main thing that keeps rolling through my head is a new kind of mantra that I find myself saying out loud to Curt and Jamie that is strangely reassuring. They are in complete agreement on all levels. "It doesn't matter, nothing matters." This little zen koan is strangely comforting despite its seemingly nihilistic content. It brings home the absurdity of existence and therefore, there is nothing to get uptight about. Jamie, despite his initial nodding of agreement, experiences my mantra in his acid-addled brain quite differently, and far more scarily. He hears it as "this is where we are and this is where we will be.........forever." Jamie is so freaked out by my repeating of the mantra, and desperate, he can think of nothing else but to find our dorm's RA, Terry, a sweet, young grad student in engineering from Cambridge, Ohio.

Jamie walks into Terry's room about three doors away with the three of us trailing behind him a few paces and says, "Terry, I'm having a bummer trip. Arnie, Curt and I dropped some acid a few hours ago. I don't think I'm ever gonna come down. Help me, Terry, I don't know what to do."

Aside from Terry's being a few years older than we are, he's a pretty unlikely candidate to help someone relax during an acid trip. I mean, he's an engineering student. So he tries by saying, "Well, close your eyes and go to sleep. Maybe that will help." It's obvious now that Terry's experience with mind bending substances is limited to drinking beer.

Jamie tries his advice by closing his eyes. "Holy shit, Terry. You just turned into a tarantula. I'm outta here." We stifle chuckles, and with that, like with a hive mind, thinking Jamie is with us, walk back into the "demon's den" or hell where Curt and I go off into something completely different by switching on Procol Harum's "Shine On Brightly."

I start feeling like we are mutually, simultaneously, but wordlessly having a conversation with God and the Devil about who to believe in, and about which entity has the most power. Not noticing Jamie back in the room at first, we think he is the Devil as his reddish, curly long hair turns a bright red and we imagine that he has a seemingly knowing smirk on his face. It was actually a look of terror. Finally noticing him and moving on from that illusion/delusion, Jamie turns into a lamb. More his actual nature without the backlit hair. We all calm down again as Curt's and my smile begins to put Jamie at ease….for a minute, a second. Because just as we are getting our bearings, a siren goes off "truly" signaling the end of the world, if not nuclear war. Elementary school drills for nuclear attacks when we were instructed to hide under our desks, comes back as an image. Except now, knowing how ridiculous it was that a desk could protect us from a nuclear bomb, we panic. Terry bolts out into the hall and blares, "Everyone downstairs. NOW!"

Curt and I join Jamie in panic and terror as we rush to the elevator, down the eight floors to the lobby, and into the street. "What's happening?" Jamie finally blurts out to Terry, to which Terry replies grimly yet calmly, "It's the Steeb Hall quarterly fire drill." Tom, our guide, who is not on acid, has had enough of all of this madness and whisks us off to a friend's off campus apartment where he says we can trip our brains out in peace, which we do for the next four hours without further incident until we come down. The evening cemented the four of us for life, with our shared connections. For sure.

The next day, still logey from the previous night's adventure, we're pretty wiped out. With no sleep to chasten us, Jamie and I share a booth for breakfast at our favorite greasy spoon on High Street, "Dirty" Charbert's Diner. Jamie's in a hurry because he has to run off to Professor Van Zandt's Intro Sociology class which is "quite intimate." Only a thousand people in a huge auditorium, not unusual fare for freshmen at this behemoth university. I ask permission, or rather, insist on coming to the class, being curious about sociology and all. Jamie is okay with that, although a bit hesitant, half remembering the previous evening's freak out which he has partially blamed on me. He seems to be holding a grudge against me for saying that "nothing matters" which threw him into a state of terror. He's pushy about my quickly finishing my home fries, awesome fries, I must admit, worrying that we'll be late for class.

Arriving at the huge lecture hall is like entering a rock concert. Two levels of seating, balcony and main floor with the din of what seems to be multitudes. Being somewhat late, we can only get a mezzanine seat, but luckily, first row. Van Zandt, the prof., is a strong lecturer, confident, and knows his stuff, pacing as he talks dramatically. He does have a certain habit. At the end of a long paragraph before beginning a new one, he mutters........"So,"... as people do to gather their thoughts. But, without skipping a beat, in my impudence and impulsivity, I yell with velocity......"Sew buttons!"

Suddenly the place grows completely silent. Jamie turns four shades of red, approaching purple, as all eyes, including Professor Van Zandt's, are directed straight to the balcony mezzanine. Jamie ducks just in time as I turn my head away. The silence is deafening and seems to go on forever. Finally, Van Zandt begins again, this time deliberately remembering not to use the word "so" as he begins, just in case. Jamie, waiting a minute until Van Zandt gets on a roll, elbows me and whispers, "Let's get the hell out of here," which we do, slithering stealthily out of the building. Jaime half goes off in anger but also can't contain his laughter.

"You fucking asshole, Arnie. "You could have gotten me in trouble, asshole."

"Yes, to the former, Jamie. What else is new? But if I'm such an asshole, why were you laughing so loud?"

"Cuz it was funny, you asshole. I don't want to be known as the student who embarrassed the professor, asshole, but the outrageousness of it all was fucking funny, I gotta admit, you fucking asshole."

This sociology incident, along with the acid trip, proved to be THE highlight of a grim, depressing fall quarter, throwing me once again into an academic hole (0.6), ladies and gentlemen. But at least, it left me with a mantra of my own.

It's deeper and more profound than my buddy Mike's "So what? " zen koan of the previous spring. "It doesn't matter, nothing matters." In other words, if you don't have any love in your life or anything else," it doesn't matter because nothing matters." This insight absolutely helped me survive the rest of the eight hour acid trip. By that 3 am juncture, I was down, exhausted, exhilarated and no less intact than before I dropped. More than that, it gave me a weird kind of confidence that I could survive any kind of internal journey, which there would be more of. Definitely the highlight of an otherwise dismal quarter.

That being said, academically at least, following my woeful 0.6, it would be "up against the wall, mother fucker-time," for winter quarter, once again. The gauntlet had been thrown. Dear old Dad says, "Sink or swim." If I don't get my grades up, I will be out of school. This sentiment is echoed and announced by OSU in a neat little form letter with my student number, and vociferously seconded by my father. I vow to swim. It's the bottom of the ninth and I'm down by three runs. I vow to focus. I register for next quarter to take Comp Lit, Intro to Philosophy, Western Civ Part Three and Geology 101. Nobody counts me out, I hear myself say with determined anger.

CHAPTER 8

Comeback City

"Up against the wall, motherfucker," time again and I'm not gonna give up and ratify the idea that I am a sick, pathetic, underachieving, nutcase loser. I think I must need the pressure or fear or adrenaline, something…as I study, focus, read the material, take notes, all the things you're supposed to do as a bona fide student. It's a ferocity and focus I haven't experienced since my heavy duty sports days when I actually cared about being the "best." Frankly, it feels good to be this focused and determined. It also helps that I'm interested in my courses. Just like when I was in my senior year of high school when I took nothing but courses I liked. Senior English, Psychology, Problems of American Democracy and Economics. Just before I fell into the abyss. This time it's Comp Lit, Intro to Philosophy and Western Civ. 1914 to the present. It's not a struggle to do the readings. It's not a struggle to be prepared for the tests and papers. Interest + fear = success. That seems to be the formula. I stay on top of these classes and have an easy time getting A's because I want to learn. It's easy to be turned on by these areas, philosophy, history, literature. It's what I care about naturally. And you know what else? I like succeeding, even sometimes if it's what my father, the Establishment or the powers that be expect of me. So be it. Sometimes it feels good anyway and strangely not like selling out. Maybe because I'm doing it for myself, too. My efforts pay off: three A's and a D...... What the fuck, I have my limitations.

It proves to be a good quarter for me socially, too. I come out of my depression, perhaps adrenalized by my fear of flunking out, which gives me the energy and self confidence to get back in circulationc with girls, to socialize more regularly, to meet new people. Guys and girls. Just feeling better. More with it. When I feel better, I think more clearly and realize that because I am pleasing my father isn't a reason not to do something. Getting good grades actually feels good on its own merits. Being authentically interested makes it easier, and fear of flunking out also seems to galvanize me. Almost as if I need to play from behind in order to get going. It's like when my basketball team, the New York Knicks, get behind, I notice they tighten up their defense, play harder and win a lot of come-from-behind games. That's me, too. Whatever it is, this combination of factors is a winner. I think of myself as Silky Sullivan, the great thoroughbred from the late fifties who could only win when he came from way behind. That's me. It worked for him, except at the Kentucky Derby in 1958 when he couldn't beat Tim Tam. But the point is, I am motivated as hell.

Toward the end of the semester, with my energy and focus back, I start hanging out at the Student Union, which is conveniently located near my dorm on South Campus. I begin to make a regular practice of going there after class around three in the afternoon. If a person wants to listen to music, they can go upstairs to the Listening Room where you can put on earphones and listen in private. Another option is the Tavern next to the cafeteria, a cozy ski chalet-like space, where students eighteen and over can swill 3.2 beer. Some of the students call it piss water, because the beer is so diluted. But there I go and listen to the jukebox filled with up-to-date tunes. The Union also supplies a bulletin board anyone can use to find out about jobs, apartment rentals, concerts etc. All this makes the Union a very busy place, yet with that calm midwestern vibe compared to the hard driving, frenetic New York pace.

It's here at the Student Union that I run into an ex-service-man-turned-radical activist named George. He's a short, dark-haired guy, mid 20's, grad student, who speaks with extreme confidence and passion about his views on politics. Turns out I met him about a year earlier at my dorm when he was on a recruitment trip as president of the campus SDS. I was in a more liberal phase then and less persuaded by the extremeness of his ideas but nonetheless, I found his views thought provoking. In the summer of '69, SDS disbanded and broke up into two splinter groups, Progressive Labor and the Weathermen. This guy, George Bohichik is now peddling a new group that is kind of an amalgam of the old SDS and Weathermen but with a Maoist tinge. He calls it the "Third World Solidarity Committee." Basically the group's goals boil down to anti war activities, breaking up univer-sity allegiances to companies involved in war efforts, pro Black and Latino studies programs, the formation of a Black Student Union and lastly, being against all university activities that contribute to U.S. imperialist activities in the Third World. Really not that much different from the old SDS, except maybe more militant. This ambi-tious agenda feels de rigueur in radical politics circles now.

Bohichik and his cronies, both males and females, have a harder edge than the liberals I'm used to associating with. More sure of their beliefs. See the world in a more black and white way. I like the clarity. Bohichik et. al. usually hang out in the Student Union cafeteria, sitting at the same long formica tables every day, amongst the peculiar array and cacophony of OSU students who are jocks, preppies, locals, farm boys, hippies, frats and Blacks. Bohichik, three of his "comrades" and I become a regular at this table. Bohichik begins to fill me in about the goings on of his committee. Because I seem to pass muster, he invites me to some planning meetings that I attend a couple of, also held at the Union, usually early evening with about 15 other people, fairly evenly distributed between men and women. All White. The Blacks at this point have their own meetings, as the Black power ethos of the times explicitly requires the racial separation for radical organizations. I feel a connection with the ideas, perspective and anger expressed in the "Third World" group, especially the anger, and definitely in agreement with their critique of the namby-pamby waffling of the more liberal minded politicos I've run into and been a part of on campus so far. Bohichik is very focused and single minded.

One afternoon, I meet him at the usual table and he is very excited and talking louder and faster than usual. He's just seen the St. Valentine's Day massacre film about Al Capone's mob in Chicago and he had a strange take on the movie.

"Those guys were scum but I admire how organized as a group they were. That's the kind of organization we need to have. Efficient and well-enforced."

"Wow," I say, listening and kind of amazed, not ever having thought of Capone as having an organization that was a well-oiled machine. But I realize how right he is, except for how anti-democratic and fascist their structure really was. I am more dazzled by how sharp and amoral George's thinking is. With George, the ends justify the means. There's something attractive about how definite he seems about everything. But the way the "Third Worlders" act with each other is very heavy handed and dogmatic. I feel like I have to watch my words carefully or I will be attacked. There is a right and wrong way of thinking. This is in marked contrast to my liberal friends from the Oval the previous spring, and my current Steeb Hall mates who seem more tolerant and relaxed, while maybe less informed concerning diverse opinions, for better and worse. Less knowledgeable maybe, but easier to be with. Anyway, this connection with the Third World group gives me a new political outlet as life on campus begins expanding into greater fullness.

The 34 committee of liberal politicos from the previous spring disbanded when the two leaders Jed and Hal graduated, although I continue to run into individual members from that group around the campus from time to time. This winter, as my social isolation and depression lifts, I have more energy and confidence. I don't shy away from people I see and have more conversations, whether about music, politics or just campus life. Especially politics.

Winter semester ends with separate appearances on campus of two counterculture political celebrities, Dick Gregory and Abbie Hoffman, who are ensconced in the Chicago 8 trial and have come to raise money and awareness for the cause. They talk about Vietnam, youth culture, Black power and the movement as a whole. I find the experience of seeing these two charismatic figures enthralling. They are dynamic and arousing speakers who know how to get an audience juiced up. It definitely works on me. But not so much that I forget about school. Not yet.

During finals week in mid March, I pull two all-nighters in a row preparing for finals, tests and papers. Then without having slept, Tom, myself and a girl from the nearby girls dorm, Sandy, head east through Buffalo, Rochester, across New York State on our way to Boston, a 16 hour drive with only a few pit stops along the way. Dropping off Sandy in Rochester, Tom and I pull into Cambridge at

11am on a Saturday morning. My New Rochelle friend, Ricky, now at Harvard, is there to greet us at the steps of his student co-op. I'm wired to the gills from not having slept but excited to see Ricky. That night we hit a kick ass party with many people whose last names are the same as many dead presidents, Pierce, Van Buren, Harding, being just some of the party revelers. The party is pretty wild. The weed smoking, wine drinking and no sleep combo plate proves a bit much. I get so drunk and stoned that after an hour or so, I puke all over my beard before passing out at the party. I conk out until 8 am the next day. It was the first and only time in my life that I ever passed out from drinking, or puked for that matter. Not my thing. Bad news. I don't recommend it. Maybe even dangerous as we would find out in the circumstances of Jimi Hendrix's death to follow later that September.

Tom, Ricky and I, upon regaining consciousness after having all fallen asleep at the party, gather ourselves and go out for breakfast the next day at the Pewter Pot, a well-known Cambridge eating establishment. Tom then leaves us to visit some other friends in Boston. Ricky and I, meanwhile, hang out for a couple more days at his dorm co-op, a glowing time highlighted by his fervent playing of Van Morrison's "Moondance" and the Creedence song "Who'll Stop the Rain?" Rick, in addition to being a great tennis player, is also a singer-songwriter and guitar player. He and I still share an intense love of rock music and always have ever since we were kids back in the Everly Brothers "Wake up Little Susie" days. Rick and I have about an 85% hit rate when it comes to digging the same stuff and enough differences to make our conversations interesting and deep. It's always great to see him despite our intense competitive vibe stemming from our early sports rivalry. The competitiveness adds a little spice to our exchanges. It's one of the main ways we show affection to each other. And it rarely gets nasty. Being with Ricky is rarely boring so that when I take the train to New Rochelle a few days later, I have that fulfilled feeling of being known and knowing someone deeply.

CHAPTER 9

Meeting of the Tribes

My folks, in part because they're pleased with my grades, allow me to have a birthday party. It will feature some of my old New Rochelle friends and newer Columbus friends who live in the NY metropolitan area who are here on break at home.

It's a wacky scene here tonight. First off, I think it's the first time since my bar mitzvah that there's been a party for me, as the guest of honor. Not that I have ever particularly wanted a party for me. Actually, my first inclination is to not want to have one. First, it seems like a lot of work to organize, and secondly, attention focused on me makes me uncomfortable, sort of embarrassed. The pattern of attention toward me in my family, especially with my dad, is extremely inconsistent. It goes back and forth between no attention, which sometimes feels like a relief, or constant haranguing attention, which feels terrible, and sometimes positive attention which feels unpredictably good. And I rarely know which one it will be. So, the most comfortable sort for me is to be left alone. And third, the logistics of how to navigate certain social dynamics between different people representing different parts of my life, who wouldn't necessarily know one another, feels awkward to me as well. I'm not a big introducer or social leader, so that contributes to the awkwardness.

A party in my honor, looking back on this occasion years later, was kind of a Rorschach of my personality at the time. Various parts are represented by my various interests and aspects of my friends' personalities that attracted them to me and me to them. The kaleidoscope of characters that I grew to like or love as our friendships tangled with our identities, created something that was a third thing when we were together. Some of the common elements include sports and politics, with music being the biggest unifying element. My key friends from New Rochelle are represented by Ricky, who I'd just seen, home from Harvard, and Mark, home from Colgate, and Colleen and Jean O'Banion, the sister duo. Colleen, who graduated my year, is attending a local college in the area and Jean, now a senior at New Rochelle High, an old flame who, despite our break up nine months earlier, never knew a party she didn't want to attend. Representing the Buckeyes, Curt Robinson and Jamie Olian, both from Plainfield, New Jersey, my 8th floor roommates at Steeb Hall and acid accomplices. And of course, Tom, our "acid guide," and sardonic metaphysical commentator, who accompanies them.

Ricky brings his girlfriend from Radcliffe, Liss, a very intense media major who, I would find out later, is manic depressive, which may explain why her vibe is so intense. Her presence makes matters more confusing and chaotic for me and I find it more difficult to bring the two groups together. She's intense and smart, with a lot to say and gobbles up a lot of the attention oxygen. Adding to the turbulent emotional undercurrent, is Jean, who I once had a fling with in 11th and 12th grade, only to be unceremoniously dumped by her on the same day as being dumped by Marla Mascowitz, my high school girlfriend, first love etc., etc. A double knockdown, a dumpage double header. Since that upsetting, soul spinning day nine months ago, I guess Jean has now decided to be on speaking terms with me again. Here again, a spike of anxiety and uneasiness comes over me because I really don't know how she feels about me. But apparently she was easily talked into coming to the party by her older sister, Colleen. It was agreed by my mates that Colleen is the best looking of the five O'Banion sisters. But Colleen had never gone out with me or any of my close buddies. Consequently, Colleen's presence must have made it safe for Jean to be at the party. Jean is polite, yet distant towards me. I look for but don't sense her rage towards me. That's a relief.

Nobody tokes up at the party, especially with my parents upstairs, not to mention the fear and paranoia that the cops could enforce the law and put us all in jail. But there is a lot of drinking, beer and hard stuff both bought and provided by yours truly and parents Milt and Barbara, possibly as a gift for me. Strange but true.

The general tenor of the party, while chaotic, is fun with lots of laughter, mostly light hearted banter with sporadic bursts of heated talking. Topics of the day include current or recent films of interest and influence on our maturing psyches: *Midnight Cowboy, Hud, Cool Hand Luke* being the films getting most of our attention. Politics, the war, and activism on campus are other hot topics, of course. The major political issues of the day are the widening war, soon spreading to Cambodia by the Nixon administration, and the beginnings of what we now refer to as identity politics on campus, Black Studies, Ethnic Studies, Women's Studies. The party chatter is like a bee hive of activity, talking about counter cultural concerns, drugs, organic food and vegetarianism. Mark and I have a burgeoning interest in third wave or humanistic psychology, now part of the new human potential movement, which has sprung up in California, particularly at the Esalen Institute in Big Sur. Mark has just finished reading

Gestalt Therapy Verbatim and is extolling the virtues of Fritz Perls, the founder of Gestalt therapy, in leading the movement toward "self actualization" through psychotherapy. Perls just died this month and so Fritz is on the minds of countercultural types tuned into that personal growth kind of stuff. The work of Rollo May, Wilhelm Reich and R.D. Laing also garners attention in the discussions among us collegians, particularly those of us preparing to major in sociology or psychology. My emotional state up to now oscillates between wary tension and then relaxation, particularly when joking and kidding predominate the overall vibe.

Then, tension erupts. It is caused by competition between one of my friends from OSU, Curt and my oldest chum, Rick, now at Harvard. Curt, LSD co-conspirator, a somewhat sullen yet humorous fellow with a prodigious album collection. Rick, my oldest friend, is majoring in Social Relations, a hybrid major combining psychology, sociology, social psychology and anthropology. Rick is in the middle of a field placement as part of the major requirement in this department. The course he is taking is called the Sociology of Misery and the assignment Rick needs to fulfill involves infiltrating a White Irish street gang in South Boston without letting on who he is and why he wants in, in order to gain access to the inner working of both the gang dynamics, life in South Boston and the various intrapsychic processes of the gang members. It is a somewhat dangerous enterprise as these gangs are into crime, muggings, theft and robbery and are not above or against using violence to suit their needs whether to service their momentary impulses, to send messages to potential rivals, or to coerce loyalty from its membership.

What I think ticks off Curt about Rick is that Rick is being very dramatic and grandstanding about his South Boston experience, hogging all the attention at the party, sort of making a bit of a spectacle of himself as he is drunkenly shooting off his mouth. Curt, being a competitive sort himself but not being very aware of his tendencies, makes sarcastic comments, shoots me glares of disgust and anger, and occasionally bates and provokes Rick, apparently trying to instigate a fight. I'm uncomfortable because I feel caught in the middle and I'm not quite sure what to do. I have allegiances to both friends and don't want to have to make a choice. I do nothing, my preferred mode of behavior, except to monitor the situation. The presence of other partygoers seems to diffuse the potential escalation. Luckily, Jamie, Curt and Tom, because they have to drive an hour or so back to Plainfield, leave at around midnight anyway before the hostile vibe can escalate and get out of control. Trying to integrate two parts of my life is like trying to belong to and incorporate two warring tribes. The vibe feels very primitive, almost as if the two sides are vying for my approval to see which side I care about and agree with the most. Weird. I'm glad I don't feel forced into having to pick. At the end of the night, my takeaway is a vow to not to have another party for a long time. It's just too stressful and not fun trying to make everybody happy. Although I like having many of my friends from disparate parts of my life in one place, at least in theory, in practice it's too much work and too much of a hassle. I realize I prefer going to parties rather than having them. I wonder if the different parts of my life are incompatible, if the near fight between Curt and Rick is an example. Whatever it is, I didn't enjoy being in the diplomatic, peace making, greeter role. I much prefer being a participant/combatant, without the responsibility.

Two days later, it's back to Columbus with Jamie and Curt, the aforementioned party combatant. What is usually a 10 hour journey turns into a 15 hour nightmare courtesy of a major snowstorm on highway 70 centered in Harrisburg, Pa. Stuck on the freeway for long periods without moving is mostly made bearable by our delicious food choices of jelly donuts, Ruffles With Ridges and Mountain Dew, as we basically chain smoke our way down the highway with our respective Viceroys and Marlboros. The intermittent whiteouts on the drive back to Columbus, as inauspicious and potentially dangerous as that sounds, will be the prelude to a momentous three months.

PART TWO

CHAPTER 10

Spring Quarter, 1970

We were young then. Most of us were the first generation in history who had televisions for babysitters. Since the early 50's, my earliest memories were less about events among me and my parents and brothers or relatives, and more about the tv shows I watched. It was a point of common interest between me and friends. It was partly how we sorted out who we liked and who we didn't. The other ways that bonded or divided us were the types of music or ballplayers we preferred, and movies or actors or books we liked. These magnetic fields were how we made our determinations. For me, it began with *My Little Margie, Amos and Andy* and the *Abbott and Costello Show*. We're talking early to mid 50's here. Also essential bonding material was Brooklyn Dodger baseball direct from Ebbets Field, before they broke all of our hearts by leaving for LA in 1957. By the spring of '70, I bet I logged over 20,000 hours of tv, ads, sports and what have you. I guess I was probably about average for my generation in my tube watching. Some kids with working class parents didn't have tvs so they didn't watch at all, but most of us did, and many of us watched a lot. I mean we played a lot, too, without the parents around. Just went out and played all day. Mostly sports, street games, low level mischief, that kind of thing. The point I am trying to make is our brains were drenched and addled and inundated with commercial messages, conventional mores, and ideals about what America was all about and I grew up believing they were true. That was until 1963. November 22 to be exact.

That was the day the covering came off the hard ball and revealed all the little disconnected threads delicately holding the ball together. There were earlier inklings and other bellwethers, of course. The racism toward Jackie Robinson, the reaction against desegregation with the Little Rock students, Martin Luther King leading the civil rights movement in the South, all manifestations of the ongoing racial inequalities stirred up questions about this supposed JUST land of ours. Let freedom ring. That's what we were told and believed. When JFK was assassinated, the innocent patina of America ended. The violence at the core of our collective psyches came to the fore and began a revisioning of the history of America, its founding and development that more and more began to reveal its uglier underbelly. Quite disturbing to my age group. The response of our parents to our hostile and loud criticism of America and its hypocrisies struck many, if not most of them, as the reactions of spoiled children. It was said that we were recipients of America's largesse looking gift horses in the mouth. Parents were not amused. They were angry, in fact, and in even the most liberal houses, of which mine was one, there were intense disagreements. In Middle America, the Midwest, South and West, it was even more intense between the kids and their parents. At least in my house, we were allowed to express our views. The 60's, after Kennedy was killed, became the decade of "ism" attacks against inequity. Racism, sexism, capitalism, imperialism, materialism. Epithets were thrown wildly by us kids, often and without regard for their impact, accuracy or context. Parents were beside themselves. We didn't care. Anger and rebellion at the bourgeois, suburban, comfortable, safe, protected lives we were raised in and that our parents had created was a major part of the core issues we criticized. We were accused, often and rightly, of being parasites on the system who had the luxury to criticize the greatest country on earth, whose grandparents and parents had sacrificed everything for them and now we stinkin', lousy, and ungrateful kids were throwing it in their faces. These were the times: 1963–1974. The Sixties.

CHAPTER 11

The Left – April 1970

It was going to be a sweet semester. Spring in the Midwest often is after the horrendous cold, frequently snowy, long and dark winters. Spring acted like an aphrodisiac on the young, hormone-pumping, libidinal minds of the Buckeye college student. And I had an academic schedule to match and enhance that were all in the wheelhouse of my interests as I eagerly looked forward to the coming quarter.

I will be taking Intro to Psychology, 19th Century Philosophy (Kant and Hegel to Nietzsche), Black History, and the popular Bernie Mehl's education class where the reading list reflects the radical edges of this moment. *The Autobiography of Malcolm X, Huckleberry Finn,* and *Soul on Ice* is a sampling of three books in Bernie's syllabus. I am intrigued. All told, that makes 18 units for this quarter, more than a full time load. I am now off of probation after my previous well performing quarter when I bounced back with 3 A's and a D. The D was in "flunk proof geology," and I was lucky to get that D, given my lack of comprehension and effort. "Flunk proof" meant you got a D just for showing up. I was up to that. Last quarter's A's were in areas that I liked or really loved. Intro Philosophy, Comp Lit and Western Civ 1914-present. My interest and efforts got me over the 2 point probation hump to 2.14. I was rollin', again. So now, once more, I thought, "All my troubles are over."

There were, however, other larger social forces crashing over the OSU campus that I was destined to play a part in. The two significant national issues in the headlines that month in the consciousness of the likes of me and my ilk were the New Haven trial of Bobby Seale and Erica Huggins, two Black Panthers on trial for inciting a riot at the DNC in Chicago, and the expanding Vietnam war, soon to be widening into Cambodia.

Upon return to Columbus, my daily routine and drill consisted of classes in the morning and early afternoon, and hitting the Student Union. This groove started towards the end of February of last quarter when I met George Bohichick of the Third World Solidarity Committee. With the beginning of spring quarter, I started hanging out at his table every day for an hour. We discussed the world events and actions the committee planned to protest military spending on campus via R.O.T.C and the planned expulsion, now with hopes of reinstatement, of the Black students who took over the administration building two springs ago. At these meetings, besides George, his girlfriend Sara, and a few others, there was a guy named John Alloway. He was a little older than I, 26 to be exact, and a VietNam vet, it turns out, who had been in the Air Force dropping bombs from fighter planes. He graduated from OSU the previous spring in social work and was now working at CYO, the Columbus Youth organization, where delinquent kids were sentenced, Juvenile Hall, as it's sometimes called in other parts of the country. Alloway had a hard edge about him that was appealing to me. He always wore Ray Bans and was a cool customer, not easily flustered. Seemed clear headed, calm and goal oriented. I gravitated toward him as well as George. In some ways, more to Alloway because he was less theoretical in his mind set and more action oriented. He wanted to do things that would make an impact on the administration at OSU. Bohechik did too, but he liked dressing it up in Maoist lingo or Marxist rhetoric which I was sort of interested in, but to be honest, I preferred the "action" part of direct action better. These guys and their respective groups began to occupy increasing amounts of my time. Not that I skipped classes, which I was starting to enjoy, not that I stopped hanging around with my dorm mates, and not that I stopped hunting for women which was an ever present preoccupation wherever I was, it's just that my focus was starting to widen. To be honest, it felt good. And I was hellbent on doing it all.

On the relationship front, I hadn't been with anyone seriously since Marla broke up with me in June of last year and psychologically I could say, in full sincerity, that I was over her. It took me 9 months. The first six were brutal. Depressed, withdrawn, lethargic, unmotivated, and disinterested in school with 3 F's and a C fall quarter for my trouble. No dating. Bupkus. Winter quarter, better grades in part because I was under the gun from Dad and on academic probation from the school. I "arose from (my) pastoral torpor" (see scene from the 1963 movie *Tom Jones* where Tom's sister admonishes him for his laziness observing Tom early in the morning, drunk and lying about in a pig sty with two buxom women), got decent grades and began to get out and about socially with my chums and started looking, and to some extent finding, some women to date.

But now it's week one of spring quarter on a Sunday night and I am in my dorm room with Curt, Jamie and Mike du Brûl, my tolerant roommate, sitting on my bed listening to Neil Young's *Everybody knows this is Nowhere* album on my record player. I have just discovered Neil Young's first two albums and am completely "into" them. The song *Down by the River* with Neil's machine gun guitar sound is blasting when I get a knock on the door from one of the yokels on the floor telling me some girl wants to talk to me on the pay phone. I have no clue. I automatically go through my mental rolodex of possibilities on my walk to the hall phone. Could it be somebody from here or could it be somebody from home? I am drawing a blank because I've been out of touch with girls from home and am not really seeing anybody from here. I'm clueless. I put the receiver to my ear and it's a familiar, friendly sort of sexy lilt.

"Hi, Arnie. Remember me?" My heart is pumping a mile a minute. Damn right I know who it is. I struggle to regain my bearings.

"Jesus. Hi," I say back," how'd you get my number?"

"Your mom gave it to me when I was home on spring break," the voice replies. It is Marla's. "How are you?" Marla asks imploringly.

"Pretty good," says I, confidently but with just a hint of hesitation and caution. "You?"

"Good," she says. "I'm at Hood College here in Frederick, Maryland finishing my freshman year. It's nice here. Only, it's all girls. Oh. Yeah, classes are okay," she continues.

"Mm," I murmur, trying to play it close to the vest.

"I missed you, Arnie," she blurts out, getting right to the point. "Are you okay?" "Absolutely," without missing a beat, "Couldn't be better. School's cool. I like the

kids here, actually. I think I prefer them to the kids in New Rochelle, if you want to know the truth."

"Are you seeing anyone? "

"Why?" I ask.

"It's just that I've been thinking about you a lot and missing you and wanted to call and say 'hi.'"

"Are you all right?" I reply now with sincerity, starting to feel some concern for her.

"Yeah," she says. "Everything is alright." Then hesitating for a few seconds, she goes into it. "My boyfriend and I just broke up. We met last summer at camp. We were both camp counselors. He's graduating from Duke this spring."

"Oh," I stammered in return, feeling nervous, excited, scared.

"Anyway," she went on, "I just find myself thinking about you a lot and missing you so I thought I would call. "

"Well," I say, "to tell you the truth, I spent the first six months since we broke up last June pretty bummed out. I couldn't get much going at school or socially. Spent most of my time listening to Bob Dylan records and getting loaded. By winter quarter in January, I started getting my act together."

"Are you seeing anybody, Arnie?" Marla cutting through my verbiage.

"Why?" I ask, tinged with a little anger.

"I don't know," she says imploringly.

"Nothing serious," I say.

"Why?" I come back, somewhat defensively.

"It would be nice to see you again," Marla mutters. I'm excited, scared, wary but flattered.

"Maybe we should start talking over the phone again and see how it goes. How about that?" Marla agrees, and I sense her mood suddenly brightening.

"Let's speak every week. And if things still feel good, maybe we'll get together this spring."

"I'd like that. Thanks for calling. So, I will speak to you in a week." I get off the phone and I think to myself. Fuck. For the first time in 9 months, I'm feeling happy. I'm feeling good and thinking that I am feeling good and thinking how good it feels to feel good and at that very second she calls me. What the fuck? What kind of cosmic fucking joke is this? Just when things are starting to feel good again. All these Rick Blaine, Casablanca-like images of Bogey in his café after hours with a bottle of scotch getting loaded bombard my brain as I envision Bogey's reaction to the return of Ingrid Bergman (Ilsa Laszlo) and her husband, Victor Laszlo after they enter Rick's. "They grab Ugarte and then she walks in. Well that's the way it goes. One out, one in." That's how I'm feeling, putting a completely romantic, cinematic spin on it. I'm nervous, expectant and excited. Luckily, spring events to come provide plenty of other fish to fry as a direction and a distraction.

Distractions aplenty. Basically, it's a four prong, activity central mode of operations. School, dorm life, political activism with the Third World Solidarity Committee and my forays and inquiries on the hustings going solo, still looking for women. I think my mood is somewhere between confident and grandiose. Exuberant. "Fuckin' A" is all I got to say. Dead in the water from June to December. Comin' back to life, January to March. High energy. Feeling REALLY good. Outgoing, meeting a shitload of people, sleeping more erratically. But loving my classes: Intro Psych, Education, 19th Century Philosophy, Black History. Reading a lot of cool stuff, like I mentioned, *Huckleberry Finn, Soul on Ice, Electric Kool Aid Acid Test*, and reading Kant, Hegel, Nietzsche, Kierkegaard, W.E. de Bois, Richard Wright, James Baldwin, Langston Hughes and Malcolm X. A very stimulating quarter and very relevant to my political interests. And that's only a small part of it.

Back in the dorms, Curt, Jamie and Tom are continuing to get high a lot and all of them are now paired up with women. Jamie, since the end of fall quarter, Curt, more recently with a move on a quiet Cambridge, Ohio girl he'd been eyeing in the cafeteria, and Tom reuniting with his girlfriend from the previous year, Debbie from Bay Village, a westside Cleveland suburb. They are fairly occupied in their duos and the foursome that we had in fall and winter, mostly just the guys, diminishes somewhat. It matters a bit to me, but actually most of my time is consumed with school, politics and looking for women. I also continue to meet a lot of different guys as well. Mostly political activist types. In addition to George Bohichick and John Alloway, I just met another unaffiliated radical type, Paul Ricciardo, who is really the most like me, less organizationally inclined, more anarchic and freewheeling, less ideological but ideologically engaged and knowledgeable nonetheless. He's definitely critical of the liberal establishment, but not completely alienated from it. We are the non-Marxist, Marxist leaning, liberalish, libertarian, libertine left, whatever that is. We're probably fairly sexist but starting to get an earful from women from the burgeoning women's movement, now about two years old, officially. Paul and I have been hanging out on a regular basis at the Union after my daily communiqués and planning meetings with the Third World Group that also meets at the Union every day at 3 after classes. By 4:30, Paul and I hit the streets, shooting the shit and "hunting." Sometimes finding. And by the end of the day, during the week, I go back to the dorm and gladly hit the books. It's a pleasure because they are courses I'm truly interested in. In true underachiever style, I'm focused in classes but don't study on my own. I'm completely into it while I'm in class. Thinking about it in retrospect, I was probably pretty ADHD on top of this undiagnosed bipolar thing. Whatever, back then it was "all good," as I didn't feel that there was anything wrong with me. High on life.

That Sunday, Marla calls again at our planned 8 pm time. The mutual tone, deeper, more romantic, more filled with longing. I am in the grips of it. But it only lasts as long as the phone call, because the next day, while still thinking about her a lot, missing her, wanting her, I am doing that Stephen Stills thing, "If you can't be with the one you love, honey, love the one you're with." It just so happened that that song was popular around then, coming in handy as a momentary theme song.

It's now the middle of April and the events are getting fuzzy because things are moving fast and furious. It feels as if everything is happening all at once. And I mean everything. So I'm going to try and slow it down and describe things one by one so as to give you a blow by blow account.

CHAPTER 12

I Wanna Take You Higher

Sunday night at 8 pm. I'm perched next to the pay phone, waiting for the ring. Ah, here it is. She's right on time.

" Hi, Marl."

" Hi, Arn. Um, I'm kind of tired. It's been a long week. How are ---- you?"

"All right, pretty good. Things are kind of heating up around here. Really, kinda cool. I'm into it."

"Huh. Is everything ok? You're not talking about the peace movement stuff, are you?"

"I am. Yeah, There's a lot goin' on. Next week there are plans for some marches down High Street to the Capital. And next week we're getting ready for a major action at OSU to oppose the corporate recruiters coming to campus. Actually, I better watch what I'm sayin' cuz the phone could be bugged."

"Jesus, Arnie. Sounds scary, crazy. Makes me a little worried."

"No. Nothin' to worry about. It's alright. It'll be all peaceful and stuff. Plus, there's a lot of people involved so I'm not one of the main organizers. It only takes up some of my time anyway. You know, the rest of the time I'm in class and I've got really interesting and fun classes for a change this quarter. Black Studies, teaching American culture in school. You know, like we're reading *Huckleberry Finn* and *Malcolm X* and then my complete favorite course, 19th Century Philosophy."

"God, Arnie. You always were so intellectual. I forgot that about you. I'm just trying to get through freshmen reqs. You know, freshman English blah blah blah. Anyway, I miss you Arnie, I can't wait to see you. Let's try to get together soon."

"Maybe I'll come down to see you at your school for a weekend or something. I'll borrow a car. I don't know. I'll figure something out. How are your roommates treating you?"

"Really great. Love my roommate. She's from the South, did I tell you? Yeah, like around Richmond. The only thing wrong with this school, aside from the fact that there are no boys, is that it's mostly White kids. Feels so weird after New Rochelle and all the different types of kids we used to hang out with, you know?"

"Yeah, it probably would. OSU isn't like that but definitely not as many Blacks on campus percentage wise as we had at New Rochelle High. It seems weird, actually. So many yahoos. You know what I mean. Farm kids."

"Yeah. What we have is a bunch of Southern belles, mixed in with some New York Jews. How do you like that combination?"

"Well, you definitely go to a different kind of place. Did you know we got 45,000 undergraduates here? It takes forever to walk across the campus. Too big. But I'm finally starting to meet some interesting people, finally. Anyways, what do you hear from the kids at home? Nancy, Lisa, Becky?"

"I speak with them all the time. Nancy and Lisa both have boyfriends up in Boston and you know Becky's close to me at American in DC. She's just dating a lot of guys. I love those guys. I miss them a lot. I'm just glad that I love my roommate, too. Otherwise, I could be pretty lonely, I think. I mean, the girls here are nice and all but you know Nancy and Lisa and Becky and me. We're like sisters. No one is as close to me as they are. What about you? Who do you hear from?"

"Actually, like I was telling you last week, I saw Mark and Ricky at a party back in March at my house. I saw Ricky and Mac up in Boston during spring break. And I think I told you, I saw Ronnie last spring at Ohio U where he goes. Plus, I think you know Lonnie and Macie both go to OSU, although I never see them. He's into the frat thing, if you know what I mean. He's got that shag haircut. I'm finding it hard to relate. And Macie, we just hardly ever bump into each other. There's a lot of fuckin' people here. But I can't wait to see you. It's good to talk to you but I think I gotta hit the sack soon cuz I gotta write a paper tomorrow and I haven't finished the reading. W. E. B. Du Bois, *Poor Folk*. I gotta write a reaction paper on it and talk about its relevance to what's happening today with the Civil Rights movement, Black power, etc. I love this shit. Feels so alive."

"God, Arnie. I wish I felt so turned on by my classes. I mean they're all right and all and I am doing pretty well, but it's just school. I don't know. I wish there was something I was learning or doing that I felt as excited about as you seem to be."

"Ah, you'll find it. Who knows. We'll talk soon. Next Sunday."

"Bye, Arnie. I love you."

"Yeah, me too."

I am exhausted all of a sudden. I wonder if it has to do with the emotional energy I'm expending from starting to get my hopes up about Marla. Not sure, but regardless, it's just too bad. I gotta do some reading. I march into my room, pick up Du Bois and head back into the study lounge, sort of bleary eyed. There are a couple of people there when I arrive. Marquis Jones and another Black guy who I am less familiar with. Oh yeah, he's that guy from the floor below us, another Panther I think. Marquis so much as affirms this. They're reading from *These Choking Times*, an underground Black newspaper, militant in outlook. They nod to me as I walk in. I try to avert my gaze and not listen to their conversation and succeed in getting into my books early 20th century screed. It's fascinating to hear Du Bois talk about "second speech," the way Blacks develop two languages, one for White ears and one for when they're alone with each other. It's been developed for survival purposes and turned into a fine art over the 350 years that Blacks have been here through, slavery, emancipation, reconstruction, Jim Crow and Martin Luther King. I sense some leeriness toward me coming from Marquis Jones who hangs with me socially, picking up women, playing basketball, shooting the shit. But there's a level between us where the window comes down. I wonder if it's a religious thing, like he's Christian and I am Jewish. Or maybe it's because I come from more money, upper middle class and he's working class, lower middle class. But possibly it has different and deeper roots. Maybe it's like Du Bois says, the gap is historical, cultural, ethnic, racial and situational. I don't know. I don't care. I do care but I try not to let on to him, or more importantly to myself. It does feel limiting, all this pretending and a bit alienating, too. But then I feel alienated from most, if not everybody I know at some level. It's just a question of at which level we're talking about, I guess. I try to pretend Marquis and his friend

Sammy are not there and pretty soon I'm in Du Boisland pretty deep. I like it here. I can forget who and where I am when I'm inside books.

I say to Marquis after an hour of being in the study lounge, that there is going to be a rally tomorrow on the Oval to protest the war and the campus involvement with war research. I tell him that my group, Third World Solidarity Committee, is making active efforts to hook up with and coordinate with his group, Black Student Union Activists and that we're all gonna try to put out a common statement expressing our outrage about the mockery of justice going on in New Haven with the Bobby Seale, Erica Huggins case. He nods, quizzically, not knowing these things as he hasn't been going to meetings in the last week, but rather spending his time getting stoned, doing school work, and the usual looking for pussy shit. He is very neutral and flat with me as is his Black friend Sammy, who wouldn't want to appear like an Oreo. I play along on the outside, even though it feels crappy on the inside. Now around 11:30 pm, I am tired and bid my adieu.

Monday April 12– Sunday April 18

Things are heating up with the political stuff on campus, yet here I am sitting in 19th Century Philosophy this afternoon. It's weird. Most of the students in the class are philosophy majors and I'm exploring whether to become a philosophy major as well. I thought I was gonna major in psychology when I got here last year but the psych department sucks. It's rats. Experimental and behavioral. Not what I'm into. I loved my Intro Philosophy class with professor Foxx. Plato, Descartes, Hume, Kant, John Stuart Mill, Nietzsche. I loved it. All the big ideas and issues in the history of western civilization.

The rational vs. the irrational, free will vs. determinism, notions of the good, virtuous life, the mind /matter problem. All the things I think about anyway. Might as well find out what the heavy hitters have to say. Definitely, more inclined towards philosophy at this point than psych. The philosophy teacher is a 5th year grad student himself, focused, and impassioned. In his class we're covering Kant, Hegel, Fichte, Kierkegaard, Schopenhauer, Nietzsche and Bradley. A little William James, the American pragmatist, thrown in for good measure. I am so into it. Only trouble is I am into it in the class, listening with rapt attention. But I can only make token efforts at reading, having trouble concentrating at the dorm and really struggling to get any papers written. My typing sucks and I can't seem to get myself slowed down enough mentally to get the papers out. Besides, the shit going on on campus is far more exciting and relevant, not to mention distracting. Today, I'm making my rounds at the Union, meeting with my Third World Solidarity Committee friends, George and his cronies. Later, I meet up with Paul for some more political conversation and chick chasing. Later tonight around 9, after I supposedly get my work done after dinner, and am back in room 812 with my dorm mates, I plan to get together with my main man John "Counter" Alloway. He gets his nickname because, as an anarchist, he is against everything organized on any permanent basis. We meet and soon he and some of his mates talk me into doing some guerilla theater for when the corporate and government recruiters come to campus next week. It's a full day. I hope I have the energy and focus to get it all done. I run through the schedule in my head. It is:

2:00–3:00 pm: 19th Century Philosophy
3:00–4:00 pm: Third World Solidarity Committee

4:00–5:00 pm: Hang out with Paul Ricciardo
5:00–9:00 pm: dorm, hang out, study, eat
9:00–11:00 pm: guerilla theater with John Alloway and stay over at his place.

That's my Monday. Then, my Tuesday will be:

10:00–11:00 am: Psychology 101
1:00–2:00 pm: Black Studies with Greg Thomas
3:00–4:00pm: Third World Solidarity Meeting
4:30 pm: Hang out with Paul Riccardo
5:30–7:00 pm: hang out at the dorm, study, eat
7:00–10:00 pm: Contemporary Topics in Education with Bernie Mehl

Wednesday: same as Monday
Thursday: same as Tuesday

It's an ambitious agenda, I realize, but I'm trying to stay on top of my studies, reading, attending classes, and going to my three regular political meetings. One official, the Neo-Leninist Third World crew, one anarchist, the Alloway guerilla theater group, and finally, my little burgeoning affinity group that I have developed all by my lonesome, with Paul and a smattering of others. That's not all. I also need to maintain my ties with my buds from Steeb, too. They're important to me as well. Then, there's getting a good night's sleep, eating decently. All that shit. It's a lot to have to keep together. But what the hay. I'm 20 and luckily have a shitload of energy. Anyways, that's my schedule for my week. It doesn't even cover my forays and inquiries with meeting women, which is ongoing, and everywhere I go on some level. Just not the major focus of my activities per se.

Recapitulating the week to bring it into sharper focus, politically there are numerous petitions and demands starting to circulate on campus connected to a variety of issues:

1. The Black Student Union regarding the expulsion of the Black students the previous year and the demand for their immediate reinstatement into the university.
2. Corporate and military recruitment.
3. The creation of ethnic studies departments.

This is the local angle connected to a larger set of national protests happening on many campuses that has been in existence since 1964 with the free speech movement, anti-war teach-ins, civil rights marches, sit-ins and administration building takeovers at Columbia, Wisconsin, Harvard and Cornell. Berkeley, of course, the harbinger of it all, continues to push the administration and town folks, most recently with the People's Park incident, when UC Berkeley tried to take over a park used by the community for use as student housing. I am staying abreast of all these events through my readings which now include *Ramparts Magazine* and the underground newspapers that have emerged here, now even at Ohio State. In the not too recent past, OSU has had a reputation for serious conservative, mainstream, frat rat, somewhat reactionary football, Woody Hayesish, militaristic, patriotic thinking. We activists are very much swimming upstream. There's turbulence in the air, and that turbulence is permeating the slow-to-change environs of Ohio in general and Columbus in particular. You can feel it. It's everywhere and now it's here. Even though it's now year 7 since the Free Speech Movement and the Beatles, this change thing, even now at OSU, bastion of conservatism, in April 1970, has finally arrived.

My group, the Third Worlders, are meeting with the Black activists and a newly formed assemblage called the Ad Hoc Group run by a poli sci grad student, Lorraine Cohen, who is trying to coordinate with the Black Student Union people and Third World Solidarity group to stage a demonstration. There are other groups involved as well. They are the longer established anti-war groups, the New Mobilization Committee and the Moratorium Committee, tending toward the liberal in outlook. These are the people who, on a national level, brought us the Moratorium just seven months ago in Washington on November 15, which I attended with my buddy, Tom. The Mobilization group has been around even longer, since the Pentagon March of October 1967, which Norman Mailer wrote about in *Armies of the Night*, which I haven't read yet.

Basically, there are now six groups involved. The three liberal groups also include the NAACP, probably the oldest of all the groups, plus the New Mobilization Committee (New Mobe), and the Moratorium Committee. The three that I am most connected with are considered more radical: Afro-Am, (the Black studies, Black representation et. al. group, which presented the admin group with 19 non-negotiable demands), my group, The Third World Solidarity Committee, which wants all involvement with companies connected to the VietNam war effort eliminated, as well as ROTC, and an end to recruiting by these companies, and finally Lorraine Cohen's ad hoc group. This ad hoc group consists of grad students, students in the leadership role, who are increasingly seeing themselves as the negotiating arm of all the other five groups. So, now things are moving beyond the meeting level into plans for actions.

On the night of April 13th, I go over to John Alloway's house on 16th Avenue between Indianola and Summit above High Street. He lives in a house called "Big Red." Yes, it is a red house, a play on The Band's first album, *Music from Big Pink*. Also, "Big Red" is not to be confused with "Big Green," another house on 15th Avenue, that houses another band of lefty communards. These people are less affiliated with organized groups, but equally involved. At Alloway's house, the dope is flowing liberally and the discussion with four other of his mates and me centers around a plan to disrupt the "Recruitment '70" campaign being held at the Student Union, featuring about 60 corporations and government agencies on campus to recruit students for jobs. These firms include, but are not limited to, Dow Chemical, the FBI, the CIA and others, many of whom have ties to the Defense Department, and are directly or indirectly tied to the Nixon war effort in VietNam. The plan is for the 6 of us to get dressed in black monk-like robes, wear red bandanas and paint our faces half black and half white, and carry a black casket with us into the ballroom where the recruiters will be presenting their wares. On this casket will be the head of a dead pig bought from a butcher's shop. Upon entering the hall, we will lead the procession protesting the "Recruitment '70" assemblages, circle the entire hall silently and solemnly, pig's head covered by black cotton fabric and stop in front of the CIA booth. We will then remove the black covering, and present the pig to the recruiters, laying it just to the right of the CIA table. When it's obvious to us that the CIA recruiters have seen the pig, we will pick up the casket and leave the hall. This is our plan scheduled for Wednesday, April 15.

At noon, the six of us guerilla theater actors, black robes and all, begin to execute the plan. Following a small demonstration on the Oval, we march solemnly to the Union. Our design works perfectly except for one thing. As soon as we deliver the pig to the CIA pavilion and exit the hall, leaving the CIA recruiters in shocked rage, a ruckus breaks out. It detonates inside the hall where the recruiters are stationed as the campus pigs, pun intended, rush into the hall and arrest sixteen students. My group gets off scot-free. Cynically viewed, albeit unintended, one could say that this is a classic hit and run job. But the die is cast. The point of no return has been reached. First, there are the already pissed off Black students, and now with these new arrests, a bunch of riled up White students as well. The arrests ensured this. Another rally is scheduled for the following Wednesday to protest the arrests of the students at "Recruitment '70" and to restate the Afro Am Committee's set of demands that still have not been responded to by the OSU Administration. The tension level continues to escalate.

Meanwhile, this weekend there's a rock concert scheduled on the campus Oval featuring lots of rock bands, all local, such as Ronnie and the Hemorrhoids and Hieronymus Bosch. It's Sunday and the Oval is jammed with probably a few thousand students on blankets, sitting together stoned or drunk, in good spirits. The campus cops are a minimal presence. They seem to want to let sleeping dogs lie given the superheated atmosphere of the campus. The event provides a good opportunity for the students to let off steam. A splendid time is had by all.

I'm there with my dorm mates and run into Barbara and Ronnie, girlfriend, friends I know from the February 21st Committee. My Oval tribe. They're all living in apartments now, so I see them less than when we were in dorms, eating in the same commons. So running into them and Hal and Jed, my first bonafide friends, and my mates from Steeb Hall, feels like old home week, like seeing family. People who I lucked upon. These are people I found through serendipity and picked because of our shared values, outlooks and probably backgrounds, different from the guys in the dorms who came from less familiar upbringings, in particular the guys from freshman year, Mike, Italian working class, Joe, Polish working class and Marquis, Black working class. The differences are probably some of what I like about these people but with Hal, Barb and Rachel, the similarities are probably what draws me. Analyzing it in my head, after I run into them on the Oval, I wonder if all these folks I've been hooking up with constitute the external manifestation of who I am trying to become or becoming. I certainly don't think that way about them very often. Mostly, they just seem like fun and interesting people to hang out with. People that I think will have my back in a pinch. My definition of friends.

The Sunday concert is fun and fun-wise, the quarter is shaping up to be a more exciting and adventurous time than I can ever remember. The only downside is that I am not sleeping so well. I take to wearing my red bandana from the Alloway pig casket caper every day with a Star of David on it, and wear it proudly. And on campus the day of the concert, while sitting with either my dorm mates or the Oval crew seated not too far away, I leaf through my paper back of Che Guevara's *On Guerilla Warfare.* Don't laugh. Maybe I'm a little bit deluded and grandiose. I read it with serious intent and ardor as if I believe that the situation in America, Cuba or South America is similar or the same. I've also got Regis Debray's *Revolution in the Revolution* in my hands, thanks to the Alloway influence. Because of the personal relationship I am developing with him, he is more instrumental in my radicalization than the Third World Committee who seems more analytical, more ideological, more rigid and less creatively action oriented. I mean they are activists, too but less yippieish. More serious, a little duller. I clearly prefer being around

Alloway and his crew. I feel much less on guard and worried about saying the wrong thing. More relaxed.

On the personal front, tonight I speak with Marla, as is our routine, and the call goes well, again, to my increasing comfort and hopefulness. She listens with interest, amusement, but some alarm to my adventures and activities of the previous week. In contrast, her week sounds humdrum to her and to me, quite frankly, although I do not say so to her. I think she is a little jealous of what is going on at OSU, but also expresses concern about its potential to get out of control as so many campuses have in the previous 5 years or so. She expresses concern for my safety. I tell her not to worry but underneath I think I like her expressions of concern for me. This feeling seeps into my consciousness and I half let it in. It feels like we are getting closer each Sunday in our weekly talks, even though we've had only four conversations. It feels as though our direction is moving toward meeting again and maybe getting back together, which fills me with a kind of expectant excitement.

While all this is true, it doesn't stop me from being "on the case" during the week. I am hedging my bets. Although I am feeling unusually friendly and outgoing, I'm not having any luck scoring, but I am meeting some really nice women. One is named Ronnie Lovler, who drives a Honda 50 motorbike and works as a journalist for *The Ohio State Lantern*, the school newspaper. She is cool, open, fun, a senior journalism major, obviously. We met at the Union and I take to hanging out with her on her journalism reporting forays. She is hot, but I think she views me more as a younger brother. She walks around braless. Not that unusual for artsy, political and hippie types but she has nice ones, too. She is covering both the political student activities and the planned events of the 100th anniversary of the university's founding in 1870. She alternates assignments. Ronnie has a lot of energy and verve and likes to drink, party, get stoned but she still has focus left over to get her assignments in before the deadline. I admire her capacity to maintain that balance. It is not something I have been able to do very well. And I wonder how she and so many other people I know and admire are successful at maintaining that balance.

Now the political things move into a crucial phase which will last for about six weeks starting with Wednesday, April 22, Lenin's 100th birthday and the first Earth Day. Both holidays are being celebrated, albeit by different groups on campus. The more liberal groups salute Earth Day with a far larger demonstration, while the TWSC committee tweak the occasion into a smaller but more vehement demonstration focused on the continued intransigence of the OSU administration toward the demands of the Afro Am and Third World Solidarity Committee. Representatives from the three radical groups, George Bohichik, Lorraine Cohen, ad hoc and Michael White, who later becomes the mayor of Cleveland, all speak at the rally expressing their indignation at the admin's recalcitrance regarding student demands. Speeches implying the intention of further actions are hinted at by the speakers. Following the demonstrations, the three main speakers and various reps from the groups go into the Union to discuss strategies for what to do if the admin's lack of action continues. Discussions about a student strike begin and the consensus of the three groups is to give the administration until Monday the 27th to respond. If they do not, then a strike will begin on Wednesday April 29th, no ifs, ands or buts.

By this time, I am hitting at best, 60 percent of my classes, and am not alone in being AWOL. It's too bad because I am enjoying my classes when I go, and the readings when I do them. But my level of distraction is too high and I'm too caught up in the ongoing political drama to slow my mind down long enough to shift gears and get back into my academics. Life at 20. Sleeping irregularly as well. In retrospect, one could say I was manic or hypomanic. I seem to cycle seasonally. Fall: down. Winter: more neutral. Spring: high. I am high. And I like it. And I'm not on any meds either and haven't been taking them with any regularity since coming to OSU, despite two brief hospitalizations and prescriptions for Haldol and Stelazine. Whatever. I just won't take them. I don't like how they make me feel. They zonk me out when they get into my system and I have zero patience for that. So I have decided to go it alone. Just me and my biochemistry. Leuchter, my psychiatrist since June of '69, is now seeing me individually as the group therapy he enrolls me in turns out to be a bust. I miss half the sessions, deliberately oversleeping and even though my old man is being charged for them, it doesn't seem to matter to me. They were on a Saturday morning, which didn't help and I got little out of them when I was there. I acted as more of an observer. So, in my individual sessions with Leuchter, I lie to him about the meds situation even though I know he is an advocate. I think, "Fuck it. I don't need his heavy authority trip, fucking fascist, Nazi pig that he is." The man fought with the Nazis in World War II. That's right, he did even though he was a Catholic and Hitler was not a fan of them either. He told me, his father pushed him into it and he only did it as a survival measure. But, it gave me ammo to not listen to this guy as if I needed any reason or reasons to rebel. My rebellion is in full swing and has been going on for 7 years and is not going to stop anytime soon as far as I am concerned. All those drugs did was make me feel like a slug, lifeless, dead. The trade off of so-called sanity as the powers that be defined it was not a good one and I am not willing or ready to make that devil's bargain. I'm taking my chances with my psyche or biochemistry, or whatever you wanna call it, particularly in the spring when I feel so energized and alive.

I digress. Expressions of tangential thinking perhaps or flight of ideas maybe. I don't give a shit. Still rebelling? Still angry? Who cares? Anyway, back to the story.

We're now into Thursday and Friday of the week of April 20- 27. Bohichik and I and the Third World Solidarity Committee, ten or fifteen of us altogether, are meeting regularly for a planning strategy for the possible upcoming strike. Lorraine Cohen of the Ad Hoc committee comes by on Friday evening to tell us that she plans to meet with various grad student reps of various social science, humanities and arts departments to assess and get their assent on going out on strike if necessary. She tells us that there is a lot of sympathy and support for the students' position vis a vis the university and that particularly Philosophy, Political Science, Social Work, English and Sociology are taking the lead. At least the grad students. The faculty is another matter. They are staying sympathetic but not yet interested in going out on strike. Events are starting to coalesce. Lorraine is a charismatic, bright, energetic person who's doing a lot of formal organizing with both her department and other departments. She is trying to coordinate with TWSC and Afro Am and has become the hub of the movement on campus. She's very dynamic, at least to me. To others I think she can be grating. Not to me. I find her dynamic, charismatic and very smart.

The weekend is somewhat uneventful. It's really about waiting for an answer from the administration. Novice Fawcett, the university president, is meeting with his people to decide on a response. We are not optimistic. I think they want to feel like they are doing what they can within their bureaucratic framework and that it is and should be enough. Their idea of a rate of change is quite different from the rate of change desired by us students, to say the least. Maybe I'm putting a stereotypical spin on it but, this is the conservative Midwest and the administration really doesn't know what's hit them. They are used to docility and are angry at the insolence of the students and are not about to let some snot-nosed kids tell them how their university should be run.

I spend Saturday and Sunday over at "Big Red," Alloway's house, getting stoned and hanging out. It seems as though the rest of the university rank and file are starting to get into the act as back at the dorm, relatively apolitical types like Jamie, Tom and Curt are all getting revved, if not politicized. The demonstration on Monday should be big. Now switching gears to my love life.

Sunday night it's the usual phone call with Marla. Still good, still warm, feeling like all systems go. It's looking like we are headed towards getting back together. She's really not on my mind so much now with all that's happening on campus. Maybe that's a good thing, maintaining a little distance. I notice that it seems to increase desire on her part. And I like to be wanted. No correct that, I love to be wanted, especially now, especially from her but the anticipation of the next day's rally dominates my mental airwaves.

Monday, April 27

The verdict is in. The administration will not honor the requests of the students. They will take their requests under advisement for further review but they do not have the money to provide for the demands from Afro Am and they don't even respond to the demands of the Third World Solidarity Committee who are asking the university to divest themselves of involvement with companies involved in making arms for the VietNam war. It's clear as dirt. There are 1500 students on the Oval today to hear Lorraine Cohen's report to the crowd about the administration's actions, or inactions, I should say. The call is for a student strike by the leaders to begin Wednesday the 29th at noon. Students are encouraged to stay out of classes until there is some positive action from the administrators. At the rally, there are two other representatives who speak, Fred Green of the Black Student Union and a representative of the New Mobe committee who also speaks about the university's involvement in the war machine and our need to take steps. There is an atmosphere of exhilaration doused with anger as the crowd disperses. Let the games begin, I say.

CHAPTER 13

Time Has Come Today
Wednesday, April 29

The word has been put out. Around noon, groups of people begin massing in two locations: one, the main and largest crowd on the OSU Oval with placards, signs etc. The signs say such things as "On Strike, Shut It Down," "Join Us," and "End Support of the War Machine." It is where me and my dorm mates, including Tom, Curt Robinson, Jamie Olian and two Italian kids from Mayfield Heights in Cleveland, Sammy Albarico and Vinnie Pescalante are hanging together. A so-called affinity group as we so-called "rads" like to call it. We're all wearing red bandannas, and refer to ourselves as "The Red Bandana Brigade." We are all full of shit and caught up in the excitement, testosterone-fueled, authority-hating intensity of the moment. The other gathering location is at 11th and Neil Avenue on the west entrance of campus where a smaller but more militant crowd of students has formed. Around noon or twelve thirty, with few knowing how the decision is made, the campus gates are closed to the outside by the protesters. After closing the gates, the protesters march with picket signs mostly saying "Pigs Off Campus" around the closed gate. Paul Ricciardo, one of my mates is down there along with some SDS types. As soon as the gates shut, the crowd gears up for the campus and city "pigs" to arrive. Ten minutes later, the sirens start to blare as thirty or so city and state cop cars begin to descend on the scene. Getting out of their cars with bullhorns in tow, they bellow, "You have 2 minutes to disperse!" In reality, their version of 2 minutes is actually thirty seconds before they charge as Ralph Jordan, another picketer yells to Paul Ricciardo, "HEE-ERE THEY COME, " in an exclamatory, ironic and sing-songy tone. And come they do, with billy clubs, tear gas, everything but bullets. The crowd disperses, most escaping. Word gets around instantly. It's on. The pigs have reacted. Like a wildfire, a full fledged riot ensues from Neil Avenue to High street covering the OSU campus from west to east with most of the action centering on the central Oval area. Soon the place is a gray haze of smoke, with the acrid aroma of tear gas filling the air and dozens of students running with handkerchiefs shielding their eyes. The scene is chaotic. My Steeb Hall mates and I are with a huge crowd of demonstrators as the cops lob tear gas. Almost instinctively, the protestors are lobbing those canisters back at them in defiance. It's glorious and scary, but frankly more glorious than scary as the crowd of demonstrators creates an illusion of safety and protection.

The large number of angry students gives me and I suspect many of us, a sense of invulnerability. It's cops and robbers writ large. Out of the dorm windows, seemingly en masse and on cue, students are playing the Stones' "Street Fighting Man" as the riot continues. The red bandana brigade, Curt, Jamie, Sammy, Vinnie, Tom and me during a temporary lull from the cops and student game of "lob the tear gas canister," hit the center of the Oval. Everyone, the red bandanna brigade included, is shouting "On strike! Pigs off campus! On strike! Pigs off campus!" Momentarily isolated from the larger crowd, we of the brigade are suddenly confronted by a couple of muscular, blonde, jock fraternity types prototypical of the scene at OSU. This one particularly burly character confronts me because I am the one with the biggest mouth and he calls me a hippie, faggot, commie whose ass he's gonna kick. I, in my usual sensible way, jacked up as I am in the euphoria and carnival atmosphere of the riot, reply without hesitation, "Come on, motherfucker." As I had been previously taught by Sammy and Vinnie, who are more seasoned veterans, in a street fight, you always throw the first punch, as you may not get a second chance. You throw that punch to end it. I learned the first part but not the second. Immediately, after yelling, "Come on, mother fucker," to the frat rat who claimed he was gonna kick my ass, I threw a Floyd Patterson style left hook. The Floyd Patterson style left hook that had left Ingemar Johannson unconscious and won Patterson back his heavyweight title. There was only one problem here. Not being an experienced street fighter, in fact never having been in a street fight at all, I reverted to the play fighting mode of my career in the basement of my family's New Rochelle home growing up play fighting with my younger brother, Lew. So, I throw the left hook and as it is about to land on the bone just below his right eye horizontal to his ear, I inexplicably but not surprisingly, open my hand as if in a slap fight. The jock is as surprised as I am but before he can come back at me, Albarico cold cocks him from the side and knocks him down. Not waiting to assess the damage, the RBB is off.

We soon head to the scene of more furious action. This time it's the mayhem on High Street where cop cars are being burned, turned over and kids are pelting cop cars with stones and bricks. The RBB, of course, enters at full throttle where soon after we, I should say I, are confronted by another pillar of American society, another frat rat jock type who says to me, "You fuckin' prick. You have no respect for anything." This confrontation, notwithstanding the fact that High Street following the OSU-Michigan football game, a meaningful win for OSU, has been the scene of several postgame alcohol-fueled riots by the jock frat contingency, with damage to property much greater than anything we students have done, plus an increase in gross bodily harm including rape than any other time in OSU history. "That's okay," as Novice Fawcett, the OSU President resident said in the campus paper *The Lantern* the day after the game, "just a bunch of guys blowing off steam." But throw in a little politics, anti-war protest, military research on campus, underrepresentation of Blacks, women and minorities on campus, students, faculty and administrators, well that's another matter.

Anywho, this time the frat rat rushes me. I easily side step the guy being quick and all and this time I throw six left jabs in a row unchecked, not enough to knock him down but enough to stun him as we move on. This felt really good. Anger and hate has found a bonafide target with a human face. The endorphin rush is palpable. The crowd mayhem continues as the smell of tear-gas pervades High Street. Now the crowds are getting larger. Not just your basic hippie long hair and Black people in the streets but now with their frat houses getting hit by tear gas, the beginnings of jock rage towards the cops emerging as well. The rebellion widens. City and state cops are everywhere as the riot enters its fifth hour. Lots of arrests. In the hundreds. Luckily, the High Street area is loaded with alleys, so if one is familiar with the logistics it makes it relatively easy to escape the grasp of The Man. My mates and I avoid the cops as we weave back and forth through the alleys then back onto High Street where the main center of riot action is, all the time picking up bricks or rocks and periodically hurling them at cop cars being careful not to aim them at cops themselves. I'm juiced and not afraid to be provocative. I pick up a softball from the alley. We're maybe about ten feet from the city and state pigs who have started to create a barricade on High and 16th. Momentarily separated from Curt, Jamie and the rest of them, I take the softball and roll it toward the pigs, yelling as I'm rolling, "This is a bomb," while off in the distance I vaguely hear Jamie whispering something to Curt. "Holy shit. Did you see what that crazy Arnie just did?" In the next instant, the cops, taking my verbal threat seriously, run to the back of the barricade another 10-12 feet to evade the "Molotov cocktail bomb / softball." God this is fun. A carnival atmosphere. Jamie and Curt cannot believe their eyes and ears. "That crazy motherfucker could have got us all killed." We then split en masse. Now Curt and Jamie, clearly spooked by what I have done, not to mention my state of mind, keep their distance from me and go off by themselves. But I'm so amped up, I don't notice their reaction nor do I think I've done anything crazy. At all.

By 8 pm, with the sun starting to go down and darkness coming upon us, the RBB crew are exhausted. Eyes reddened, depleted from all the cop dodging and brick throwing, Vince, Sammy, Curt and Jamie make their way back to Steeb Hall without me as I head through the alley to "Big Red."

As my Steeb Hall mates slither into the dorm lobby, they watch in disbelief as the events of a few minutes ago are aired on the local tv station. Actually, not just the local Columbus station, but the CBS evening national news with Walter Cronkite at the helm. Jamie and Curt are freaked and worried...for me. They decide that I'm really fucking nuts and dangerously unstable and know I haven't been taking my meds, because I confided to them about it. Having been regaled by tales of my Nazi doctor, they go to the Columbus

Yellow Pages and find my shrink's name and number. There is only one German sounding one in the Yellow Pages and they call him. They inform Leuchter that they have been with me today during the riots and that I've done about as stupid and crazy a thing as they have ever seen. They believe correctly that I've stopped taking my Stelazine. Dr. Leuchter is taken aback by this news as he is under the impression that I have been. Leuchter leaves a message for me at the dorm lobby but I will not pick up that message for three days as it's that long before I check my mailslot. In the meantime, unaware of my Steeb mates' goings on, I am bobbing and weaving away from the cops through the Columbus alleys, the great escape hatch. Finally, as the sun starts going down around 8pm, I arrive at "Big Red" where my affinity group and guerilla theatre mate, John Alloway, lives.

Jamie:

"Fucking Arnie. That guy's a fucking lunatic. I mean he's a great guy and shit but his judgment is minimal to none. Can't believe what he did today with that fucking softball. Could have got himself and a bunch of us who were near him killed. What the fuck is the matter with this guy? Fucking crazy asshole. Scared the shit out of me. Curt and I, once we got away from the mob, decided Arnie is completely unhinged. I know he's not taking his Thorazine or whatever it's called. Not that that guy doesn't have a whole shitload of them. Sure, he's not taking them. We got so worried that something terrible was gonna happen that I decided to get a hold of his shrink, the guy with the German sounding name that Arnie makes fun of. Oh yeah, Leuchter. That's it. So I go into the Columbus phone book and find the shrink's number. Left a message with his secretary, saying that Arnie is doing some self destructive shit and could get himself killed. The shrink called me back in ten minutes, alarmed at my message and said he would leave a message for Arnie to get in touch with him, which relieved me some. Look, what's going on here is fucking exciting and scary. And dangerous as hell. I'm gonna try to be more careful. Cops have guns. We don't. That crazy motherfucker.

Arnie:

A great party is happening. "Big Red" has balconies great for viewing the action. I put on "Let it Be," "Let it Bleed" and "Bridge Over Troubled Waters" in consecutive order as the distant noise of the riots, the whistle of tear gas canisters and the blare of cop cars pierces the night air. I light up a j and take it in with the euphoria of someone who feels he has had a part to play catalyzing the "all hell breaking loose of the day's events." It's cathartic. Feels productive. For too long, the powers that be, content in their lazy hegemony, have set the rules of the game. Now the freaks, losers, outsiders, minorities, will be vindicated. From here on, there will be fairer representation of Blacks, women and minorities in important campus decision making. A message has been sent about the university's blasé attitude toward war and weapons research. The lazy Midwestern, football soaked, 3.2 drinking apathy days are over. Or so I think. Or so we all think. Good fucking riddance.

The blare of "Street Fighting Man" by the Stones, "Time Has Come Today" by the Chambers Brothers, and "No Time" by the Guess Who is heard from apartment and dorm windows. The atmosphere is festive but not without a touch of danger, rage in general, but not a lot of fear emanating from this reporter. But that's part of the problem. I move towards the danger and action. If I were smart and sensible, I would move away from the potential violence or actual violence. But I am strangely and powerfully attracted to it, like a moth to a flame. This is how it feels. Like a potent opiate. The closer to the danger and violence I come, the calmer I feel. Certainly, very alive, but also strangely peaceful. Sort of like the paradoxical "Kill For Peace" slogan, only slightly less extreme. Instead the feeling is to throw bricks for peace. To be honest, if I slowed down enough from my manic non-stop moving and talking, and stepped back from the situation which I was not wont to do, nor did I, for the entire week of rioting to come, I could have made other choices. When I could think about it from a place of some distance, I could see that I was actually putting myself into dangerous situations. But there was no fear to serve as a check on my actions. And it was being noticed by my friends, by strangers, and even to a tv audience of millions. It could come back to haunt me.

CHAPTER 14

Street Fighting Man
Wednesday night

I spend the first night of the riots, Wednesday the 29th of April, 1970 at "Big Red," getting stoned and sleeping for 6 hours. The next morning at around 9am, dressed in my uniform from the previous day, blue jeans, blue work shirt and red bandana, Converse All Star low whites, I head back to the dorm for a bit. There, I meet my red bandana brigade mates, Tom, Curt, Jamie, Sammy and Vinnie, dubbed "The Steeb Hall 6." While they are all gung ho in an emotional sense about the day's happenings and ready for more, today we unanimously decide to be a little more low key about the coming demonstration beginning at 10. Wait and see is the attitude. We all head up to the Oval. Curt and Jamie are being a bit more reserved toward me, but I barely notice it. Maybe they are feeling guilty, maybe fearful. I'm so caught up that I don't pay it much mind.

Amazingly, by 10, the action has already begun, just minutes before we arrived. There, cops and demonstrators are continuing their back and forth lobbing of tear gas canisters. Only today, the cops have upped the ante. Now, instead of tear gas, they are using pepper spray. It stings the eyes and stinks, making the students nauseous. We see several students passing out gas masks and the smart, more seasoned demonstrators out on the Oval have kerchiefs to protect their noses and mouths from the fetid smell of the spray. There seems to be even more students out today and the vibe in the crowd is much more chaotic and angry. By 10:30, as I stand behind the make-shift barricade demonstrators erected with bricks and logs near the entrance of Arps Hall, the psych building, about 10 feet from me, a fellow student, a female, suddenly is felled. And not by the tear gas and not from nausea but by a bullet. Suddenly, some nurses appear and immediately make arrangements to get an ambulance for her. It looks like she has been shot in the thigh, bleeding; she just lays on the ground, very still, while the nurses and nursing students attend to her. They quickly enlist the help of some other students who lift her and carry her to safety into Arps Hall while they wait for the ambulance. The sight of this brings home to us who are near the girl, that this is real. Not just a game. The cops, and OSU administra-tors mean business. It does not have a frightening effect on us but rather galvanizes our anger even more. FUCK THESE PEOPLE! FUCKING PIGS!

The rest of the morning sees a continuation of advance and retreat from the contested area of the campus Oval. The cops charge and fire pepper spray. The students run in retreat, retrieve the gas canisters and throw them back at the pigs. This goes on for a couple of hours. By this time, I've lost track of my mates. We've gotten detached from each other. I don't know where they are. I am out in the mob by myself, though not feeling uncomfortable but rather feeling a part of something good, something larger. But, at the same time, I'm becoming aware that this rioting and back and forth with the pigs is not really very productive and not really affecting anything positive, although it's sort of fun. I think to myself, what would have an impact on these pigs? Boycott. Everyone stays out of class and the workers and support staff at the school should be encouraged to go out on strike in solidarity with the student strike.

I immediately head to the Social Work department where I search for John Behling, the faculty advisor to SDS, who is a pariah to the university administration and an idol to the campus liberal and radical community. As an associate professor of Social Work he is protected by tenure, but has been punished by his department by getting terrible course assignments: statistics and a horrendous schedule. He has to teach classes at 8 am and 5pm. He's a bit pissed at the department but he loves his work, loves the students and is politically impassioned. It turns out he is in his office talking to students. I've only met him once at a meeting of the Third World Solidarity Committee which he attended once to inform us of procedures if we were interested in becoming a formal campus organization. We weren't. He clearly seemed sympathetic at that meeting to our cause, which was primarily anti-VietNam war, anti-military research, anti-military recruiters, anti-ROTC, anti-corporate military recruiters and solidarity with the Black Student Union and Women's Liberation Group.

Behling vaguely remembers me from the meeting as we talked briefly afterwards about his views on the rupture within SDS from the previous June when SDS went in two directions, Progressive Labor, a pro-Maoist group, doctrinaire, sympathetic to Mao's cultural revolution and The Weathermen Brigade, a direct action, militant group that was frustrated by nonviolent means of creating change and thought that insurrection was the only way to make a significant difference. Behling expresses to me that he is dubious toward both

131

groups, seeing the SDS break up as a desperate move representing the worst in the radical left: the rigidity of the PL contingency and the lunacy of the Weathermen contingency. He seems weary but not entirely disillusioned. He detects a lot of passion in the White and Black students he has had contact with, and also understands that the civil rights and anti-war movement has moved into a more militant phase than in the previous 5 or 6 years. He tells me that he observes a lot of impatience on the part of the youthful members of the movement and a hardening recalcitrance and backlash on the part of the political establishment, now in the hands of the Republicans, Nixon in Washington and James Rhodes in the governor's office in Ohio. The Republicans, particularly Nixon, are about stoking the politics of resentment with the White working class and they are very good at it. Behling comments that the country is as polarized in April, 1970 as it has been since the Civil War. This is Behling's analysis and it makes good sense.

I visit Behling this Thursday as a self-appointed, unofficial representative of all the radical groups, to talk with him about introducing a university-wide boycott. First, I want his input on how to get the OSU blue collar workers and staff, who keep the school afloat, on our side and second to support, if not strike, in solidarity with us striking students. He has a skeptical look but speaks sympathetically about our desires. He sees a big class divide between the campus workers and students that will not be easily bridged. Additionally, from a self-interested perspective, he opines that these folks need their wages, not all of them are unionized, many in fact are not, and they would risk losing their jobs, livelihoods for what? Some abstract cause? No, Behling says, it would take a lot of work to enlist the support of these folks, not that it isn't not worth the effort, but that it's a long shot. He thinks a better way to go would be to help facilitate the student groups to make sure they're all united in goals and actions so that they speak in one voice. That to him seems to make the most sense. Behling is a veteran of the Korean War, and had been involved in union disputes before getting his doctorate in social work, so he had the experience to back up his opinions, I thought. Plus, he was a likable, warm and sympathetic guy. Not brusque or patronizing to either students or staff. A real "mensch-y" guy, so I trusted his opinion.

I find that the meeting with Behling is salutary, calms me and makes me feel more in control, at least intellectually, about the cyclone of events happening around me. I leave his office and head back to the dorm to mellow out. It's clear to me that the violent, militant stuff, while gratifying, isn't going to accomplish our goals. If anything it could be counterproductive and probably make the university admin people less willing to negotiate, or so I am thinking now. They need to be brought to their knees where they hurt and that is in their pocketbook. But as Behling pointed out, the idea of getting the campus workers and clerical staff behind the students is probably unrealistic. So, like so many of my fellow activist students and fellow rioters, I am left without a concrete plan. Events would have to evolve as events would. As I hang out back in Steeb Hall, I realize that I am exhausted. Exhilarated. But exhausted.

I call my parents on the phone wondering if they have heard about what was going on around campus. They had. In fact, my mother informs me that she not only heard about what is going on at OSU, but actually saw me and my red bandanna on the CBS evening news with Walter Cronkite. It's worrying the shit out of her. I can hear the shakiness and tightness in her voice. I picture her lower lip trembling a bit as it did the day I was hospitalized at the IOL.

"You could get killed," she told me. "You should be very careful. Even though Dad and I support a lot of the issues you and your fellow students are protesting, the violent methods, rioting will only bring on a repression and get someone killed."

My father is just as emphatic. I yes'd them both, having realized a long time ago, especially with my father, that it is impossible to get them to completely understand my perspective. They are too invested in their understanding and way of seeing things based on their childhoods and experiences of the Depression and World War II to understand how we Boomers in general, and me in particular, relate to the world. They believe in working within the system, and if possible, making change from there. They are good liberals. My mother is an old-time Henry Wallace and Stevenson Democrat, my father a Stevenson Democrat and more recently, a precinct captain for the Eugene McCarthy for President movement in 1968. I respect the courage of their political convictions. I just have a more radical orientation about what makes America tick and what to do about it. I guess that my perspective originates from my nuthouse experience of those 9 months in '68, and four more weeks of nuthouse time in '69. I know what it feels like to be incarcerated, even if it was voluntary for me. I know what it feels like to be a second class citizen, even if many of the problems I had were of my own making. My sympathy and anger is with the underdog, Blacks, especially Blacks, the poor, the mistreated, the losers of the American game of capitalism winner-take-all competition. My anger is given voice in the slogan we chant at demonstrations, "Work, Study, Get Ahead, Kill." I didn't realize at the time that while these sentiments, anger and sympathy for the underdog, composed a valid political critique of American society, it also served as a rather elaborate and overarching rationalization for my continued lack of success on an individual basis. I was too juiced, grandiose and deluded with the idea of toppling the system to see how my euphoria might serve as a distraction from my own personal problems. But, hey, give me a break, I am only 20 years old here and just trying to make my way on my own with limited input from my parents. The political situation on campus is heady stuff and I am completely into it.

It's Friday, May 1, 1970 and all is relatively quiet on campus. There is a sizable police presence and the National Guard has been called up by Governor Rhodes, and they are making their presence felt. Everywhere you turn there are armed guardsmen, many my age. It makes for a weird scene. Although the day is rather quiet on campus, nationally, the day becomes quite newsworthy. Nixon announces his invasion of Cambodia which sets off a spontaneous reaction on several campuses around the country. Berkeley, Wisconsin, Stanford, Michigan, Wash U- St. Louis, are some of the places that flare up. Many schools in Ohio erupt as well, including Kent State, which the next night, with their sizable Weather brigade, sets the ROTC building on fire.

A couple of my friends and I along with "Big Red" mates, John Alloway and Pablo Ricciardo, are tuned into the radical scene at Kent and other campuses and decide to make the journey up to Kent that Saturday afternoon after we hear of a rumor from local Weather people that there might be a kind of direct action that night. We want to witness this and participate. We drive in Alloway's VW bug, arriving in Kent by 5 pm Saturday night where we meet up with some Weather people that Alloway knows. We go to the demonstration, which rather quickly, turns ugly resulting in the torching of the ROTC building, which is the obvious symbol of the militarization of universities. We witness this in glee as students cut hoses to prevent fire fighters from squelching the flames. So long ROTC building. It's only partly destroyed, not burned to the ground. Oh well, you can't have everything. Alloway, Ricciardo and I stay at Kent that night with some Weather people and drive back to Columbus on Sunday. Again, I'm exhilarated and exhausted.

CHAPTER 15

Gut Punches, Bolo Punch

I spend this Sunday at the dorm hangin' with my Red Bandana Brigade mates, watching TV, napping, and listening to music. Lots of Jefferson Airplane, "Volunteers," Stones: *Beggar's Banquet's*, "Street Fighting Man," and of course, the Chambers Brothers', "Time Has Come Today," the anthems of revolt. It's Sunday evening and I call Marla excitedly as she listens to my tales of the previous week's events. She is supportive, though worried, not wanting me to get hurt or arrested. I try to reassure her telling her that I know what I am doing. I completely believe it. I'm not sure how convincing I am. We plan to meet the following Saturday in D.C. where there will be a huge anti-war demonstration protesting the war. We both look forward to meeting with eager anticipation. Perhaps this meeting will cement our getting back together. I think. Then after getting off the phone with Marla, as is my usual ritual, I phone my parents.

My mom says in a quiet, yet plaintive voice that there is something she needs to tell me. She continues, "On Friday morning, I woke up coughing blood and was quite alarmed. So Dad and I scheduled an emergency appointment with a pulmonologist and we are awaiting the results tomorrow." I'm instantly alarmed, but try to sound as reassuring as I know how.

My father, when he gets on the phone, tries to sound nonplussed, saying it is at worst a case of pleurisy. "Mom will be alright." Something in his voice doesn't sit right with me, but he is a doctor and that part of me has an almost blind trust in his capacities, skills, and knowledge in this department. I'm inclined to want to believe every word he says and I tell them I will call tomorrow. They inform me that the situation in Madison, where Dave's in grad school, is also quite tumultuous with riots having broken out there as well. Dave and Cherise, while active politically, are not directly involved in the fracas the way I have been down in Columbus. Things start to feel like they are coming unhinged. The feeling of calm and perspective I had when I left Behling's office has evaporated. There's too much going on right now and I can't get my head around all of it. It's too overwhelming, so I try not to think about it all. I put my worry about my mom and the excitement about seeing Marla out of my head and stay focused on the political situation at OSU.

Monday, May 4, 1970

Another rally is scheduled for today. The central topic is the events of the past week, local and national. The agenda: What to Do? The strike is continuing and many professors in solidarity with the students have stopped classes while some have not. Unsurprisingly, it breaks down along departmental lines. The physical sciences, agriculture and engineering schools, which tend to be more conservative, are against the strike and in favor of continuing classes. They support the students who want to get an education and who want to continue coming to class. The humanities, arts and social science departments, particularly philosophy, social work, poli sci and english are the most sympathetic to student demands. They vote in support of the strike. Other social science/humanities departments are sympathetic, but less outspokenly so. These include psychology, econ, sociology, history and education. The professional grad programs, law, medicine, and dentistry, do not take a position but basically continue business as usual as much as they can, without committing either way. It's the graduate TA's who are the most supportive and militant, particularly, philosophy, poli sci and english. Poli sci and english produce some leaders like the aforementioned Lorraine Cohen (poli sci) who leads the ad hoc committee that oversees my group, the Third World Solidarity Committee, as well as New Mobe, Black Student Union and Women's Lib. Dave Lidera, a grad student from philosophy, a sharp and clear thinker, does a lot of behind the scenes organizing of all the TA's and gets the support of many of them in the social science and humanities departments.

Out of all of this, there are no surprises except one, Bernie Mehl. He's supposedly the most radical of all the professors, although Behling from social work and Kettler from poli sci could make a strong activist case. Mehl, while in his education classes expounding an essentially anarchist ideology, civil libertarian, libertine-sexual politics, pro-Black power, anti-war, when push comes to shove, chooses to keep his class open. Some of us are appalled. His so-called rationale is to provide an instructive forum for addressing grievances in a safe place while continuing to provide the education that many students have paid for and deserve. What a lame-o, scab-motherfucker. It ends my brief but intense idolization and romance with

Bernie. Although I do take another class with him and still find him more interesting than 95% of the other profs, the goo-goo-eyed idolization of him dies the day I hear he is keeping his classroom open. Fuckin' scab.

Bottom line, the campus is divided between faculty and students, certainly, but the administration, even more so. They see us as the "barbarians at the gate," unkempt, unshowered, profane and vitriolic. They are basically united against us striking students and sympathetic faculty. By Monday, with news of Nixon's invasion of Cambodia, the trial of Bobby Seale heating up in New Haven and the events of the previous week here at OSU have the place electrified. 15,000 students show up at the Oval for the demonstration early in the afternoon. Maybe the biggest demonstration in OSU history. Both faculty and students speak. For the faculty, David Kettler from poli sci, and John Colinveau from the Biology department (ecology wing) are present. They speak in passionate support of the strike but equally so in passionate support of a nonviolent approach to making demands. They vociferously argue that violence is counter-productive politically and practically, not to mention that people get hurt, which would deflect the movement from its goals and make the focus about means not ends. They argue forcefully for militant non-violence. Continuing boycott of classes. Picketing of buildings, enlisting the support of campus workers and clerical staff and developing solidarity with other university student and faculty groups also on strike. In Ohio, by this time, most, if not all, of the campuses are on strike. And this combined with a Teamster strike in Toledo has exhausted the entire supply of the Ohio National guard which has been mostly called out to quell the violence on the campuses, OSU being the largest disturbance, then Miami of Ohio and Kent State being the next two largest disruptions.

After Colinvaux and Kettler speak, Fred Green, Black Student Union representative, Lorraine Cohen of the Ad Hoc Committee, Suzie Jamison of Women's Liberation, Dave Goldman from New Mobilization, and yours truly, believe it or not, representing Third World Solidarity (yes!) make speeches from our various perspectives, making pleas for unity on the issues, Black and women's faculty representation, Black and women's studies, reinstatement of expelled students, ending military research, ending military recruiting, and corporate recruiting, in short, each of the already presented demands to the administration and university president, Novice Fawcett. We reiterate our support and exhort the strikers to hang tough and not capitulate to compromise or thuggery. I am the second to the last person to speak and I focus my harrange on the apathy of the non engaged members of the student body. Those students who, while professing their support in private, in public conform to the rules of administration. Mostly, I am addressing frat rats, the moderate, non committal, opportunistic types who change their positions depending on who they talk with. I challenge them with my profane rage, to take a stand, stick their necks out and stop playing safe. The people I'm pitching to are the people who will one day rise up the ranks of the business world, the people who know how to "play the game." They disgust me. My speech is a deliberate provocation to "join us, join us, join us," the words I use to end my 5 minute speech.

The last speaker, Bernie Donnenberg, former president of SDS, is not currently a student but still involved, and is the most articulate by far of all the "student" speakers, second only to David Kettler in eloquence, but more impassioned and more dangerous. In his speech, Bernie dives into the history of protest activity on the OSU campus, beginning with nascent stirrings from the civil rights movement in the early sixties up to and including the shift to Black power, and the miniscule, but cohesive anti-VietNam war protests in the late sixties, to finally, the attempt of Black students in the late sixties for a Black studies department and more Black students and faculty on campus. He also includes, of course, the regrettable incident of Feb. 21, 1968 when 34 Black students were arrested for a sit-in at the admin building and expelled. Donnenberg talks about how the campus has changed and matured rapidly, particularly in the past couple of months. What was formerly a couple hundred students, at most, involved in political activism, is now in the thousands. He highlights how inspiring it is to him and then takes a dramatic pause, marking a shift.

He says, "We now have the makings of a mass movement. We are powerful. We are dynamic. We can change this university and we can change this country. But we need to do something today. We need to do something right now. About a quarter of a mile from where I speak, there is a military building where the university trains students to become officers once they leave OSU and join the Army, Navy, Air Force or Marines. It is called ROTC. Right now there are students, down there, playing soldier. They are marching, they are drilling. What we need to do and what we need to do right now is go down there and show them and their bosses how we feel about their presence on our campus. If we want to be powerful, if we want to create change, this is a small step we can make now. I say, Enough talk. Let's head down there now."

And with that, the crowd is roused up and disperses as a good couple of thousand people head west to the ROTC building and fields where the student soldiers are practicing their drills. Two thousand of us head there and see a group of maybe 50 ROTC students in uniform. We enter their field, yelling, mocking and tormenting the soldiers, our fellow students. We do not care. We are right. They are wrong.

It is now about 2:30 and moving through the crowd there is suddenly a murmur and then an outcry. Word has come that 4 students at Kent State have been gunned down by the National Guard during a demonstration on campus. The mocking, jocular vibe now begins to turn ugly as students pick up stones and fling them mostly at the building but at some ROTC students as well. By this time, most of the ROTC students have fled to safety inside the building, so the stones are then aimed at the building and the windows facing the field. The rock throwing lasts about 20 minutes until the National Guard finally make their appearance, standing in formation in front of the building as the protestors, which includes me, disperse back to the main campus. We then retreat to High Street. This is our version of cops and robbers, undergraduate college student style. I'm sad and enraged but do not throw any rocks.

The night on High Street is a frenzy. Throngs of people on the street, stunned and angry. I run into Paul Ricciardo and John Alloway, my anarchist comrades, as we knife into the crowded, smokey, dank but comfy Larry's Bar on the north campus side of High Street. There we run into one of my history teachers, a grad student working on his Ph.D. on insurrection in Central America in the late fifties and early sixties and American efforts to stifle that cause in their support of military dictatorships. Lieders is his name. It turns out he is an "out" gay which provides him with part of his personal raison d'etre for his outrage at the system. He sits with us at our table as a friend of Paul's, Sam Greenwood, from Kent State, walks in. Paul flags him down and the five of us sit together at a booth, in all its torn red naugahyde glory. The vibe in the bar is raucous and angry. We listen intently as Sam tells us of the day's events at Kent. He was a prime mover in the protests, he says. A member of SDS and later their Weather Brigade, he was one of the people instrumental in instigating the ROTC building destruction there at Kent. Sam says this with burning pride. But it's also obvious in his description of today's events that he is badly shaken and at times is tearful. He has just arrived in Columbus from Kent and leans into the booth to tell us his story. He relays that he is from Pittsburgh and went to high school with one of the four kids gunned down. In fact, more than that. He dated her. Actually dated her heavily in high school and some her first year at Kent. He is talking about Allison Krause, a beautiful, socially conscious young woman. Allison was a good student, counter culturally oriented as well as politically involved, although not as much as Sam. Nevertheless, she was highly sympathetic to the student anti-war cause on campus and was there today at the Kent demonstration when she and three of her fellow students were stupidly gunned down. The word on the street is that Sylvestor DelCorso, the leader of the Ohio State National Guard, gave the word to shoot to kill. He, in turn, was given the directive by Governor James Rhodes, a conservative Republican, law and order scum bag. Rhodes, so the rumor goes, was given the go ahead by none other than Tricky Dicky at the White House to teach those, in the words of Spiro Agnew, "nattering, nabobs of negativity… those hooligans," a lesson. And a lesson we get. In this country, no one and nothing is safe in the defense of property or the status quo. Your freedoms, your desire for equality, your desire for justice, your desire that the country or the world be a better, more fair place for everyone, not just the few, is unimportant. If you want those things then you had better be prepared to die for it. It is not going to be given to you. You have to take it.

The politicians, Democrat and Republican, are tools of the moneyed interests, and they are only going to go as far as they are pushed. They need pushing. And Nixon, now that he is President, is cultivating a counter offensive, with his push for the Silent Majority to start talking back to us youths, Blacks, disenfranchised, women and other disempowered minorities and peoples. This is their country and they are going to take it back. It is here that the culture wars of the 60's polarization really begins and continues, to this day. It is not that there hasn't been a long history of cultural and political division and conflict in this country dating back to its founding. It's just that the intensification of the divisions are reaching a new height with the social insurrections that began in the 60's. The Silent Majority is striking back at the civil rights, Black power, anti-war, women's lib movement, burgeoning environmental, flower power, free love, back to the land organic food, gay liberation, consciousness expansion through psychedelic drugs and/or eastern mysticism movements. Nixon is stoking the counter offensive and he is doing a good job. These are the days of the return of the white hard hats kicking hippie ass on Fifth Avenue in New York City. Governor Reagan first stoked this politics of White backlash in his run for governor back in '66 when his campaign in California centered on an attack on law and order by those "anarchistic, outside agitating, Cal Berkeley students." It worked as he was able to defeat two time governor, Pat Brown. Then Nixon used it in '68 to get elected President, exploiting the fears of people alarmed by the riots in Watts, Detroit, Cleveland and Newark, alarmed by the demonstrations and riots at the National Democratic Convention in Chicago, and playing on Americans' sentimentality for the good old days of the *Leave It To Beaver* and *Ozzie and Harriet* America. The America that none of us had grown up in, but somehow thought we had, while inhaling the cesspool of propaganda, tv.

This is our reality on Monday night, May 4, as Sam tearfully describes Allison to us and how the scared, literally shaking in their boots National Guard on the Kent campus lost discipline, reacted in panic and fired. We White students, for the first time, have a small taste of what it might be like to be Black or brown in this country. We revel in our victimhood and righteous indignation. We drink to Sam, we drink to Allison. We drink to the martyred four students. We drink to Fred Hampton, Black Panther killed by Chicago cops who entered his house without a warrant and shot him in his bed. We drink to Bobby Kennedy. We drink to Martin Luther King. We drink to Che Guevara. We drink to Malcolm X. We drink to Jack Kennedy. In short, we drink and drink until it hurts no more. John Alloway and I stumble back to "Big Red" where people are milling around and then we go into Alloway's room. He crashes on the bed and I crash in a sleeping bag on the floor, falling into a fitful, drunken sleep.

The next day things get even more intense. The National Guard look different from the way they did the previous few days. They look tense, sort of focused, a little scared. It is a big change from the impression they gave off days earlier when they appeared more relaxed, easy going, with an almost jovial attitude towards the students and the protestors. Now they look like they mean business. The rumor is that the Nixon to Rhodes to Del Corso message "shoot to kill" now applies to all the campuses protesting, striking or rioting in Ohio. It is as if Nixon is doubling down now that the four students have been killed at Kent. My comrades and I thought he would go in the opposite direction, thinking he thought a mistake had been made. But this is not what we are hearing and we are not believing anything we hear in the papers, on the tv or radio. We're tuned into the underground, or the rumor mill. Sometimes we are right, sometimes we are wrong. Clearly, we radical protesters are paranoid or suspicious enough that we are not going to listen to any info funneled through the mass media. It's clear to us that they are simply tools of the power elite and corporate plutocracy. Not to be trusted.

Students spontaneously mass around the Oval at noon to hear more speeches from Lorraine Cohen about the negotiations with the admin. The atmosphere is scary, angry, and chaotic. I, on the other hand, am feeling no pain. I am lovin' every moment of it. In a state of euphoria, sleeping little, hopping from event to event, like a chicken with its head cut off. Operating on pure instincts. Now, the Red Bandanna Brigade breaks down into two units, the Steeb Hall crew of Curt Robinson, Jamie Olian, Sammy Alberico and Tom, one prong, and Paul Ricciardi, John Alloway and me, the "Big Red" crew, the other prong. We are not communicating, just doing our separate things. I'm not even staying at the dorm any more, having taken up temporary quarters with Alloway at "Big Red" or, at times, staying with Ricciardo at his place on the south campus near Chittenden and High. It's my way of saying that I am done with dormitory living. It feels freer and a lot more grown up.

So, Alloway, Ricciardo and I hit the streets and end up at the Oval at noon, listening from the periphery of the mass of protestors as Lorraine talks about her frustrations with the admin and their reluctance to seriously negotiate and address our "non negotiable demands." Fred Green, the head of the Black Student Union, a freshman, is equally blistering in his diatribe, tying in the plight of Blacks in America, the plight of Blacks on the OSU campus with the anti-war demonstrators, particularly the four White students killed yesterday at Kent. "We're all niggers now," he says. His talk is both stirring and inciting.

The rally lasts at most for 45 minutes and then we strikers head to various sites on campus and try to block buildings so that students can not get into their classes. This is patently illegal. But my mates, and many others of us, clearly at this point don't give a shit. We are done. Paul, John and I join up at Denny Hall, an english humanities building, while others team up at some of the other more popular buildings, the mostly liberal arts halls. We steer clear of math, physical sciences, engineering and agriculture buildings thinking that that could create head-on confrontation with the pro-cop, pro-admin, pro–law and order crowd, who might be aching for a fight. We figure we'll hit the places where we might have success and relative sympathy. And mostly we do, for about a half hour until the Guard comes. One or two students attempt to bypass our efforts to block entrances to buildings. I get into both of their faces like a bully, but know that I have Paul and John as back up, and succeed in getting both White male students to back down and leave the building's entrance. But almost immediately, the Guard, comprised of maybe 30 in single file, rushes in with bayoneted rifles pointed at the protesters as we three hop onto the retaining wall at the side entrance to Denny Hall and jump through a window seconds before things get ugly, which they immediately do. Two hundred more students are arrested, several dragged away. Now, for the first time, I have the feeling that I could be killed. The looks on some of the Guards' faces are fierce. Their faces have morphed from scared young men to the stony look of attackers. And they have guns with live ammunition, by the way. We are unarmed. The equation has changed.

We hang in Denny Hall until things cool off with the Guard. They move on to another building and this is pretty much how the day goes. Cops and robbers, hide and seek. Not a game but feels like one, even now. The situation with the strike is really starting to fragment. The situation is getting out of control. Our leaders are exercising minimal authority over their minions. The cops, Guard and admin are fiercely reactive, trying to bully students through force to get us to capitulate. Things are more and more chaotic, almost like a war zone. Nothing's making sense. Negotiations are a joke. I finally decide, whether out of fatigue or a sense of futility that I've temporarily had enough of the craziness, and I return to Steeb Hall, get my clothes, take a shower, and call home that night.

On the phone, Dad informs me that they have found something on Mom's lung. But, it is not cancer he insists. Which, of course, makes me think that it is. His insistence has the feel that he is trying to convince himself as well. His manner seems grave. Mom sounds subdued, a little sad, but trying to put on a brave face about the news. She tells me she has stopped smoking. In my discomfort and a sense that mom is also uncomfortable, I change the subject and offer that the campus situation is getting increasingly out of control, particularly on the heels of the Kent State shootings and venture a guess that the campus will likely get shut down. They express their sympathy with my situation but their primary reaction is one of worry. I then tell them I plan to get a ride to D.C. to see Marla and participate in an anti-war demonstration the following Saturday. But Dad, when he gets back on the phone, is not having it. He is insistent that if the school shuts down as appears imminent, then he wants me home. He says that Mom and the family need me. No, ifs ands or buts. I agree. I recognize that the priority is to be with my mom but I'm also feeling disappointed that I won't be getting together with Marla. I am beside myself with upset, worry and sadness. My mom's well being is my "given." She's always been accepting, warm and there. Always was, and so I thought always would be. It is a real shocker. I feel scared, an emotion I rarely allow to surface.

I get off the phone and promptly call Marla to tell her that the campus is probably going to be closing tomorrow and that I can't come to D.C. to see her as planned because of my mom's situation, so instead I'm going to have to go back to New Rochelle. She says she understands. After hesitating for a moment, says she has some news of her own, telling me she was going to call me anyway to tell me there has been a change in her plans. It turns out, and her voice begins to quiver, and slow down, that she and her boyfriend, Saul, have talked, on the night of the Kent State shootings to be exact, and on the heels of that conversation, have decided to get back together. "I'm extremely sorry," she says, "but that's kinda the way it is. "......... I am blown out of the water, staggered but say I understand, saving face. But I'm on the ropes.

Truth be told, I'm crushed. Two and a half years of being in a relationship with her. Her calling it quits with me after breaking up with her three times. Her breakup with me was brutal, almost vicious, but sort of understandable, then 6 months of depression for me and veg. city following the break up, then three more months starting to feel back to my old self, neutral town, then rising expectations of getting back together and now this. Fuck this shit. I feel like I've been kicked in the stomach. No, actually, not kicked in the stomach, but in the face. And I didn't even see it coming. As I said, I am as polite as I can be to Marla for the rest of the conversation as she inquires and expresses her sympathy about my mom whom she has always liked. But, once again I'm on "queer street." I'm fucked up.

I hang up the phone, not really having a sense where I am. I need to get better at taking a punch, I tell myself. This is not a good day. Not a good day at all. So, without thinking, for a change, I put on my work shirt and bandana, my street fighting clothes, and bolt back onto the street. I find Ricciardo and we stay up all night getting drunk and stoned while looking for women, the ultimate salve for my devastated feelings.

Wednesday, May 6

More of the same. Chaos, tear gas, hide-and-go-seek games with the Guard. Ricciardo and I are having a running dialogue about the events, their significance and political theory the events could best be subsumed under. Ricciardo is a poli. sci. major so he has read Marx, Rousseau, Plato, Machiavelli, Lenin and Hobbes. At some level, he thinks it is all bull shit but he's fairly knowledgeable and into the conversation. He has a good sense of humor and a dramatic mimicry of the intonations, regional accents of his profs and is constantly aping them, leaving us both in hysterics. Ricciardo and I take turns lecturing each other with our half-assed theoretical knowledge and even less practical experience, all of which we make up for in youthful energy and ardor. The governing statement we have for each other in our non-listening to what the other is saying is, "If I want your opinion, I'll give it to you." This could be the mantra for the whole campus at this point given the absence of communication between all parties.

By 5:30 p.m, Novice Fawcett has had enough of the hijinks, mayhem and disorder. He declares the university formally closed until further notice. We are all jubilant as if we have won some kind of prize. We have succeeded in shutting the school down but, as of yet, haven't won any of our demands. With a mass of mixed feelings, I get on the phone to TWA and book a flight to La Guardia for the next day.

I am wired to the gills. Giddy, exhausted, overwrought, euphoric about the events in Ohio. So much so that these feelings, for the time being, override the deep sadness and worry I have about my mother's condition, not to mention my hurt, disappointment and rage about the could have been, should have been, future with Marla based on the previous months' phone calls with her. I am a mess, only I mostly don't know it. I am manic, having a good time, feeling good, feeling no pain. It's incredible how my mind protects me from pain sometimes; understandable how people become drug addicts, alcoholics, overeaters or gambling addicts for that matter. Anything to just not feel the pain, or anything for that matter.

Marla's Version

Wait a minute. I feel like I'm getting bad press here. You people are only getting part of the story here. You see Arnie, he was my first boyfriend. High school sweetheart.

First love. I cared about this guy a lot. Through thick and thin. Stood by him. He was a lousy boyfriend but I loved him anyway. But, the summer after Arnie and I broke up, I met this guy at a Jewish camp in the Blue Ridge mountains in North Carolina, where I was a camp counselor. He was a counselor there, too. I was pretty raw at the time from having just graduated high school and still being really pissed about Arnie. Pissed about his treatment of me. Pissed about his "flipping out" and pissed about his abandoning me. Tired of loving somebody and not getting the love I needed and deserved in return. So you might say I was ripe, in a way, to meet somebody nice. And there he was on the first day of camp in the mess hall, orienting me and some other girls about the rules and expectations for camp counselors. This guy, Saul, that was his name, seemed nice and also smart. A few years older than I, he seemed to know where he was going. Premed. A good student. A solid guy. But sweet and warm, too. I needed that after the roller coaster ride I'd been taking the last few years with Arnie. And Saul was interested in me, too. I liked that. And of course there was this attraction and he was into being Jewish, too. I think I was ready to be influenced in that way. I was always Jewish, but not "that" Jewish. But because he was into celebrating the rituals, Shabbat, the candles, the prayers, you know that kind of thing, well, I think I took to it, first because Saul was into it but later because I kind of really liked it a lot for myself. So, being with Saul was really nice that summer. We hung out a lot and became an item throughout the summer and into the fall. He was in his senior year at Duke, applying to med. schools and I would be a freshman year at Hood College in Maryland horse country. All girls. That last thing was partly my parents' idea. Actually, mostly their idea. In a lot of ways they were pretty conservative. But I went along. That's how I was.

Then during the fall semester, Saul and I continued to talk frequently and see each other on occasion. We were exclusive. But by winter of the next year, the physical distance started getting to him, for him more than me, because in early March, Saul found out he was going to be going to Emory, in Atlanta, for med. school. His attitude towards me grew distant until one weekend during a visit on the Durham campus at Duke, we had a long talk. Saul was having doubts and I must say I was too, but I didn't want to rock the boat since we got along so well. And well, it felt so comfortable with him. But Saul was, I guess, feeling it more, and said he thought we should take a break, maybe see other people and find out if it was the real thing. I was against it mostly, but what could I do? I was upset and cried a lot. I left the Duke campus, back to Hood and then a week later, home to New Rochelle to visit my folks.

Suddenly alone without a boyfriend, really for the first time in almost four years since I was 15, I felt miserable. And intensely lonely. For some reason, I found myself calling Arnie's house kind of knowing Arnie wouldn't be there but I got Arnie's dorm phone number from his mom. I found myself missing Arnie.

I was very angry with Saul and hurt for sure, but mostly angry. Arnie was my first love and although he treated me like shit a lot, he was also a lot of fun when we were together and I needed that connection. So, when I got back to school, I called him. He was distant at first but then "into" it, like he wanted to see if we could get back together, too. I was "into" it also. With those old loving feelings returning as we talked on the phone each Sunday, I hoped we would get together in D.C. at an anti-war demonstration, as we planned. It would have been a perfect time for our belated reunion. I was really looking forward to this and feeling close, in some ways closer than ever as we talked. He seemed more mature, although so passionate about the political thing he was into. It was a bit over-whelming. But intriguing.

And then, the night of Kent State, I remember it vividly because my roommates and I were crying, upset, Saul called wanting to know how I was doing, saying he missed me. Saying, he thought he made a mistake breaking up and wanting to get back together. I was torn. Starting to feel close to Arnie again, but when I thought about it, Arnie was really a blast from the past. Saul kind of got me in ways I had never been gotten and I needed that. Being with Saul felt hugely important but I also felt awful about hurting Arnie and really bad about what I was gonna say to him. But I needed to be honest. I know it may come across as cruel to Arnie but I really wasn't trying to lead him on. I was trying to be real with him about how I felt. It's just that things had changed and I needed to be fair to my heart. And my heart said... Saul.

CHAPTER 16

It's a Family Affair
May 7–May 18, 1970

I get on a plane the next day from Columbus to NYC. I'm in a grandiose and aggressive mode and nearly miss my plane. I'm not paying attention to the time. Very caught up in the present. I'm disorganized and distracted. I try to fast talk my way onto the plane because I arrive at the airline check in counter with only ten minutes left before the flight and they don't want to let me on the plane. I go ape shit. Yelling and cursing at full throttle. They nearly arrest me but after I calm down, they allow me on the next plane which luckily is leaving in half an hour. I momentarily calm down once on the plane. My dad picks me up at LaGuardia and as we head back to New Rochelle, I can see he is doing his best to cop a more hopeful attitude. He emphasizes that it is important to be upbeat around Mom, to keep up the impression that she has pleurisy. In fact, my dad won't say she has cancer either. The dreaded C word.

Arriving home at Daisy Farms Drive is a mixed bag of sensations. I am sort of relieved to be home and glad to see Mom. She looks about the same, maybe slightly thinner. I notice she has stopped smoking but has a chronic low level cough. She greets me with her usual, "Hello, pussycat," and makes an effort to sit and listen to my various and sundry goings on of the last few weeks, what with the riot business, Kent State and especially the bull shit around Marla, stuff I am in the habit of sharing with her. I always have felt her solidarity with me while also knowing I was going to get a fair hearing with her. She would tell me when I was off base and when the other party was wrong. She has always been like that. Fair, practical and a really good judge of character. It's part of what I love about her as a person. She is also my mom and I feel her unconditional care and concern. That having been said, I am at this point of my life, impossible to manage or govern by her, my dad or anyone. Probably my dad was better at it than my mom as he is not afraid to be heavy handed or a prick when dealing with me. So my dealings with him have always been more conflictual. My mom is just basically more accepting, understanding, but I must say, so much more easily overwhelmed by my "schtichlach" (yiddish for a particular type of craziness.) Especially now, I don't want to burden her with my shit too much. Just enough to keep her apprised.

With Dad, I have a tendency to share the more negative just to provoke the asshole. I am good at it and know what buttons to push. I'm good at getting him to bite a fair amount. Not always. I get a bunch of lectures from him about nonviolence, staying focused on school, Nixon and the repressive Moral Majority, the Silent Majority's counter reaction to the youth culture antics of the last bunch of years. So, not wanting to be lectured, I keep any information brief and mostly focus on Mom. After being around her for a while, I notice that she is clearly weaker than when I saw her last. It is upsetting, to say the least.

I will stay in New Rochelle with them for 10 days while OSU is officially shut down from the strike and riots until I hear they will be reopening on Monday, May 18. I stay close to the house during this time, as my New Rochelle friends are still away because their schools have not shut down. Harvard, B.U. and Colgate are still open despite the disorder on all of their campuses. Dave and Cherise are still in Madison, despite the turmoil. The University of Wisconsin hasn't shut down either. It's more used to protest as the school and its students have been up in arms dating back to the fifties and is now one of the major anti-war campuses along with Berkeley and Columbia, with their protests ongoing since '64, '65.

OSU, unlike these other colleges, has no tradition, no history of liberal or radical protest. The admin people, the cops and the state have no background or experience for dealing with students and it shows in their primitive, draconian responses. The campuses of Berkeley, Madison and Columbia, well, there, at least the students, faculty and administration, not to mention campus cops, city cops, state pigs, as well as National Guard are much more astute and experienced. Much less reactive. It takes a lot more to get them stirred up. Though of course, eventually even there, they get reactive, it just takes more to get them there.

The notice to return back to school comes in the mail. I am informed that all classes for spring quarter could be taken pass/fail since too much time was lost due to the strike and the shutdown. We will be returning for week 7 of the 10 week quarter system. I had taken 18 units, two education classes for 8 units, an intro psych class for 5 units and a 19th century philosophy course. I decided to major in philosophy after the winter quarter. It was psychology first, now philosophy, but I had not formally declared anything yet. But this is where my interest lies right now.

CHAPTER 17

What Goes Up Must Come Down

(May 18–June 10, 1970 – Finishing up spring quarter)

A big campus rally is scheduled for Thursday of this week now that everyone has had a chance to cool down during their week off. Students, faculty and administration representatives are invited to speak. The featured speaker is one Charles Woodrow (Woody) Hayes, the famed Ohio State football coach, a noted orator of the populist school, William Jennings Brian variety. It is by far the biggest rally of this whole three month period. Must be 20,000 students massed on the Oval today. School has now been back in session for four days and the strike is still officially on. But during this period, there was some movement from the administration in terms of their willingness to negotiate with the student groups. There is a call for a meeting by Lorraine Cohen with student groups this weekend to end the strike, as she seems to be feeling more optimistic that some demands were possibly going to be met. Included in the meetings are the Black groups, Third World Solidarity, women's and New Mobe contingents to discuss the status of the negotiations and to decide whether to continue or end the strike that was planned for Saturday, the 23rd of May. But the vibe today is a little different. The students' opinions are more up for grabs, less unambivalently pro strike compared to when the rally began, more willing to be persuaded by the powers that be. To be more accurate, the crowd is divided into three camps: the unabashed pro-strike folks in the majority, the all out anti-strikers, the minority, and lastly, the mildly pro-strike and fence straddling middle, which is probably thirty percent of the crowd. 50 percent pro-strikers, 20 percent anti-strikers, and 30 percent fence-sitters. That's my rough appraisal of the crowd's preferences today as the rally begins. In some ways, it will be up to the speakers to convince the 30 percent which direction it wants them to go. There are reps of all camps doing their best to persuade, from left to right. The Woodman (Woody Hayes) is the master of ceremonies. The legendary OSU football coach starts out by saluting and celebrating all the students who have been active participants in the past month's strike. He celebrates their passion, their concern, their desire to make the school and country a better place for all people. He congratulates and praises the student activists in their burning convictions regarding racial justice and equality, gender equality and even the students who are ardent in their beliefs opposing the war in Vietnam. At least, he intones, they are willing and able to participate as active citizens in our thriving experiment in democracy, this country of ours the U.S. of A. So far, so good. But it is here that the Woodman's speech tone takes a hard right.

"Democracy," he declares, "depends on its citizens and its leaders to honor the rule of law; to follow its tenets and to exercise one's

freedoms and rights with civility in as peaceful a manner as possible."
He then admonishes the students for their unwillingness to follow the
rules of law, as well as their unwillingness to express their grievances
in an orderly, civil fashion. The students must do this if they have any
chance of gaining a fair hearing, he opines. In addition, the rights of
other students to get an education must be respected or the protesting
students will, once again, bring on themselves the wrath of the law
enforcement authorities. Undoubtedly, an amazing speech that for
the first ten minutes has the crowd spellbound, until Woody makes
his turn, somewhat subtly at first, into expressing and supporting
the position of administration. It doesn't work. His manipulative
attempt is seen through for what it is. The crowd, initially pacified
for most of the rally, begins to shift. Incensed by his transparent
attempt at manipulation, the crowd grows angry and shouts epithets
at Woody. The usual stuff. "Fascist pig" being the most popular.
People begin rising en masse from their lotus positions on the Oval,
like an ant colony with a hive mind. Pretty soon throngs of people
have, as they put it, had enough of the bull shit, as we ants head
over to High Street and begin trashing the place, smashing storefront windows. The scene is ugly. Protestors are partially provoked
by Woody's speech, but mostly expressing frustration and anger at
strike's not producing any meaningful progress. The trashing of High
Street turns out to be the denouement for the strike. It turns off a
lot of previously sympathetic students to the strikers, so that within
the next week or so, the strike basically peters out as students resume
classes for the last two weeks of classes and finals week.

But not for me. I, along with a cadre of what has become a dwin-
dling number of protesters, are not done protesting. There is now an
ongoing curfew on campus after 8pm that is imposed by the campus
police. This has been the case since the last days before the campus

shut down the first time in early May and is still the case once the campus opened up again in late May. It is referred to as a "cordoned off area," by the cops.

So on this night, after the High Street trashing following the massive demonstration and speeches, I find myself on the Ohio State Oval with a bunch of co-protesters who I know only casually from the protests of the previous month. There are about five of us. A Black guy, two White women, a White dude, and me. The curfew is 8 pm and as the 8pm curfew nears, people start to disperse. All except the five of us. We are determined to stay as the campus cops appear promptly with the clock striking 8 on the University Hall clock tower. Without much effort, they round us up, simply by drawing their guns and haul us into the van to take us down to the Columbus City Jail. I'm pissed, but mostly at myself for being so stupid. "Why the fuck didn't I just leave earlier, you idiot?" I hear myself say. But while in the van, I find out that the two White girls and White guy are tripping on acid. There's a lot of cackling interspersed with "wows" as we ride downtown. As we are being booked en route to the bullpen, where freshly arrested folks stay before arraignment, my tripped out companions are having very vivid visual hallucinations.

The cops, fitting the chunky and fat stereotype, are "perceived" by my three tripped out companions as actual pigs. This perception produces great hilarity all the way around which makes me feel that this was gonna be another interesting "experience." Interesting, sure. Dangerous and scary, definitely. The novelty and fantasy that we're all being heroic adventurers wears off after a couple of hours. My three tripped out friends are soon released on bail, leaving only me and my Black acquaintance, John Flowers, behind bars. He informs me he was incarcerated at Mansfield State Prison for third degree murder and as he is a veteran of these environs, will protect me from the other "bros," so that nothing untoward happens to me in this almost completely Black populated bullpen. Flowers says to a couple of bros he knows in the bullpen, "This honky's cool. He's with me. Don't mess with him," which seems to work for the three, four hours he's there until he, too, is bailed out leaving me, myself and I to my own devices which are pretty limited in this arena.

I'm scared and extremely wary of being in the bullpen with angry felons who are not particularly partial to white skinned dudes or interested in my radical-liberal politics. I keep my distance and interact minimally. I try to sleep, but being scared, I start to worry that I will never be bailed out. At this point in my fear and despair I start to cry. I am left alone, but can hear commentary from the bros, like "white punk motherfucker," "bitch" and other complimentary epithets that accompany my crying jag. The sobbing, which lasts a while, proves purifying. It cleans me out emotionally, serving to clear my head, leaving only my anger. I am now ready to do what I have to do to survive, including fight, if it comes to that. But luckily, it does not come to that, because soon after my crying jag stops, I am allowed a phone call. I call the OSU Switchboard, a student clearinghouse designed to provide bail money for arrested protesters. But the fuckers are out of money. "Fuck," I yell. But scrambling now, I persuade the pigs to let me make another call. I convince them that the first one didn't count, that I got the wrong number. I then call my shrink, Dr. Leuchter, who goes into action, immediately calling an attorney friend. An hour later at 9 am, I am released on bail, just missing jail breakfast.. Another "experience" for the record books.

I go home and sleep the rest of the day. The final act of a topsy-turvy spring. The lawyer my shrink hired ultimately plea bargains my case down to a misdemeanor, and I receive two years of non-reporting probation, which will not go on my record, assuming I keep my nose clean. I don't even have to appear in court. Things will quiet down significantly following this last stupid, and in retrospect, self destructive event. I'm relieved and quietly grateful that my shrink has come to the rescue, and begrudgingly tell him so. Maybe the old Nazi ain't so bad after all, I think. And, to be honest, he actually came through when the goddamn Student Switchboard which I donated to, which was supposed to bail us protesters out, didn't. It's lucky I had the shrink, old Nazi that he was. At least he cared enough to get me out of jail and get me a lawyer to make sure the arrest was erased from my record. It's more than most Blacks and my White friends without money had. I feel lucky and not without more than a heaping portion of guilt that I have had the protection of my shrink and his lawyer contact. But that's how it is. But from then on, the political activities on campus really quiet down. Almost eerily back to normal. Almost.

I am secretly glad that things are less intense. I am tired, though on another level, sort of pissed that things are starting to decelerate. I loved the excitement and thought we could make a difference. But I have to get back to my life. My classes, my social life, my mother's illness, my emotional reaction to the Marla business. My problems. Everything I've been avoiding. The last three weeks have been sort of like coming down from an acid trip. I feel edgy, agitated, grumpy and irritable. But socially, it's been kind of interesting. My social horizons have greatly expanded during the previous two, three months and I continue to meet lots of new people as the social environment on campus for the last three weeks of spring quarter, though quieter politically, is unusually open. People are meeting each other and falling into deep and profound conversations about important subjects: sex and politics, feminism, organics, human potential, psychedelic drugs vs. eastern spiritual non drug practices, existentialism. Strangers, acquaintances, definitely relating in a different way to each another than they had ever before. And this openness, surprisingly for me, extends to my own ethnic group.

I decide to start meeting Jewish girls again. Now that Marla and I have broken up for the second time in nine months, for some reason, I become reinterested in Jewish girls. This is a departure from my first 18 months at OSU when I made a deliberate choice to avoid Jewish girls, in fact, most girls from the east coast, period, but especially the Jewish jappy types from Long Island, New Jersey, wherever. Now I feel an urge to return to the fold. I find myself frequenting Taylor Tower, the mecca of freshman and sophomore Jewish girls. To my surprise, I meet some cool Jewish girls. Ones I can talk to. And some of them are very attractive, but I'd always known that. But now I find them refreshingly open, bright and fun. I'm not sure what has changed for me, just that it has.

Sue is one such girl who takes a liking to me, and me to her. She's from Beechwood, a predominantly Jewish Cleveland suburb. She's sweet, pretty, hippie-ish, frizzy hair, heavily into the Beatles and Stones and pretty sympathetic to the strikers but she believes in non violence. Basically a liberal. She gets pissed at me when I go off on my negative, angry militant rants about The Man, etc, etc. In retrospect, I don't know if I blame her, but then I find her annoyance with me annoying and another excuse for my usual reaction of feeling unknown or not understood. When I get like this, I get this hangdog look on my face which says, "Keep away." Kind of a mean look, some have told me. Sue has her limits, she's not a perfect fit for me but she is fun, attractive and affectionate and we start seeing each other somewhat regularly, but not formally. Meaning we're not an item. Not exclusive, which leaves me plenty of time to roam the streets.

I'm pretty much getting all passes or A's this quarter so there is little pressure on me to do academic work, except for my philosophy course where I can't get my concentration together to write a paper on Kant's "Prolegomena To Any Future Metaphysics," the prelude to his "Critique of Pure Reason." The course is fascinating to me but I've missed too many classes, didn't do enough of the readings, so I have no sense of how to write the paper, nor the focus to stay on the ideas I have for the paper. I don't get it done and I have to take an incomplete for the course which I will have to make up the following summer. I use my time the last three weeks of the quarter reading books I am interested in, for a change. *Making of a Counter-culture*, *The Greening of America*, and *Politics of Experience* being the three that stand out. But I digress. Getting back to the all important roaming of the streets.

One night in early June, being on my own and eager for social connection at around midnight, I fall into the affectionately named High Street greasy spoon "Dirty Charburt's." I say "fall into" because half drunk students often trip on the five sticky stairs leading into the restaurant from street level. I'm sober though. It's a hipper hang out than the frat and sorority infested "Clean Charburt's" on the corner of 15th and High. I'm just sitting at the counter, having just ordered breakfast of eggs, bacon and homefries, from one of the surly Black waitresses. Their standard gruff query to the students when they come in is "Whatchu want, honey?" I can't say that it's a friendly tone, but more like a growl, but not exactly hostile either. Mostly, it's funny in a business-like, down home way. Anyway, as I turn around to head to the bathroom, I spot these Jewish chicks. I'm pretty sure they're all Jewish, except for one maybe. They're in a booth, laughing and giggling. Two of them eyeball me, smile and seem to be communicating that they would not be averse to my coming to their table. Cute as hell. I make eye contact with them and smile. Upon return from my men's room business, newly washed up and toweled off, I see these two cuties eyeball me again. Well, that's enough for me. I stroll over to their booth and casually ask if any one of these women has a cigarette, my standard come on line at the time. The one with the easiest smile, Charlene, sporting a huge blonde Jewfro, says, "yes" and offers me one of her Newports. She's sweet and open. But I am after other bear. There are two other brunettes with straight hair, dark haired beauties, while friendly, are a little less open initially. But very interesting. Hippieish, but not overly. They nod when I ask in my usual forward style if I can join them. Gretchen, the fourth girl is there having tea, having just gotten off of her shift at the Jolly Roger Donut Shop and she says she's tired and is heading back to Taylor anyway, so I can have her seat. So I sit down with these three lovely women, Charlene, Jeany and Lyndy. It turns out they are all from Dayton, Ohio and the three of them ARE definitely of the hippie-ish variety, into the Beatles, organics, flower power, smoking dope, back to the land stuff, just as I thought. Sort of political, but less hard edged than some of the politico women I had been hanging with these past months. They are softer, warmer, more fun to be with. Much less abrasive on an interpersonal level. Charlene is the most talkative, the most open, the most out there. Into astrology, tarot cards, I Ching, and all manner of mystical stuff. Jeany and Lyndy are more grounded, more organo types, make your own clothes, macramé, artsy, earthy types. And they speak with almost a southern drawl. Soothing after a lifetime of New York hard edged accents. They are completely sweet. But it doesn't take long for me to find out that they are attached, Jeany, to a guy named Jeff, a New Jersey Jew into the arts while Lyndy is hooked up with a rock musician named Ted. Apparently, Lyndy and her high school sweetheart, Tom, who she almost married, had recently broken up because she felt his politics and values were way too conservative for her, a different kind of fall out from the political and countercultural sea change. So this Ted guy is intriguing to her. She says they share a love of George Harrison and eastern mysticism. I stay at their table for fifteen minutes or so and then bid them adieu realizing that this conversation, while pleasant, is not gonna go anywhere for me in the romantic realm.

Jeany, Lyndy and Charlene commence to comment about me upon my exit from Charbert's.

"He was funny," Jeany comments.

"He was cute and funny," Lyndy adds.

"Very skinny," Charlene observes.

"I could go for him, but he's pretty intense, and I'm already hooked on Ted," Lyndy again.

"Yeah. East coast. Sorta like Jeffrey," is Jeany's comment.

"Guess you can't have 'em all. Maybe he'll just have to be the one who got away," Lyndy concludes.

"Oh well," I think to myself as I head down High Street back to Paul's apartment. They were nice, albeit not available. I would meet other women that spring but I dare say, none as nice as those three, pound for pound.

John Flowers

I've already talked about John Flowers, the "brother" I got arrested with on the Oval and who I went to jail with, but not how I met him. So, there is this guy I run into on the first night of the riots when I momentarily get disconnected from my red bandana contingent mates who serve as our mutual protection. This event happens around 8 pm on that first Wednesday on the 29th of April while we're going in and out of the alleys, evading cops. This guy, Flowers, proves to be instrumental, educational and entertaining for me during the next three years. He's a guy from east Columbus, the Black ghetto of Columbus, a Vietnam vet, now attending OSU as a sophomore himself, only he is 26, whereas the average age of us politcos is about 20. He turns out to be one of the funniest, streetwise dudes I would ever meet. John Flowers is the dude's name, a "blood," the affectionate term used those days.

We meet at sundown on the first night of the riots. It turns out that we are both in the same area searching for bricks to throw and are about ten feet apart when firing them. Both of us are aiming at cop cars and after a short time, get into a non verbal contest over who can hit the unmanned cop car the most times. We wink at each other every time one of us would thump the "pig" car. After a half hour of this, I think I'm winning, but the score is close, maybe 7 hits for me and 6 for him. He has a heave it, shot put style throw while mine is more of a honed baseball overhand fire. We're both a little tired as our mutual grunting expresses, and the dude approaches me to say he admires my throwing arm. I, in turn, express similar admiration for his athleticism. He says his name is "John, John Flowers," and I tell him mine, "Arnie Brucher," but he can call me "Bruch." He then says he has a bottle of Almaden, a higher end, student-grade wine, and offers to share some of it with me. We have an immediate chemistry.

He has a warm smile, easy demeanor, great sense of humor with entertaining patter. I can be pretty witty myself and we hit it off quickly. Sharing the jug, we get pretty loose in a hurry but as we are drinking, keep an eye on the pigs, in case they make a return appearance. Pretty soon, the two of us become very unwound, and

John starts demonstrating some boxing techniques to me. He boasts that he is so fast, that he can tell me in advance when he's gonna hit me and I still wouldn't be able to defend myself. I take him up on his challenge and am found wrong. With utter bravado, John announces his punch, and I'm powerless to stop it. He nails me on the button, i.e. my chin, and boom, I go down. It hurts a little, but mostly my pride is wounded. But more than that, I find the whole thing completely amusing and soon the two of us are rolling in laughter. God knows why. We agree to get together at a later date to go looking for women together, which we do, on and off for the next three years. I receive quite an education in picking up chicks, ghetto style. White and Black, although, mostly White when he and I are together. Definitely a cool dude. Luckily, Flowers is with me on the night when I get busted, and his knowledge and experience of prison life makes at least the first few hours of incarceration entertaining, tolerable and relatively safe. Because as I mentioned earlier, right after he leaves, being in jail no longer felt entertaining. In fact, it gets down right scary.

June 1–15, 1970

The quarter fizzles in an anti climax. The last two weeks, students are back to school and the strike is over. This quarter, I get a Pass, two A's and an incomplete in 19th Century Philosophy. It's a ridiculous quarter for everyone academically as most of us are in classes only about half the time if you add up days missed during the strike. I mostly return to hanging out at Steeb Hall with my bandana mates and Sue Kahn during this period. The atmosphere is eerily quiet. I fly home after what passes for finals week and spend ten days with Mom and Dad and brother Lew. My mom appears slightly thinner. It's somewhat alarming but she's still with it mentally. We talk about my OSU adventures, the goings on with the political situation on campus and in the country, my grades, social stuff, girls, pretty much everything except drugs. She and my dad think I still take the phenothiazines that the shrinks prescribed to me since the IOL, the private Hartford nuthouse from '68 and other hospitalizations at Upham Hall at OSU the summer of '69. I do nothing to dissuade them from that illusion. I try not to lie, but when I am asked point blank by my father if I am taking my medicine, I do. I also deny any street drug usage. It's easier. They don't understand. I don't need the hassle and my mother doesn't need to be worrying about that crap now.

I see Rick, who's home from Harvard, and Mark, home from Colgate during this period. Separately, we go drinking a couple of times and have a good time reconnecting. They share tales of life on their respective campuses as I relate what has been going down at OSU, this spring at Kent State, protests about Cambodia, feelings about Nixon and the actions of the National Guard. Even though my conversations with Mark and Rick have a somber and serious tone, I find our camaraderie uplifting compared to how I feel when I'm at home with my folks.

It's depressing to see my mom in her weakened state and I try not to let it bother me. But bother me it does, as all things of importance do, if not right at the moment, then immediately soon after like I am having a delayed reaction. I am sensitive, for better or for worse. I feel things very intensely, that's why I guess when I am not feeling stuff, my distraction and denial abilities are pretty intense and well honed. I vacillate between feeling intensely or not feeling anything at all. Fairly extreme. Not much middle ground there. It will be a relief to get back to campus, I think to myself, although not without a snippet of guilt.

CHAPTER 18

Summertime Blues - Eddie Cochran Version

June 15, 1970 - August 28, 1970

I'm taking two classes, English 103, the third course in the three part sequence, and Intro to Film. I'm signed up to be living on the north campus where the dorms are open in the summer at OSU. But I live there in name only. My buddy, Paul Ricciardo, has a two bedroom apartment on south campus and his roommate is mostly gone for the summer, so I have a crash pad whenever I want it. My buddies, Curt and Tom are in the same dorm but the two of them seem kind of bummed out. We are spending a lot of time listening to James Taylor's new album, *Sweet Baby James*, which has a pretty depressing vibe in a lot of its songs, particularly "Fire and Rain" which is the most dismal. I find out via *Rolling Stone* record reviews that it is about a girl James Taylor knew when he was in the nuthouse at McLean's who suicided. I mostly stay away from Curt and Tom in my attempt to not get too bummed out myself, although I still love these guys a lot. They are my main men and there's a lot of affection and camaraderie between us. We've been through a lot by this time. Acid trips, riots, women. The whole nine yards. Even hangin' out on the east coast and with Tom in Cambridge and they even made the effort to come to my party, which kind of choked me up. They are basically my best friends at OSU but Paul and the aforementioned John Flowers and I are starting to become tight. John Alloway, my guerilla theater buddy, has faded into the wood work since the riots because he's not a regular student at OSU anyway. He spends most of his days working at CYA, the residential facility for juvenile delinquents, so I hardly see him any more. This summer it's one part Tom and Curt. Two parts John and Paul. John and Paul are much more into looking for women anyway. So much more fun. They're more out there. You could say Tom and Curt are more like George and Ringo, solid and dependable, maybe somewhat less charismatic, possibly more introverted.

The summer is a blur to me. It's not even like I am smoking that much weed but I sure as hell, my attention is not dominated by the two courses I'm taking, although, I'm not adverse to them. Actually I'm a bit more into school than I've been in awhile since the winter quarter and the spring riots. Feeling a little more cerebral, I read all the assigned materials in both courses, staying ahead of the game in assignments and getting B's in both courses without breaking a sweat. I don't care that much about getting A's, particularly if it means any extra effort or undue sacrifices on my time. I have different priorities at this point, having long ago abandoned my fantasy about being a serious student, getting straight A's and transferring to Harvard.

This summer with the academics so easy and the politics of the previous spring abruptly subsided, what's left is getting high, listening to music and trying to score, my main preoccupation, particularly now that Marla Mascowitz has let me down, not so gently, twice in a year. Heart broken, heart hardened. In the words of my buddy Paul Ricciardo, "(You are) now looking for a meaningful relationship and/or a blow job." Not necessarily in that order. A bit crude perhaps but true nonetheless. The man has a way with words.

Paul, John Flowers and I are busy gentlemen. Every night, particularly Thursdays, Fridays and Saturdays after 9, we hit the streets. When not with them, I'm on the case on my own. I actually have better luck scoring on my own, but I dare say, it's not as much fun. These guys are a barrel of laughs. Paul, the Sicilian from Pepper Pike, is from a suburb in Cleveland, parents perhaps connected to the mob, unclear. John, from east Columbus, street smart to the max, lyrical, poetic, ridiculous, very funny.

I get laid three times this summer, once, meeting a girl at an open house the first week of summer school while hanging out at my supposed dorm on the north campus with Curt and Tom. Her name is Shirley, she is friendly, outgoing and ready to boogie. We meet, she responds to my invitation to check out my vinyl, and offers a so-called "back rub." The rest is funky history. That was a one time only encounter. The next is with Shelley on a weekend when my two old Oval Cleveland mates, Hal and Cal, who are up in Cleveland for the weekend, invite me to hang with them, only they could not provide transportation. I have to get there on my own. So, I hitchhike up highway 71, and catch a ride from a guy on a motorcycle who takes me most of the way. My old Oval buddy, Hal, said he knew people at Case Western who told him that there would be a frat party at Sammy house. These friends of Hal's tell me to look up these two Yids, Jack Golden and Will Wolfskin and they'd grease the skids so I could spend the night at the Sammy (Sigma Alpha Mu) house. They'd meet me on Saturday for the party, and we'd hang out on Sunday. I am game and arrive at the Sammy house by Saturday at 4 when Jack, one of the dudes, greets me and shows me where I can stay.

The party begins around 8. By this time I am already ripped from beer and pot. It's a sizable party of about 40 people, half girls, half guys. Music is deafening. It's the summer of the band Chicago and "Ball of Confusion" by the Temptations. It doesn't take long to meet this stoned, recently graduated high school senior, soon to be a freshman at Antioch, Shelley Friedman of Cleveland Heights. Clearly hippieish, frizzy hair, no bra, peasant blouse, bell bottom jeans. Out there, fun, ready to boogie. When we meet, she seems carefree. We eyeball and smile at each other and immediately begin to fast dance. A half hour later we are making out. She spends the night with me in the room they had set up for me at the frat house. Shelley was sweet but I never saw her again, inquired as to her whereabouts, or got her address or number. And she never told me to call her. It was simple, a discrete event, with a beginning, middle and end. No muss, no fuss.

The third and last Schtup City this summer happens about a month later into early August, about two weeks before the end of the quarter. My mood is starting to shift at this point, and I am becoming more introverted, quieter, less boisterous. I'm that way when Paul rounds up a woman on High Street and invites her to stay over, hoping for "Schtup City" for himself. Only it doesn't turn out that way. Debby likes me better. She is a divorcee with a three year old daughter who is traveling with her and is staying at Paul's, which was informally my place too, as I started giving him a portion of the rent. Debby and her daughter Rachel, crash in our room. Actually, one time when Rachel falls asleep in her little sleeping bag, Debby, Paul and I, Paul in his bed, Debby in her sleeping bag, me in my sleeping bag are left awake. So commences a conversation, clearly geared on Paul's part to connive, scheme and manipulate Debby into his bed. It is not working. I'm not trying too hard. A half hour into this "lights out" verbal joust, I turn over ready to go to sleep. The next thing I know, I'm surprised to find Debby on top of me, taking off her shirt, ready to roll. More experienced than I am, she needs no instruction about how to pleasure me or how to get herself pleasured. She is a hot patootie. Fun to fuck. And gone the next day with daughter Rachel, never to be seen or heard from again. The fact that the little girl Rachel was in the room while the deed was happening, suddenly dawned on me. More importantly, as far as I knew, it never dawned on Debby. In retrospect, a careless and irresponsible act, but such was the way of things, especially when it came to matters of a sexual nature.

That was the last of the fun this summer. From now on it gets grim. Depression is starting to rear its ugly head again. Sex, while it lasted, was a temporary balm from the emotional pain, but only in the short term. My mood starts to darken, concentration starts to go, and I feel myself starting to withdraw again from people. Luckily, classes are done and I am able to get through them, all except the 19th Century Philosophy incomplete from last spring where I cannot, for the life of me, get it together to write that fucking paper on Kant. So my incomplete becomes an F which only adds to my depression. But my deeper issues are my worries about my mother's health and the pain and hurt I feel from Marla Mascowitz having broken up with me, now twice. Despite my deepest wishes to have the break up not affect me, it still exerts an emotional hold on me. It is now almost four years since we first started to go out. I ruminate and obsess about her even as I intellectualize that we aren't really compatible, but my wounded pride moons for her. It sucks and I sink into a moderate to severe level of depression. No meds. No focus. Lots of sleeping.

Lethargy. Languor. Torpor. Sloth. Reduced verbiage, lowered self esteem, the usual. It lasts and gets worse as the end of the quarter approaches. It's now August 23.

By this time, my dad, who's already under heavy stress from my mom's illness, gets a call from my shrink, Dr. Leuchter, who sees me getting more and more depressed and is unable to convince me to take my meds. My dad now has to come out to Columbus to check in on me and meet with me and Leuchter.

The old man is under stress and is angry at me. I'm angry at him, but still want his approval. But by this time, my pride and rebellion are so entrenched that I will NEVER admit this. So, a meeting we have. Leuchter, though heavy handed and authoritarian in his own way, and also empathic in his own way, knows one thing and that is that my old man is a major problem for me. At the meeting, Dad pushes his angry critique of me, and calls out my laziness, lack of focus and bad judgment. And I, in my depressed, weakened state, have a hard time pushing back. But Leuchter, the old Nazi, can and does. He basically says my feelings for me that Dad is a Sherman tank, doesn't take "no" for an answer, and is not being helpful to his sensitive son. Leuchter also says that Columbus has worn out its welcome and that classes are probably a waste of time, but that being in New Rochelle is probably not good for my mental health either due to the negative effect he, my dad, has on me. Calling my dad repeatedly a "Sherman tank" who has a hard time listening once he's made up his mind, suggests that maybe it might be a good idea if I do take some time off and go live in Madison with brother Dave and Cherise, just to get a break from school and not be home. So, it's decided and I head back temporarily to New Rochelle in a pretty serious depression. My third August in a row where I'm fairly seriously depressed. It's getting to be a cyclical thing, a pattern, and it feels like it has control of me. I hate it. And hate the thought that something inside of me has control of me. My feelings, my moods when they take hold run the show. There ain't a damn thing I can do about it. It seems to happen so fast. And I hate the fact that simple functioning, all of a sudden, feels excruciatingly difficult. I just fucking hate it.

Back in New Rochelle, I can see that Leuchter is right. My father is a frantic mess and what's worse, my mother is starting to wither on the vine, although she's putting up a brave front. Dave and Cherise, home for the summer from Madison, being the strong ones, keep my dad and Mom afloat. They are helpful to Dad both emotionally and practically, doing their best to keep him focused and to my mom, putting in lots of time just being with her. Now Dave and Cherise have me to contend with, for a change. I have the uncomfortable thought that they must see me as quite a piece of work, which I am, of course, as erratic and inconsistent as they come. Clearly, the family's consensus, at Leuchter's urging, is that I've worn out my welcome in Columbus, at least for now. None of them liked the place. They didn't like the fact that I got busted and that I've had two, if not three relapses psychiatrically speaking since the IOL back in '68. Perhaps, OSU is not the place for me. Perhaps, college is not the place for me at this point and I'm not in disagreement and too depressed to argue an opposing point of view either at Leuchter's office or at home. Will-less. It is decided and I go along with the decision, albeit somewhat passively, that I will drop out of OSU for a quarter and go live and work in Madison to be near Dave and Cherise while I get my "head" together. Then, if I feel better and get more motivated, I can return to OSU and finish college. It's now a done deal. Of course, it feels like another defeat but that is how it is. All that's keeping me going at this point is a kind of blind faith that things have to get better and a stubborn unwillingness to give up the ship. That's all I got. My Silky Sullivan soul. Pure instinct.

So Dave, Cherise and I drive to Madison in late August, and arrive a couple of days after the infamous Army Math building bombing on the Wisconsin campus by the Armstrong brothers, militant, angry and increasingly desperate members of the radical left. The anti-war movement's violent turn is in full swing now. Everywhere.

CHAPTER 19

Lower Depths Redux Madison, Wisconsin (Fall 1970)

Bummerland has followed me to Madison. Jim and Cherise have been given unofficial custodial care over my health and well being mentally and physically. Dad is back in New Rochelle overwhelmed and consumed by my mom's illness. Grappling with upset and frustration by my mom's pleurisy, as he refers to it to the world, and to my mother as well. He refuses to call it the C word but everyone knows and assumes it's cancer but are afraid to say it, particularly my mother. This is the strategy now in dealing with cancer patients, to not tell them their actual diagnosis. The secret adds to the edginess and anxiety around the house. But everyone is doing their best to cope.

As far as my situation, I don't really understand the reasons for my bummerhood. The art and science of psychology and psychiatry, like most things of this kind, must be a combination of genetic, biochemical factors combined with a cyclical feature that cannot be treated by the phenothiazines, the antipsychotic medication, I have been taking on and off since January '68 for my so-called diagnosis of paranoid schizophrenia. However, I'm not content with this explanation as it seems too out of my control, so I keep looking, and frequently finding, environmental causes and stresses. This time it's my mom's illness and the break up with Marla. It also occurs to me that I often confuse cause and effect, like, is my low self esteem because of my biochemistry or is my biochemistry changed by my low self esteem. It feels impossible to know. Regardless, in the academic arena, but not just, but definitely when it comes to sensing how my dad feels about me, approval wise, my self esteem is affected. Of course, that is when I give a shit instead of assuming my macho, Bogartesque bravado. Actually, underneath the Bogey façade lies the heart of Montgomery Clift. Scared, hurt, tortured. Not gay though, which was well known about Clift by this time. At least I didn't think that about myself, despite a few experimental forays to see what all the ruckus was about. After trying it out with a couple of Black dudes, for some reason, one on the OSU football team, I conclude that I am turned on by women. I have to say that in looking back that I was pretty out there, open to shit, more than most, some of which was clearly potentially self destructive, but I was definitely willing to take more risks than most, many times to my detriment.

Back in Madison, the depression is fairly thick. I'm back in my hardly talking mode. Dave spends a couple of days with me helping me get set up with a place to live in a rooming house off Lake Mendota, close to campus and then helps me to get a busboy job at Hoffman House, a restaurant closer to downtown Madison than near campus. My hours there will be six days a week, 7am-3:30 pm. I know no one in Madison except a couple of guys from New Rochelle, John Turner and Peter Zeughauser, but I am in no mood for socializing. Isolated, withdrawn, down on myself, and self conscious, I hide from others. Being around people is painful. I do it minimally. At work, I try to be as helpful and friendly as possible with customers, which isn't very much. At the campus area eating co-op, the Green Lantern, where I have my meals, I help out with food prep, eating with strangers, who are a radical bunch of students. Even though they are very much my kind of people, talking is agonizing and I hit it off with no one. I've lost my wit and speed of comeback which have formerly been my specialties. I am a veritable vegetable at this point in time. Minimally functional. I spend most of my off hours back at the pad, reading or hanging out at the Wisconsin Student Union, especially on Monday nights when I watch Monday night football alone with Howard Cosell, Frank Gifford and Dandy Don Meredith doing the announcing.

I do get a lot of reading done during this period, which actually lasts about three and a half months. The *Great Gatsby, Tender is the Night, The Far Side of Paradise,* a veritable Fitzgerald festival, Thomas Wolfe's *Look Homeward Angel,* and Steinbeck's *Grapes of Wrath.* If nothing else, I am reading some good shit and actually relieved to know I'm not so depressed that I can't read or concentrate. TV, no surprise, is easier to focus on. It requires a lower level of attention, and reading is more of a conscious effort at concentration. Also trying to figure out my major, so I haven't given up all hope about finishing college.

At this point, I have taken a psych class and thought possibly about majoring in it, especially during my first quarter. Of course, by now I have gotten sidetracked by interest in other subjects and by my second year considered philosophy as well. Basically, on a practical level, I don't know what the fuck I want to do although when I think about it, I actually like all of those subjects on an intellectual level and I'm starting to see the way these various subjects might be related. It's really cool when I think about it that way, like the myriad of ways you could look at the problems of race in this country. You could look at it psychologically, sociologically, economically or historically. Just different angles on the same thing. For some reason, this realization was a turn on. But now, while being depressed, none of this seems to matter.

I make no effort to contact or get to know the four other residents in the rooming house who are all Wisconsin undergrads, and after minimal verbal exchanges with them I decide they are not my cup of tea. I'm withdrawn with my fellow employees at the Hoffman House as well, which I am finding is a weird place to work. The place gives me the creeps. I later find out it is renowned for its union busting efforts, which makes me feel like I'm on enemy territory. My boss is a guy named Hans who is also the chief waiter, busboy and manager dude. During my shifts, I'm under the superficially cheerful supervisory eye of Dot, the hostess, and part time manager of the place, whose claim to fame, as far as I'm concerned, is her use of wonderful and foreign-sounding euphemisms in her patter. She uses, "hooseywatsis" or "thingamajig" for tools or when she refers to an object or process she has no vocabulary word for and employs "the deal" as a stand-in, for mostly anything. Hicksville Central. Working in this kind of milieu does not help my mood. I am there for your basic pay check "deal" or "whatchamacallit." Dot's "sophisticated" vocabulary is strangely amusing in a stupefying way, but not enough to turn the tide on my depression.

Even though I'm in a foul, depressed mood, of course, once again, I do not take the prescribed medications, and do not see any shrink, thank the Lord. The no meds allows me to maintain some semblance of a libido. I indulge in onanistic activities. If you don't know what that word means, look it up. I like saying that more than just jerking off. Believe it or not, I am still pining for Marla, (What the fuck?) but have sexual fantasies for other women I remember back at OSU. You betcha. Trying to break up my loneliness and deep isolation at least in fantasy. After a couple of months of this, I can't take it any more, so I decide to give Sue Kahn, my old mini-sweetie from OSU, a call. And she's as sweet as she could be, and glad to hear from me. She and I speak for fifteen minutes and she agrees to spend the weekend with me in Madison sometime in early November.

The weekend together is really nice. She flies in, takes a bus to campus from the airport, and meets me at my place that Friday night. No brainer. I call in sick for the next day so we can be together on Saturday and half of Sunday. She's great. Sweet, warm and understanding about the situation with my mom and also my situation vis a vis Marla. Affectionate, too. We sleep together, but don't have sex, or other activities other than kissing and minor groping incursions. "That's fine," she says since she is on her period and I am not sure I can get it up that weekend anyway given my state of mind, so it's fine with me, too. I am completely in her debt for showing me kindness and concern, which I verbalize. Seeing her makes me feel like I want to get out of Madison and go back to Columbus and school. But unfortunately, my decision comes a bit too late because I miss the winter quarter deadline for OSU registration. But I decide at this point that I will go back to Columbus anyway and so in a couple of weeks, it so happened just after Thanksgiving, I am given the heave ho by the Hoffman House folks.

Management tells me some customers had complained about my surly, unfriendly attitude. Yeah. It fits. One customer even asked me how come I never smiled. My reply was probably not an example of good people skills. I said, "What is there to smile about?" Hans and Dot got wind of it and were not happy. They give me a warning for this and inform me that if my attitude/demeanor doesn't pick up, I am going to be out of there. They have a business to run and customers to please. "Sieg heil, mein Führer." Well guess what? My demeanor doesn't improve. It isn't because I'm not trying, which I sort of do, but because it is the best I can do at this point. I am depressed - mother fucker. They don't know from or care about that shit, nor do they want to hear these kinds of excuses. They do have a business to run. So I really can't blame them...... that much. Anyway on December 6, I am given the axe.

I am secretly happy and tell Dave and Cherise about it. They are understanding, because they are in agreement that Hoffman House is not a good place to work, for anybody. I tell them that since Christmas break is only ten days away, I'll hang in for the time being in Madison having already decided to go back to Columbus for the winter and spring quarter even though I haven't been able to register on time. My plan is to work in Columbus winter quarter and then re-enroll for spring. These last ten days in Madison, I am actually starting to come out of my depression a bit, brightening up, at least socially, a bit. I hook up with my old New Rochelle friends still here in Madison, John and Peter, and hang out with them, and slowly feel a bit more outgoing again, now that I've decided to get back to Columbus. It's actually nice to be able to sleep in so I take advantage of it and when Dave and Cherise and I drive back to New Rochelle in the middle of December for the holiday break, I am ready for something old/new again. A fresh start back in Columbus.

Christmas in New Rochelle: Winter in Columbus, Ohio

Back On Campus Again

So, in December of 1970, my mom is now sick with her so-called pleurisy/cancer for about 7-8 months. Cherise, Dave and I drive home, doing the full throttle 15 hour drive from Madison through Chicago, into Cleveland, across Pennsylvania on Interstate 80, in crappy cold 20 degree weather, with occasional snow flurries in Ohio and western Penn. We hit New Rochelle around 6 pm on Wednesday the 20th of December, just in time for dinner, actually in time for my dad to pick up take out from Tung Hoy. At his request, I go with him to pick up the food while Dave and Cherise visit with Mom and Lew. Zora Lee Hill, our housekeeper, is there, too. It feels sorta good to be back home in an odd, familiar, warm way. After all, I've spent thirteen of my first eighteen years in that house on Daisy Farms Drive. I've only lived the first five years of my life elsewhere, Brooklyn, that is, on Fenimore St. in lower Flatbush near Ebbets Field, the old home of the Dodgers, before they betrayed me and millions more by moving to L.A. I have a certain affection for the Daisy Farms house. It has many nice memories for me, even though the house itself is really nothing special, kind of modest actually. The backyard is nice and has a terraced rock garden that Dad and we three boys, mostly Dave and I, helped cultivate. We gathered rocks and boulders for it from the street of the new Stratton Heights development that we lived in when we first moved there. Then it was so new that parts of the area were uninhabited when we got there and often the developers would leave the excess rocks and stuff in the street, ripe for picking, before waste management came to haul it away. So I guess I have some pride or stake in the rock garden and the way it looks in the backyard. Besides, Dave, Lew and I spent endless hours playing wiffle ball back there, not to mention stickball in the front driveway against the cement stone wall. These are the things I am fondest of back home, that and the den, home of the old Zenith black and white, scene of my baptismal into Bogart, Clift, Brando and Newman movies and all the gangster movies of the thirties, the Warner Brothers Studio- Cagney, Robinson, Muni classics. I think of the den when I think about my movie memories, and my bedroom for memories of Murray the K and later WOR/WNEW FM underground rock on my transistor, that got me through my youth at home. Music, film, tv sports and books were all the mainstays of my life. They sustained and nurtured me at times when people couldn't, wouldn't or didn't.

So, yeah, I do have warm memories of Daisy Farms Drive even though returning to it and seeing my dad in his bummed out condition and my mom in her weakened state are bitter pills to swallow. I spend the holidays hangin' with the family and relatives at home mostly. On one or two occasions I go out with Ricky, my Harvard buddy, drinking at a local watering hole on the border of New Rochelle and Scarsdale that always seems to be filled with a preppier rather than hippie-ish scene. It's all right. I can blend in anywhere if I need to, although by this point, it's not my preference. Rick, for his part, is pretty Jew-froed out, hippie-ish in both looks and musical tastes.

He and I share similar proclivities in regard to movies, music and sensibilities. We're still very competitive with each other, but this mostly comes out on the sports field, tennis and basketball courts. We hit the Y one day and play a little 1 on 1. At this point I'm better than Rick in basketball and baseball because at 14, Rick chose his specialty, tennis, and in his dedication he rose to #1 in the East by age 18. In fact,

Rick has achieved a lot. He appeared on Johnny Carson with his rock band, the Valhalla Chemists, played competitive tennis on a national level, was 12th grade school treasurer and is now in his junior year at Harvard. Next to him, I am this underachiever-like kid with an unremarkable baseball and basketball career at New Rochelle High School. I had a promising freshman year as a track star in the long jump and 220 yard dash, but no follow up as I found track boring and monotonous, particularly the training part. I quit playing basketball and baseball in tenth grade for a couple of reasons. I didn't like being the tenth man on the JV basketball team where I was one of two White guys, so I quit mid season. The Black kids ahead of me in the line up were probably better and I didn't see a way I could move up. The coach was not particularly thrilled with my skills either. And I didn't like my asshole coach on JV baseball in tenth grade either. He was an ex- marine, always acting mean and nasty. I got kicked off for sunbathing during a game when I wasn't starting. He didn't like that. Also, I didn't make the first string on varsity in 11th, so I was relegated to the Varsity B team where I was a star until I broke my ankle trying to steal third in a game. By the way, they called me out. Part of me thought stupidly that if I was safe, the broken ankle would have been worth it. Finally, in 12th grade, I missed the entire baseball season due to my mental illness. So no glory there. On the music front, I made a few spot appearances with garage bands back in 9th and 10th grade at Temple dances as a lead singer, so no follow up in that department. I tried my hand at acting in 9th grade after Mr. Feist, our high school acting coach, called me the next Marlon Brando. I signed up for his new acting school in New York, "The Roundabout Theater," but had homosexual panic in my attempts at acting in the city with Mr. Feist, so quit that. And lastly, pretty lackluster as a student. A's and B's in english and history, B's and C's in Spanish, math and science, your basic B- student in a high achieving A student body. Thems the facts on the ground through high school and two years of college.

I admire Rick. Don't really begrudge him as clearly he worked hard for his success in addition to having natural gifts. The difference between us is that we had a similar level of natural gifts, but I squandered my talents due to my psychological problems, insecurities, fears and what have you. The result was I ended up at a third rate academic institution, Ohio State, with nothing to show for it in the areas of my passions, sports, music or theater. Now, in my latest incarnation, I'm a fanatical radical activist who uses his passionate intensity more than his head. So, maybe even here I am a failure. I don't like looking at things this way or feeling this way about myself. It's easier being mad and rebellious. But hanging with Rick carries these undercurrents for me, which I occasionally dip into internally. It's interesting that I can think about my problems more clearly and honestly when I'm not depressed as I was starting to become again. But when I am depressed, all I can think of are things to do or not do to help me feel better. My thinking when depressed just cycles off into self blame and recrimination. So when I do start to feel better, I am able to think more clearly with less self blame. I have more perspective and can see my positives, not just my negatives. Maybe a slightly more balanced view.

My two week Christmas vacation passes. I try to spend as much time with Mom as I can. She is visibly sinking, having lost about 25 pounds since I last saw her, now hovering at about 103. Looking gaunt, starting to spend at least half her time in bed. We spend our time together watching Dick Cavett, Johnny Carson or *Laugh In* and occasionally Walter Cronkite. She is still quite politically involved with the day to day goings on in the nation and world, with Vietnam, Nixon, the racial situation, even curious about the countercultural and especially the burgeoning woman's movement. In that arena, she spends a lot of her time discussing these facets with Cherise, a bona fide feminist at this point, and a woman exceedingly well read on all the up to date literature and issues on the subject. In general, being with Mom is depressing and sad but I try, and hopefully succeed, in not letting on. I don't think I cry even once in her presence and I have a reputation for being quite the crier. But I keep it together for her, and try to be positive, stoical and tough for her. It makes me feel better, too. It feels a little more grown up. I must confess however, that when New Year's Eve comes around I am glad that the vacation will be coming to an end in two days as I secretly can't wait to get back to my life in Columbus.

New Year's is spent at Peter Zeughauser's house, my Madison cohort's house in south New Rochelle. This is the kid from Madison who, believe it or not, I had only seen once in the entire four months I was in Madison. That's how bummed, isolated and withdrawn I was. But now I'm feeling somewhat better and I can mingle more. New Year's Eve at his house is filled with other college kids from my high school, most of whom I am only acquaintances with, but kids Rick and Peter had known as classmates. They're a more academic, nerdier, Ivy League crowd than my natural affinity group. But it's fine. It doesn't matter. Everyone is nice, but more low key than I am used to. Not as much flirting, getting stoned or even excessive drinking than I'm used to. Much less rowdy. Even Rick gets kind of bored with it. He branched out socially at Harvard, into a wilder, artier, druggy-type scene. The intellectual trip there is more well rounded, less nerdy, even less preppy than this crowd. But you could certainly find both types up there. Rick is now clearly countercultural, all the way. Year one, he had been tres political and joined SDS but got disillusioned with that fast. Turned off by the black and whiteness of radical politics. By year two, he started to get into a much grittier focus on street life and into his music, heavily. Van Morrison, Credence, the Beatles, Dylan and the Stones, of course. Tom Rush, a particular favorite. Rick is clearly in a harder-edged phase, quoting a lot of Paul Newman lines from pictures like *Hud*, *Cool Hand Luke* while I chime in with some of my favorites from *The Hustler*. Hangin' with him is really the best, most fun, entertaining part. We've known each other since '58 so we have quite a backwater of experience and memories.

The next two days are spent preparing my leave back to Cols. and hanging with Ma. It's low key, the weather sucks outside anyway. I watch a little NFL football and then hop an American Airlines flight to Columbus. It's hard leaving my mom, knowing the shape she's in, but I try my best not to think about it too much. It's too painful and scary and I need to carry on with my life, no matter what, I tell myself. So I try to focus on the matters at hand, which are looking for a place to live and a job to support myself until spring quarter when I can resume classes again.

PART THREE

CHAPTER 20

Your Final Jeopardy Answer

I land in town on a Sunday night in early January, the usual cold freezing weather for this time of year. I immediately call Jamie Olian and Curt Robinson. They're already informed of my situation, that of having no place to live. They know that John T. Moore, a former roommate of theirs from Steeb Hall, from our old dorm that past spring, just lost his roommate. The roommate flunked out and John is looking for someone. I might be in luck. John's a very easy going guy. Mellow. My buddies give me his phone number and I call him. He's very interested and tells me he has class the next morning but that I can come by and check the place out at noon. I thank him and tell him I will. The place is 69 Chittenden Street, on south campus. So, hopefully that takes care of my housing concerns. But meanwhile, where am I going to stay tonight? Luckily for me, while I am walking around with my duffel bag at 10:30 pm on High Street, I run into John Flowers's roommate, Whit, a guy I had hung out with as well but who I liked slightly less than John. He liked me well enough and offers to put me up for the night if I buy him a drink, which I am happy to do. So, it turns out my housing problems immediate and long term get fixed pretty fast. This could be a good sign about my fortunes changing. Whit and John put me up for the night, no questions asked, and the next day John T. Moore shows me his two bedroom apartment which I like well enough and agree to pay the 50 dollars a month rent. That evening I move my duffel bag into the pad. Now, I am all set. The apartment looks homey despite the shabby brown sofa and dilapidated lazy boy chairs surrounding the couch. The place has a messy but not dirty look. I think I will be happy here.

Housing situation in place, with John T. being the very mellow guy I remembered him to be, I now have to figure out what to do about a job. Not really caring what I do so much as needing a certain amount of money because I am really just biding my time until spring quarter when classes resume. Nevertheless, I have to do something. But at least for the time being, I have shelter and enough dough to get food for a few weeks from what's left from my earnings back at Hoffman House and some that my dad gave me to live on to tide me over until I find work. Dave and Cherise are back in Madison. Lew, the youngest, is back home in New Rochelle with Zora Lee, Mom and Dad. The family, all safe for now. Rick, back in Cambridge, Mark, at Colgate and Mac, in Boston. Some stability for me and the important people in my life, at least for now.

Tom, Curt, Jamie, my former roommates, are now living in apartments here in Columbus. Paul Ricciardo is in the same apartment on south campus. John Alloway, still working at CYA in Columbus. Sue Kahn, now a junior so therefore she's liberated from the requirement of dorm living and is living the life in an apartment. My basic social network. All present and accounted for and intact. Obviously, having a stable, enduring social network of friends remains important for my feeling of security given my failures in other arenas, and my worries about losing Mom and my actual loss of Marla, now twice in a year and a half. Only Marquis Jones from year 1 and 2 at Steeb Hall is gone. Transferred back to Jersey, going to Rutgers, Livingston branch. Too bad, I liked that dude with all his intensity, music-wise, politics-wise, hunting-for-women-wise and basic vibe-wise.

But these next three months will be different from before in that it's my first time in Columbus not enrolled in school, just as being in Madison working also had been a first. First time I dropped out. Actually, I took a gap semester before starting at OSU in the fall of '68 which was spent as a voluntary inpatient at the Institute of Living, the high class nuthouse for upper middle class and upper class lunatics, that I keep referring to. So, in fact, I've had two gap semesters already, in two fucking years. So, I guess this is the second fall back position (retreat) in a row, although at a different venue, and I construed it as a continuation of Gap 2. Gap 1 nuthouse. Gap 2 Madison - Columbus, (fall '70 to spring '71). I like to keep my chronologies straight. What the fuck. It helps with the coherence of my internal narrative, not to mention my mind. Provides a feeling of order. The feeling. The feeling. Being employed is part of making it happen, so I'm getting back to the job search.

With John matriculating at OSU for his junior year, majoring in political science, he is out of the apartment a fair amount. He's without a woman, which bothers him a little, but he's not the bemoaning type. Not your Cary Grant looking kind of guy. Kind of shy but really nice, funny and kind. Not kind of kind, but kind. Smart, too. Loves to play with words. We fuck around with language while pacing late at night in conversations, always trying to find ways to get the words "plausible" and "feasible" into our dialogue. Conversations revolve around words with ambiguous meanings. "Conceivable" versus "doable." "Plausible" versus "feasible." It depends on how you use the words in a sentence and what you're trying to convey. I don't know, it was more humorous than serious. It was one of the chief ways John and I amused ourselves and related when we did.

I take a couple of days to get my bearings before I go store to store looking for work. Landing at IHOP, I am able to garner a job there as a dishwasher. I immediately call my father and tell him I've got work. Being productive is his major preoccupation with me if I'm not going to be a student, so hearing I am employed, he is relieved. Dad being off my back about a job, takes the pressure off for me and enables me to relax some. I find something and that will, for the time being, allay his worries about me and his pocketbook.

Money has always been an ongoing source of anxiety for Dad, despite having more than a decent income from his cardiology practice in Manhattan. He alternates between being extremely generous with me and my brothers or being exceedingly cheap. I know enough about his personal psychology to realize that his rapid and unpredictable fluctuations have nothing to do with reality but rather part of his kind of moody personality and/or his reaction to the trauma of the Great Depression and what happened to his father in 1929 when his dad's business went belly up overnight. Anyway, the man is relieved to hear his middle son is employed. It is one less thing for him to worry about. Now he can focus his energies on my mother. She is really not doing well. Has lost 25 pounds, is down to about a hundred, starting to really look bad, although she does not complain that she feels bad. I think she is on a lot of drugs. The only treatment she's had has been radiation. No surgery or chemotherapy, if that gives some idea of how far her disease has progressed. Dad is beside himself, both as a physician who has prided himself on his knowledge and ability to get folks better, and of course as a husband, who is quite attached to my mom, despite his occasional distasteful behaviors toward her. He could be quite insensitive, overbearing, controlling and impossible with her. He always seems to want to get his way. Often, he has been flirtatious with other women, either in front of her or in her absence. In his defense, my mother has not been the most demonstrative or affectionate person, and I have the feeling she is either very shy and inhibited or really turned off by my father. Or both. It was and is distressing to me, observing this as a kid, a young teenager, and a person in my late teens. That dynamic never seemed to change the entire time I was growing up. It disturbed me and my brothers and became a topic of conversation among us as we got older.

It makes me think they have a bad marriage, or a good marriage in appearance only. You know, in tact, functional on the surface, sort of respectful and caring on the one hand, but on a deeper level, affection, passion-wise, fucked. I am sure my brothers perceive both levels about their marriage, the practical and the deep emotional.

I think their marital issues affected us in varying degrees, both then as kids and now as we are getting older. We've made vows to ourselves to not have marriages like our parents have. The current zeitgeist is that women want careers and even more importantly, equal or egalitarian spousal relationships. My brothers and I feel the same way. We also want women who have careers, earn their own money, so we can, at least in theory, have egalitarian marriages. We can talk the talk even though we might not be able to walk the walk. Whether we as young men are ready for the changes women want from us men in our daily lives is another story. But we are willing to try. Cherise, Dave's wife, exemplifies the women's lib ethos. Very opinionated about how men and women should relate in the workplace and at home, she pushes Dave for a more sharing, less rigid, traditional gender role managing the household. Other women of my generation are demanding changes as well. What it boils down to with the Brucher boys is we want different types of marriages than our parents have, and the time is ripe for it. Even my mom is starting to appreciate what the women's libbers are saying and starting to see how she, like so many other women of her generation, is stuck in dependency roles with their husbands. When I think about this, it makes me feel good but sad as well. Good that Mom is starting to get how she is trapped, but sad that she might not live long enough to do anything about it. Consciously, I say to myself that I can't allow myself to get bogged down in my sadness and fear that Mom might die. It's an impending reality that I refuse to acknowledge for very long. It's too painful and scary. Now back in Columbus, I tell myself I need to focus on my life. No matter what.

I start my new job as a dishwasher at IHOP and work 5 days a week 40 hours per week. The work, while grueling, also pays shit. But as always, especially in the beginning, I am reliable. I show up on time and follow through, that is, for three weeks until Super Bowl Sunday, when Dallas and Baltimore have an epic, tightly fought game with Tom Dempsey kicking a field goal with no time on the clock to win it for Baltimore. I get so immersed in the game that I don't show and don't call IHOP. They don't like that shit. What employer does? So they fire me. Bada bing. Now I'm fucked. Now I have no means of support.

But Paul Ricciardo steps up and comes to my rescue. Paul, it seems, knows of people selling and dealing hashish and knows where I can buy some, break it up, sell it, and make a profit. Any anxieties I have about the illegalities regarding dealing are easily overcome by the apparent ease and convenience of this activity. It is early

February and I have to get through the next six weeks before going back to New Rochelle for spring break, where once again, I will be dependent on my dad's financial largesse for school. So I take Paul up on his business offer. I buy the hash. It's in a chunk. I pay $300 to an associate of Paul's and proceed to become a hash dealer. Another skill I can put on my growing resume. Hahaha. It is quite easy, actually. Breaking up the chunk into eight parts, I charge a sizable markup so that when all the hash is sold, I double my money from the initial investment. My profit, $600, is more than enough to make rent, buy food and pay for entertainment for the next six weeks. After all, rent is only $50 a month. Food maybe another $100 a month. So the rest is for transportation and entertainment expenses. Now I understand for the first time, from an economic standpoint, the lucrativeness and simplicity of dealing. It really is quite easy and if a person is careful, safe. I basically enlist the interest of people I know, friends or close acquaintances who get stoned and I get rid of the stuff in 6 days. After breaking up the hash, I sell it to six people, with two people buying two pieces. The whole thing takes less than a week and I don't smoke any of it myself. It's not really my thing. Pot or hash for that matter. I am an acid man myself based on the couple of times I did it, believe it or not. It is easier to prepare for. You know you are gonna be psychotic for 8 hours, whereas with pot and hash anything could happen. Beer is good, too. Good old predictable buzz. Haven't done coke or speed, or shot up anything. No. I am basically straight with some minor extracurricular psychedelic interests, spiritual and metaphysical. A little bit hedonistic too, if I'm being honest. You know doin' stuff just for the fun of it.

Having made all the dough I need, I have a lot of free time on my hands. Don't really have to work. It is cool. I take the time to read a lot of books of my own choosing. Politics, psychology, sociology books. A few novels as well. Hermann Hesse, William Styron's *Confessions of Nat Turner*, Norman Mailer's *Armies of the Night* and my all time sociological favorite, Phillip Slater's *The Pursuit of Loneliness*. Psychology wise, I read Reich's *Listen Little Man*, Perls's *In and Out the Garbage Pail*, his autobiography, and spend a lot of time hanging out with John T. Moore, my roommate, Paul Ricciardo, my riot buddy and red bandanna brigade mate, and John Flowers, my Black friend and jail protector. These are my three mainstay guy buds. No women are on the scene at this point. Sue Kahn and I have mostly evolved into a friendship, as she is not that turned on to me and vice versa. It's okay. Not really tense. We see each other on occasion and it's more brother-sister than anything else and it's nice in its way. She's very sweet and caring. My other main female contact at this point is my other old friend, Tom's ex-girlfriend, who as it turns out, lives two houses away from me. She, also sweet, interesting, is from Chagrin Falls, just outside Cleveland. I definitely have the hots for her but I'm conflicted because she was once a good friend's girlfriend. I had a rule. Never sleep with a friend's girlfriend, even if it was in the past tense, a policy I practice 100 percent of the time, so I resist my libidinal lust for Stacey, even though she stops over a lot and we hang out quite a bit. It stays platonic. After a while, I think it sort of gets to be a little too much for her and she stops coming by. She must know how I feel about her although we don't talk about it. I think she is attracted to me as well, but probably senses my mixed feelings about making a move. She doesn't seem to want to make a move on me either, even though she seems less conflicted about getting libidinally involved with me then I do with her. So, she simply bows out after a few weeks of hangin' with me for 2- 3 nights a week. She might have been waiting for me to make a move on her but that was not gonna happen.

By now, I am a horn dog, majorly. Haven't had any real sex in 6 months. Once again, I find myself thinking about and pining for Marla Mascowitz. So, one night while in an all night stay up with Jamie Olian and John and, after much pondering and vacillating, I decide that in two days, on Thursday February 21, I will hitchhike to Frederick, Maryland where Marla is in college. I don't even consider that it might not be a good idea. I decide that I'll just surprise her. Thursday at 7 am, two days later, I hit the road as planned, and head east on highway 70 looking for a ride, destination Maryland.

CHAPTER 21

Marla Mascowitz (Your Final, Final Jeopardy Answer)

The weather today isn't too bad, around 40, cloudy. Parking myself at an entrance to highway 70, I quickly get picked up by an Oldsmobile Cutlass driven by a man in his thirties on his way to Harrisburg, Pennsylvania. He sees my sign, which says "Frederick, MD." That was a good ride. A 5 1/2 hour ride. I wait about an hour in Harrisburg for ride two. A trucker picks me up and takes me all the way to the Maryland border, all of this taking about 7 hours. A first for me in a semi. It's kinda cool. It's now two o'clock in the afternoon. The rest of the way is tough sledding. Nobody picks me up for about 3 hours until it's 5 o'clock and darkness is starting to descend. I'm starting to worry about being stranded in the middle of nowhere with the thought that maybe this wasn't such a good idea momentarily enters my mind. Luckily, just then, a guy in his early twenties picks me up and after hearing my story, goes out of his way and takes me not only to Frederick, Maryland, but right to the entrance of Hood College. He's definitely a romantic. After multiple exuberant thank yous, I get out right in front of Marla's dorm.

I am nervous as hell. I mean I haven't seen her in 20 months. Really haven't spent any time with her since January of 1968. Because after January of '68, I was in the hospital for nine months, then off to Ohio State for 6 months, then she had broken up with me in June of '69, and then no contact for 9 months, then those out of the blue phone calls in April of '70 for an intense five weeks of weekly romantic phone contact. Then she breaks it off on the day before Ohio State shuts down when I first hear of my mom's cancer diagnosis. So really no in person contact then either. Yeah, really minimal contact since Jan. '68. The bulk of our contact took place my junior and half of senior year. I knew this woman intensely for exactly 16 months from October '66 until February '68, but had never schtupped. Not that I keep an exact record of our time together. I wouldn't want to imply that. (Yeah right). We were high school sweethearts with not that much in common, with an intense sexual attraction that had never been consummated, love and concern for one another, but not much to talk about beyond friends we knew, family, soul music. That was about it. A pretty paltry connection when one thought about it with some objectivity. But as a 16 year old and now as a nearly 21 year old man, given that I had not had any other serious relationships since Marla, in my moony, longing for state, it seems like a lot. I love her for her loyalty and love for me during my illness. She was great. She was true blue, called, wrote and visited me in Hartford, at least a few times. For this my gratitude would be lifelong. This much I know.

But back to the story. It's now 7 o'clock and with my backpack in tow, I land right in front of Marla's dorm. I have done my geography homework about the school prior to leaving so I know where she lives. This women's school requires students to live on campus, for two years, similar to OSU. Only, Hood has about 2000 students at the most. Probably more like a thousand. Many from the south, Virginia, Carolinas. Not too many from the east. Marla, sort of in the minority there. Anyway, I bound carefully up her dorm steps walking into the lobby. There, I speak to the dorm receptionist, an older girl who confirms that Marla does live there. I ask if she could be contacted by phone, that she has a visitor. The receptionist, a romantic sort herself, complies with my request that she not mention who it is. I want it to be a surprise. I fill her in on who I am. The receptionist student is excited herself and gladly goes along with the ruse. Five minutes later, while I am seated in the lobby lounge chairs, trying to be as incognito as possible to maximize the surprise, Marla hits the lobby.

But as she enters the lobby and is talking to the receptionist, she looks over to where I am and in the same instant shouts, "I can't believe it. I can't believe it. This is too much. Bruch. I can't believe it." She rushes over and we hug. "Arnie, what are you doing here?" tears begin to stream down her face while still in our embrace. "This is so unbelievable. I can't believe you're here. How did you know where I lived ?" I, too, am startled and shocked but it's by how good Marla looks. Actually, better than ever, a real grown up woman. Hot, sweet and awesome. I must admit the hug really feels good. Like old home week, in my viscera.

She starts to weep a little more. I am dazed. We sit in the lounge chairs and just look at each other for a few minutes. She can see that my hair is pretty long. Longer than the last time she's seen me. Marla's hair is longer, too. I can't say she's filled out as she was always pretty filled out. She looks sexier but in a less girly, more sophisticated way. I am still attracted and can sense Marla is still attracted to me. Still in love with me. It is sort of amazing actually. Bizarre, surreal as well. But oddly comforting to be in each other's presence for the first hour or so. Kind of like the reunion scene in that Tom Hanks movie *Marooned* when he goes to see his wife, after she thought he was dead. She must have thought I was dead or hopelessly crazy, I think to myself, otherwise why would she have moved on. I would soon find out……. Saul.

"It's so hard to make love pay, when you're on the losing end, and I feel that way again."—Neil Young: "Everybody Knows This is Nowhere" Side Two, Song 1.

Comforting and homey. Yeah, that's what I would say it felt like. She suggests that we go out and get a bite at a local diner in town. She has her own car. A Pontiac Firebird. She is a good driver and I sit close to her as we head to the diner. There we go into our separate stories about what has happened to us both since the last time we spoke in May of '70 and the reasons for the break ups again. She tells me that she and Saul, her boyfriend, now a medical student at Emory university in Atlanta, had broken up in March of 1970 after meeting in the summer of '69 at a Jewish summer camp in the Carolinas. She doesn't really give me a clear answer as to why the two of them had broken up in '70. It was something vague like he still wanted to see other people and maybe she did too, but like I said, it's pretty vague. I am also trying to get to the bottom of why she decided to call me at the end of March in '70. I understood then that she and Saul had broken up. But I wonder who had initiated it. It is important to my ego that this wasn't just a rebound thing on her part for having been dumped. By this I mean, I don't want to feel that I was the closest port in the storm. Really the only other boyfriend she'd ever had, and I didn't want to feel like she'd call me as more of a security blanket to assuage her pain for having been dumped. I wanted to feel that she missed me, wanted to be with me and realized that I was the great love of her life. I can't say that the conversation led me to this conclusion. Nor can I say that it led to the opposite conclusion either. Actually, it's only contributing to the furthering of my confusion as to her motives and true feelings.

In the way Marla relays it, it makes me feel that when she and Saul got back together in May, maybe she HAD been dumped and that he had realized the error of his ways and was wanting back in and that she chose him over me. I am thinking that that was the case because if she truly wanted me, she would have said no to him and continued to pursue me. Alas, that did not occur. But again that was nine months previous. I want to see where she is "at" now. As I think about this, I can see that this is a massive ego trip on my part. I wanted to be wanted. I wanted to be chosen. I wanted to be the guy she picked. Now nine months later, as we sit at the diner eating breakfast at 10pm, again I am picking up mixed vibes. Saul, now a first year med student in Atlanta, has asked Marla to transfer to Emory to be with him and finish college down there. It sounds like she has decided to do it. It also sounds like he is probably going to ask her to get engaged soon, too, like part of the package in the request. So, it is all settled for her. So it seems. Yet, there is still something I pick up between us. Warmth, love, and definitely sexual tension. After all, we'd never had sex, only heavy petting and that had to be part of the underlying feeling between us. Plus, we had been each other's first loves and you don't ever get over or forget first loves, even though it is now over four years since we started going out and 20 months since we broke up for the last time. Despite the passage of time, the feelings are still there. It isn't just my feelings for her either. I could tell in the way she looks at me and touches me, hugs me, even kisses me that the feelings are still there. It's nice. But kind of sad, too. She calls her roommate and asks her if it is okay if I stay in their room with them. Her roommate, Sally suggests that she could stay with her friend down the hall if Marla so desired. Marla thanks her for her consideration, and so we go back to her dorm.

It's a funny night. In an all girls college, in a girls dorm, on an all girl floor. I am obviously used to more coed arrangements as even the conservative OSU was starting to be affected by the changes the sexual revolution had wrought that resulted in male/female arrangements in dorms. But these are really secondary matters to me tonight. What matters is that Marla and I are together really for the first time 1:1 since I came home from college two years earlier. It's not something I am used to. As we continue to talk, she puts on an old Temptations album because she knows it is something we shared together as highschool sweethearts, but it only served to highlight the ways we have changed. She's become more Jewish, more conventional, a bit more materialistic, but still nice, sweet, with good social skills, diplomatic, definitely still very bubbly and effervescent. I've grown angrier, and politically pretty radical. Pretty intellectual. Pretty unconventional, yippie/hippie. Definitely not focused in the way Marla and her boyfriend Saul are, on getting ahead, pursuing career ambitions, thinking about marriage and kids, etc. I am pretty far from that and still feeling pretty experimental regarding my life in general, wanting to change the world, still searching, clearly not in a hurry to find a career, settle down or any of that stuff. But those are the clear cut differences. She dresses more preppy. I am more grungy. I take a shower before going to bed, as I can tell by Marla's reactions that that might be a good idea. She is still really good looking and sexy. Doesn't overdue the make up. And still really a nice, sweet person. I definitely want to sleep with her but like always I don't want to push it. I want her to want me as well. But if it isn't right or the right time, I don't want to do it. We spend another two hours until 1 am talking, sitting close together, holding hands and occasionally kissing. She is clearly ambivalent. I am not, but I am taking my cues from her. She clearly feels committed to the relationship she has with Saul, as she keeps pronouncing, while on the other hand her body and behavior, non verbally, are saying something else. I don't think it is manipulative. But make no mistake about it, I think Marla gets off on being the object of desire. And it is clearly flattering to her vanity that two men want her at the same time. She definitely knows how to be titillating, consciously or unconsciously. Maybe a little of both. She does have this haughty, teasing side. It both turns me on and makes me angry. The feelings are reminiscent of how I felt when we were juniors and seniors in high school. Tantalizing. By 1:00 that morning, I say I am getting exhausted and would like to sleep in her bed. In my bargain, I promise not to touch her if she doesn't want me to. But it might be nice to "cuddle" a little if she wishes. She says fine. And so we do and I honor her request and neither of us violate the terms of my sleeping next to her in bed. No moves are made below the neck.

The Next Day

We awake in a spoonlike position with a less than fully restful sleep. Yet I can't say it is a fitful sleep either. I kept waking up in the middle of the night with a strange disoriented sensation but then would fall right back to sleep. This happened maybe three or four times. But, having my arms around Marla, even though we weren't completely naked, was strangely comforting. It was not something I was used to doing with her and the reality of that experience rendered obsolete all of my prior fantasies about what it would be like to be fully embracing her in bed. Of course, all of my active fantasies had been sexual in nature, with some imagining what her body, skin, contact with my body would feel like. The reality matched the tightness or hardness of our contact. It also matched the squishiness in the places I had previously imagined it would feel squishy. Like her hips and tush. However, unlike in high school, her breasts and genital region were off limits, so the experience itself, while somewhat sensual in a certain tactile and olfactory way, lacked that full throttle, flat out sexual component which had been a part of so many sexual fantasies, particularly when she was no longer available to me after she broke up with me 20 months earlier. Not being able to have her unleashed intense sexual fantasy unlike anything I felt the previous 32 months when we were together. Then, I simply took her for granted, and focused my fantasy, ardor, and longing on other girls/women in my high school. And a lot of them were friends of Marla's, it turns out. Lorna, Becky being two examples. They just happened to be two of the three best friends Marla had in high school and sure enough I fantasized and wanted them. I also wanted other women/girls in high school, but once Marla and I had some sexual contact, even though we had not fucked, she stopped being the sole object of my lust. It was like the old adage, wanting what I couldn't have, not wanting what I had. Kind of neurotic, if you asked me, but what did I know? I wasn't a psychiatrist or psychologist but by then logged enough time as a patient to know something was askew. In other words I wasn't just "psychotoman," I was also "neurotoman."

Anyway, the next day both of us wake up in mutual states of disorientation from the strangeness of having spent the night together. After getting dressed and washing up, Marla suggests that we eat at the diner we went to the night before. She says it is the best place for a greasy spoon breakfast. In a matter of fact manner she tells me, because it slipped her mind the night before, that she has to drive up to New Rochelle today, Friday, for the weekend. She has her cousin's bar mitzvah to attend Saturday and had told her folks that she would drive up for it. She asks me if I want to drive with her as she knows that my mother is pretty sick and maybe I would like to see her. I say sure, somewhat crestfallen. I know this means that the chance for the two of us to sleep together in the literal way, not metaphorical way, is probably doomed. I say yes, because in part I do want to see my mom, and in part because I still want to be with Marla even if it means driving for three hours in the crappy, winter weather of late February.

So after breakfast, off we go up highway 95, and soon are in Pennsylvania. And we are back in familiar territory. In a car together listening to top 40 radio. Only this time it is not nearly as fun and exciting as it was when we were high school kids. It's kind of depressing. The song "Just my Imagination," the latest Temptations hit, comes on about 3 times during the drive. Marla likes that one. She still likes her soul/Motown music. I'd grown somewhat tired of a steady diet of Motown a long time ago, although I still like some of it somewhat. Marvin Gaye and Stevie Wonder had yet to peak in terms of their epic-like, socially conscious albums *What's Going On?*, *Talking Book*, and *Inner Visions*. I am much more into psychedelic music, Crosby, Stills, Nash and Young, Creedence Clearwater and the new guy, Elton John, who has a smoking ballad out, "Your Song," his first big hit in America. I especially love Linda Ronstadt's song

"Long Long Time." It evokes my painful longing for Marla and the feelings I had and still have for her, now dashed by the ill-timed, poorly handled mistakes of my youth or something to that effect. The trip is a bummer. Not only am I disappointed that we aren't going to be together romantically or sexually, I am also, at the same time, sort of bummed out by what made me so enthralled about her in the first place. My feelings for her, although clearly unrequited or unwilling to be consummated on a gonadal level on the one hand, are in conflict with my sense on a more intellectual or interactional level, that we are really two very different kinds of people. It is as clear as day. She could be a sorority chick for what that is worth given her interests, values and basic conventionality. I am definitely not your basic frat boy kind of guy on any level. I had been through too much for that shit to make any sense to me, and I'm not really that ambitious conventionally, or career-minded or interested in fitting into the "fakakta" social structure that she so easily swims in. I don't fit in her world and I don't want to. It was never so clear than on our ride back to New Rochelle. We have nothing to say to each other after the first half hour. We pass the last couple of hours almost soundlessly except for the ubiquitous radio. By the time she drops me off at my house, I am relieved to get away but I respect her for having the decency to come into my house and saying "hi" to my mom toward whom she has affection for and vice versa. Then we part. I'm completely bummed and feel empty but glad to see Mom.

By this time, my mom is quite emaciated but still has her good sense. I don't withhold much pertinent info from her, particularly on the woman front. She's always in my corner, fairly nonjudgmental of me, and has a great sense about people. I can count on her for honesty when push comes to shove. Almost immediately, after hearing about the circumstances of my visit with Marla and her "marital status to be," Mom has an almost seering look on her face as she asks me with some degree of venom, "Hey, Arnie. You know why would she allow you to spend the night with her? What is she? Some kind of tease? I mean that was kind of mean. Don't you think so?"

I can't disagree even though it doesn't feel good to hear that my mom's assessment of my being a sucker is accurate. It stings, the sting of truth. Yet, it must be said that in my ardor for Marla, I put myself in a position to be rejected, so clearly there is blame to go all around. But, now that is over. It's not to be. I spend the weekend with Dad but mostly with Mom when she is awake and up to it. She is emaciated and I try not to let on to her how horrified I am by her physical state. I also vow both to my dad and to myself that I will not let myself cry in front of her. It just doesn't seem fair to her. Privately, when I leave the room, when I am sure she can't hear, I shut the door of my room and let it out. AAGHH!

I fly back to Columbus on Sunday night, glad and sad to have spent the weekend with Mom. I spend the next three weeks in Columbus, registering for spring, reading and hanging out with friends. Then I head back to New Rochelle for ten days. They are to be the last ten days I will spend with my mom and in the back of my head, I kind of know that this is the case. Mom is looking gaunter and gaunter. Under 90 pounds now. The cancer kicking her ass big time. She mostly sleeps and though she tries to hide it when I'm in the room with her, I can tell she's in some pain even though she is taking pain pills at this point. Dad is a mess. Lew, almost sixteen, is trying to maintain a strong front, but privately informs me he is doing a fair amount of pot and has begun taking psychedelics. Jim and Cherise are on semesters so their break won't be for another week or so. So I hang out in Mom's bedroom watching tv with her when she seems half conscious. The rest of the time, we just commune mostly in silence.

The vibe in the house is very solemn and a sad gloom looms over the place. It feels like a thick darkness has descended over the house even though spring is beginning to break through with one or two sunshiny days. It doesn't seem to make a dent in the mood or feel of the house with the heavy weight we are all carrying, knowing Mom is dying. March 26, my 21st birthday would normally be a happy occasion but not this year, not by a mile.

The day after my birthday on the 27th of March, I say goodbye to Lew and Dad then go into Mom's room to say goodbye, with an almost certain feeling that I am saying goodbye to her for the last time. Determined not to cry, I hug her. She's all skin and bones and I kiss her cheek. I watch her give me a brave smile as she says to me, "Take care of yourself, Pussycat. Do well in school. I love you, baby."

"I love you too, Mom," I answer back and reflexively say, " I'll see you soon," although I know it is a lie, but I can't help myself, not wanting to give up hope or have her give up hope. She nods and sends back a loving smile. Then she shuts her eyes as I walk out of the room, sinking and sobbing by the time I get to my bedroom a few feet away.

Dad is waiting downstairs to drive me to the airport. The drive is mostly deadly silent. I give him a big hug and tell him I will be alright, not to worry about me and that I'll be in touch. He tries to put on a stoical act, smiling one of his reflexive jovial smiles, but he doesn't fool me. He is in hell.

CHAPTER 22

Four Way Street
(Spring Semester '71)

End of March, beginning of April, it's the first two weeks of spring quarter. So it's Intro to Sociology, an education class, English 103, and History of the Reformation. It's fine. I have my mojo back. The experience with my mom, going to see Marla, and simply the passing of time, has strangely helped to lift my depression of last summer and fall. Kind of counter-intuitive if you ask me given my current circumstances with my mom at death's door. Maybe, it's all biochemical. Who knows? I am back to my old/new aggressive, assertive self. Not afraid to initiate conversations with people. Hyperfriendly. Every spring and summer for the past three springs it seems I go into this "manic" phase while every late summer August then until February, I go into a "depressive" phase. It's as though I have some kind of seasonal thing. Who knows? I'm not taking medications or getting any psychotherapy. I've been on a med and therapy hiatus since August of '70 since I went to Madison. Now that I'm back in Columbus, it feels good. Eight whole months without therapy or meds. It's the first time since December '66 that I've gone this long without some form of psychopharmacological/psychother-apeutic intervention. Well, whoopee freakin' do. Once again, despite my mom's illness and despite the fine "how do you do" meeting with Marla in Frederick, Maryland, I'm feeling surprisingly good.

I've got my "mojo working" to quote Muddy Waters, a bluesman I saw a couple of times in high school and now that song "I Got My Mojo Working" will forever stick in my mind. I thought it stood for sexual energy. Am I wrong? Anyway, I have it back. For the next couple of weeks, I am meeting "chicks" left and right. And I actually get laid. After an 8 month hiatus, I meet this woman, Marylyn at The Tavern, the Union lunch place. I do my usual "bum a cigarette" routine and she lets me sit down with her where I go into my usual 20 questions interview schtick. She likes the attention and is open and forthright in the way these Ohio women are, particularly the ones not from Cleveland. She's from Sandusky, a nearby industrial small town on the shores of Lake Erie. Turns out she lives about two blocks up the street from me on Chittenden and invites me for dinner tonight. Actually, for a traditionally greasy Quiznos pizza. Before I know it, with a little Three Dog Night's, "Celebrate, celebrate. Dance to the music," on the turntable, we start making out and the rest, as they say, is history.

Marylyn is sweet and likable in that Ohio, unpretentious way that I have grown fond of. Not sophisticated, but genuine and straight forward. Likable. She is attractive enough to me, a 7. Meets my minimum attractiveness standard. I mean I figure I am a 7 so I can attract at least 7 and more easily a 7 or less. Even though on a good day, personality wise, I can do even better. Maybe even bag an 8 or a 9. Afterall, I had gone out with the prom queen, Libby, in 12th grade, a bona fide 9. In my book, there are no 10's, a level of perfection that nobody hits, and very few come close. The best you can get in my book is a 9+. I've seen only a few and met even fewer. Even Libby was only a straight 9. Never went out with a 9+. Don't figure I ever will, don't really need to. And I have fairly generous standards. Anyone 5 or up, given my mood, is qualified . Most women, I figure 84% on the normal distribution curve are 5 or better, so most qualify on any given day with me. On a picky day, only 16% qualify. But most of the time, when I am out in public, particularly now, two out of three women are attractive enough. Maybe it's a reflection of my self esteem that I can't afford to be picky. Perhaps. But mostly, I like women, thinking that most of them do their best to look good even if they don't have outstanding natural attributes and feel that most of them deserve to be given attention. Why not? Even the ones I'm not attracted to deserve to be treated with respect. What the fuck. I'd like to say I am like this all the time but when I'm in a bad mood, which I have been a fair amount of on and off for a long time, my views narrow. The anger comes out, things suck and I become very negative. Then, it becomes a matter of 7 or up. Only 16 percent qualify and I tend to ignore the rest. As far as how women treat me, I have the feeling that most women, once in conversation with me, will give me the time of day. Five out of 6. That one out of six, well they are tough to bag on any given day, good mood or bad. So they take some extra work and honed skills. And I am interested in honing this particular skill. I've always had a general interest in how and why people behave with each other, in one to one situations and in groups. After all, I am a sociology major, just declared. I could see after my forays in psychology, philosophy and history that none of them, as taught at OSU, would meet my bill of fare. I need something broader, and more comprehensive, people/groups wise. Sociology, the subject area, seemed to meet that desire. And part of that is trying to understand what things attract people to one another.

So sociology, it is. This spring I will be taking Intro to Sociology, but I have already done some reading in "soche" as we call it. I particularly like what they now call micro sociology. The sociology of small groups, in vivo sociology. Street corner society- sociology, that kind of thing. I love observing the group dynamics on the Oval, where tens, if not hundreds of small groups, gather daily. I was first fascinated by this when I met my Oval friends a couple of years earlier, and my interest only intensified during the riots. Except then, it wasn't just small groups, but large ones, too. I wonder what makes them tick. Who is allowed into these various groups? What's their power structure and how do the members get close or remain distant? Thinking about this is one of my favorite pastimes in the whole world and gets me excited, intellectually and viscerally as well.

Anyway, the first two weeks of spring quarter are going pretty well, although in the back of my mind, I am thinking about my mother, but also trying not to think too much about her. When I do, I entertain a wish that she will get better, but I know she won't, but that thought is too painful, so I go about my usual routine, looking for distractions and excitement and communal activities. On Friday, April 9th, the end of week two of spring quarter, I hit Pearl Alley Discs, the hippie record store, to get the new CSNY live album *Four Way Street* that just came out today. It features live versions of all of my favorite songs. They're, by far, my favorite band. Love their harmonies, love their lyrics, love the way they infuse them with politics. I feel in tune with their sensibilities: hippie-political, California west coast, nature, idealistic vibe. In particular, I love Neil Young's solo rendition of "On the Way Home," his Buffalo Springfield hit from *Last Time Around*, Springfield's last album in January '68. It, of course, reminds me of my last days at the Institute of Living and the infamous softball game in November when we inmates beat the doctors and data processing people. But mostly, the song reminds me of that certain New England fall smell of burning leaves, colors changing, crisp air. The best. "...smoke ring day when the wind blows." A seeming paradox. Neil Young's plaintive voice intoning "On the Way Home" pierce through the stereo speakers as I am in full reverie mode, back in Hartford, off in some idyllic mellow spot when the phone rings.

Hearing brother Dave's voice, I instantly know what the call is for. In fact, I have had a funny feeling all day and Dave's voice on this call speaks volumes. "How's it going? ' " he wanted to know.

"Oy," I thought. "Fine," I said.

"I've got some bad news. Mom passed away this afternoon. I'm calling you from the hospital, Flower Fifth. Dad, Cherise and I are here. We're going to need you to come back. Can you make it tomorrow? We're going to have the funeral service on Sunday."

"Yeah, sure. Of course," I reply. Still shocked, still stunned but pretty present nonetheless. "Yeah, I'll get a flight back to New York tomorrow. I'll stay here tonight. Ok?"

"Well, I will pick you up at the airport. Tomorrow."

"How's the old man?" I inquire.

"He's a wreck, but we'll get through it."

"Yes. How are you holding up?"

"It's rough," he stammers. "Cherise is pretty upset, too, but we're hangin' in there as best we can. The old man's gonna need our help. He's in bad shape right now."

"Okay, I say. I'll be there tomorrow." And the call comes to an abrupt halt. Being there by myself, I am too stunned to cry immediately. But I am clear that I need some comforting. Immediately, Sue

Kahn comes to mind and I call her. She is sweet, warm and nurturing and invites me to share Passover with her. It is the first night of Pesach and Good Friday, just by coincidence, tonight. I gather my stuff, pack, and at 6 pm head over to Sue's for seder dinner with thoughts of heading back to New York tomorrow.

Sue Kahn. She and twelve of her friends, Jewish and otherwise, are there and we do the seder service with wine, the Haggadah and a little bit of marijuana, which I pass on. Sue and I share a bed that night, no sex, just cuddling. That's fine with me. It's probably what I need. Sue is kind and sweet. And the next day I fly back to New Rochelle. Saturday April 10, my brother Lew's sixteenth birthday.

Arriving back at 280 Daisy Farms Drive, on an unusually warm day for April, Lew, Zora, Dave, Cherise and Aunt Mary, my mother's oldest sister are all there. The house smells of that warm, welcoming aroma of bacon and eggs. Zora, anticipating my return, as soon as I come in the door, inquires whether I'm hungry and quickly drums up my favorite breakfast. Milt is a mess. Doesn't know what to do with himself. Crying a lot. We all huddle together mostly in the living room and kitchen. Everyone is looking for something to do, dishes, garbage but mostly just being with Dad and one another. We are all stunned. Mary, in her way, is going through the worst of it. Just two months earlier, she weathered the care then the passing of her older brother, Lenny, from prostate cancer down in Florida, only weeks after finally retiring from 40 years as an executive secretary at ex lax Inc., the laxative company. To put it mildly, she is beyond burnt just from her years at work, but now at 65, there is no rest for the weary. First Lenny in February, now Barbara in April, and a senile mother she's taking care of at her condo in Fort Lauderdale. It is just a little much. Yet, she soldiers on, mostly stoically, although she seems to get her feelings out by having plenty to say about this or that person given the opportunity, mostly distant relatives but also about some of the so-called friends of my mother, who have suddenly disappeared when word of my mother's lung cancer got around .

Zora, too, is quite sad. She had genuine affection for my mother. It was easy to do with my mom and I know the feeling was mutual. Zora is attached to my father as well and seems quite concerned about his present state. Milt is bereft. Dave and Cherise, while sad, both appear fairly rock solid, trying to be helpful on a practical level and consoling others on an emotional level.

Fairly soon, the place starts to fill up. Cousin Raymond Brucher with his lovely wife Meg. Herb and Vilma, Dad's brother and sister in law. Raymond, their son, all come visiting in the living room for an hour or so. Lew and I exit the downstairs scene fairly quickly, having had enough of this part of the family and we bolt up to Lew's

room. He has a stereo with a decent album collection of current stuff. I put on the CSNY album *Déjà Vu*, side one, and get through the first song "Carry On" okay. But the second one, "Teach Your Children," hits me hard.

"You who are on the road, must have a code, that you can live by. And so, become yourself, because the past is just a goodbye. Teach your children well, the father's hell, will slowly go by. And feed them on your dreams, the one they pick, the one you'll know by. Don't you ever ask them why. If they told you, you would cry. So just look at them and sigh and know they love you."

It gets to me every fucking time, but never more so than now. Mom is gone. There will be no more lessons from her. She is not here anymore. I miss her already. Something vital is gone. But Lew is not expressing his sadness so much, at least not on the outside. Stolid. Not a crier, hardly, but I am, big time. Have no shame about it. Actually like the fact that I feel as deeply about stuff as I do.

Although, my feelings did and do still get me into trouble. Particularly my anger, but you gotta take the bitter with the sweet. The manic with the depressive or some shit like that. That song really sets me off. The impact kids have on their parents and parents on their kids. CSNY. They get to me on a deep core level. Even more than the Beatles, particularly right now. I'd have to say Cat Stevens', *Tea for the Tillerman* album is second in terms of hitting me deeply on an essential emotional level. Those two, the biggies, plus Joni Mitchell's *Ladies of the Canyon*. Yeah, they are the top three in terms of feeling like they are talking directly to my experience regarding love, sensibility, world view, politics, even spirituality. Everything. I go into a different state and place when listening to these artists. Heart bullseye. But it's also true that thinking about my various lists is one of my favorite ways to NOT FEEL, especially now because my sadness and grief is too heavy to bear and making lists gives me a mental, emotional break.

While Lew and I hang out in his room, relatives arrive in dribs and drabs, peep in to say hi and wish us condolences and see how we are doing. One in particular rankles the shit out of me. Herb and Vilma's son, Ray, comes up by himself to show, but I think feign concern and "heartfelt sympathy for (our) loss." The guy is as phony as a three dollar bill, the kind who straightens your tie without permission at more formal family occasions when you're wearing a tie and jacket as if it's his "divine right" as the oldest cousin to straighten you out. Condescending douche. Anyway, Lew and I make short work of the dude and he lasts about 45 seconds, makes his perfunctory appearance, and then adios.

On a brighter note around five, Ricky Sidelman pops over by surprise without me even having called to tell him about my mom. Dave must have called him or something. At least I don't remember calling him. Immediately, he and I hit the basement and the ping pong table. Scenes of yesteryear are evoked where we spent our youngest years, age 8, 9, and 10 hanging out, competing with mad intensity. In those days we played for domination of planets and solar systems. We were very evenly matched, at ping pong and in general. We also both intensely were into rock 'n' roll and now, increasingly, Rick is sharing my passion for film and I'm sharing his passion for psychology. His major at Harvard is social relations. Mine sociology. When Rick and I compete, he goes into his announcer voice, narrating the contest as we play. He and I were particularly enamored of Les Keiter, a New York cult sports figure whose claim to fame was reconstructing Giant baseball games off the ticker tape. Basically making it up with sound effects, fake crowd noises and lots of drama. Rick has a keen sense of our respective competitiveness with each other, particularly when I am engaging in bravado. With Keiter's voice, he mocks my braggadocio. It is the perfect elixir for what I need at this moment. Rick is sensitive, yet also a tad indirect and circumspect about emotions, his and others. I can tell he is mindful but also trying to be very respectful. It's cool. It puts me in a slightly more cerebral place, which is okay. I need a break from the raw emotion I was feeling up in Lew's room with CSNY and such. The ping pong with Rick gives me a needed emotional breather. He stays for an hour or so, putting me in a better mood. The rest of the night is pretty low key. A few more family friends arrive but don't stay long, mostly to see Dad. After they leave, we all hang out with Dad in his bedroom, eating Chinese dinner, watching TV. Communing together. It feels warm and close.

Sunday, April 11
Easter Sunday: The Resurrection

The whole family heads out by car to Riverside Chapel in Manhattan for Mom's memorial service. Rabbi Shankman, our house rabbi from New Rochelle is officiating. By the time Mom passed away, she had become pretty embittered with the whole "religious bit" as she called it. Angry that she had gotten lung cancer although she didn't talk about it that way very much. She was mostly angry with Rabbi Shankman and Temple Israel for its pro-war, pro-American stance on the Vietnam war. That, she found unforgivable, so much so that by 1969, she and my dad basically stopped attending shul even on the High Holy Days. Mom found their position on the war disgraceful and basically decided that they and their cohorts were a bunch of posturing, sanctimonious hypocrites. Besides the horror of the Holocaust, for her, the whole "geschichte" of all religions, including Judaism, was a bunch of phony baloney bull shit. My father, a man of science as he liked to put it, basically got his spiritual sense from being in Nature and observing beauty. He was a self described pantheist. God is in Nature, everywhere. He, too, didn't get much out of the prayers, service or rituals of Judaism.

Dad was far less impassioned about the hypocrisy of religion than my mother who, I got the sense, had grown disillusioned with lots of stuff, particularly when she got sick. She was very angry with certain friends who disappeared when she got sick. No call. No show. And when some of the no-shows finally called 6 or 7 months into her diagnosis, although she didn't say anything directly to these folks' faces, when she got off the phone she would invariably say, in disgust, "They woke up, the war is over." Now the war is over and we are having to bury the dead.

The day is a blur. I do a lot of sobbing and it's cathartic as far as I am concerned. It's pretty emotional for her two remaining sisters, Mary and Janice, and her mother, Becky who just recently outlived three of her children, Barbara, Lenny and Flo. My father is an emotional mess and needs a lot of support from us. He breaks down especially when some of his old army buddies come to comfort him at the service. Buddy Lyons, Harry Teebrock, Irv Bagadanno, his oldest mates. Lyons, Teebrock and Moe Bloom, also in attendance, all had been through the Italian Campaign together in WWII. Seen the worst of it in Sicily, Monte Cassino and Anzio. Seen more than their fair share of horror and death as physicians and surgeons during these sieges. Now they are attending to a comrade. I find it touching to watch actually. I've liked these guys throughout the years, although I mostly remember them inebriated at house parties drinking up the J & B or Cutty Sark, talking loudly, laughing and occasionally triggering war stories which they relayed with sardonic irony and humor. Never heard them talk about the horrors of war they saw. Real out-there characters and they buffett up my dad on this saddest of days. Somehow we all get through it.

It happens to be Easter Sunday, resurrection day. I'm into that symbolism. Don't know why. Maybe it's half rebellion, and half honoring my contract with Jesus for helping me survive my first psychotic episode during its deepest throes. I threw my lot in with him the night I was in a paranoid, delusional state and petrified that if I fell asleep, I would not wake up. In my desperation, I promised Jesus that if he saved me and allowed me to survive, I would do him justice and be forever in his debt. I must have meant it because from that time on, my relationship to Jesus, but not Christianity shifted. He remains my "push come to shove guy" when the chips are down. When all else fails. Just another "fox hole" religious guy, I guess. It's not something I give myself a hard time about, however. Not after what all I've been through so far in my short 21 years. If I need a little Jesus, even a little acid once in a while, so be it.

We all head back to Daisy Farms Drive after the memorial for the beginning of shiva which will last a week and provide me and my family with our very much needed opportunity to mourn Mom with the respite from the day to day, and the distraction and care it provides. It helps me and everyone else there. The togetherness is a comfort. Dave, Cherise, Mary, Dad, Lew, Zora and I all hang out and hang in through the fairly continuous paying of respects. After the moirologists depart, we change gears and shift into what becomes a ritualistic tongue lashing toward those who came "after the war was over" and those weakass lowlifes who didn't have the guts to come at all. It's pretty much a group affair with Aunt Mary leading the way which provides much needed levity and hilarity. Mary is unsparing in her bitterness and resentment, particularly toward Mom's New Rochelle so-called friends who abandoned her when she was diagnosed. The post-game, post-mortem adds to the bonding. I feel very close to my family. It's very warm, nice.

There we were that week with the well wishers coming and going, reminiscing about my mom, what she was like as a little girl, a teen, the whole "geschichte." Very warm, deep, sad but full. Some of these Jewish rituals have some merit, I guess. So, the family rides out the week together and I head back to Columbus for week four of spring quarter, dazed and torn up, but determined to carry on.

CHAPTER 23

New Morning, Carole

It feels strangely good to be back at OSU, back into my life, after the grief and sadness of the previous week. I am weirdly energized and eager to resume.

My first day back after attending a couple of classes, Intro to Sociology and English 103, (my third stab trying to pass it), I make my usual field visit to the Student Union, to The Tavern, where I make my daily afternoon rounds either meeting up with friends or hanging out alone. Usually when I'm on my own I'm on the prowl. Today is no exception. I must not be in the mood to be solo, not to mention the usual horn dog stuff, because I see this dirty blonde-haired woman sitting two tables away making furtive eye contact and all the while lighting up what looked to be Lark cigarettes, my mother's brand, although I really didn't make too much of the connection at the time. Being out of cigarettes, which is pretty typical for me, provides me with a convenient pretext for bumming, particularly from attractive women. Somehow, I frequently get a cigarette, but sometimes a surly, flat out contemptuous rejection, and sometimes a get the fuck a way from me cigarette, and once in awhile a green light, yes you can sit down if you want to response. Well, today I'm golden. Maybe it is because I don't really care what response I get, which somehow frees me up to be myself, or something. I don't really know why it works this way, but I know that it does. It seems to work in all manner of endeavors, work, sports, creativity, sex: the less outcome oriented I am the better. The more I do stuff just to do it, the better. But paradoxically, I can't be too self conscious that that's what I'm doing or I'm going to get caught up in another web of being aware that I'm doing something to not have a desired effect. It gets complicated.

But certainly, she is friendly. And it turns out that she knows who I am, sort of. As she informs me, I am known in her circles as "Little Yippie" to be distinguished from "Big Yippie," another campus protestor who was about six four. I'm 5'10". The thing we two yippies have in common, besides our interest in campus unrest, protest and speechifying, is our bandanas. Big Yippie wears a bandana, only it's usually white. I wear a red one, with a Jewish star, a modification of Che Guevara's five star bandanna. So, as we get to talking, it turns out this young lady is an education major, who also had been heavily influenced by one of the most popular and controversial professors there, a guy named Bernie Mehl, a teacher who prides himself on provoking freshmen and sophomores on their preconceived notions concerning race, class and religion. He draws huge crowds, is very stimulating and generates lots of reaction from his students. The class is more like a free for all than anything else, which pleases me along with his book assignments: *The Autobiography of Malcolm X*, *Soul on Ice*, *Huckleberry Finn* and *Growing Up Absurd* being some of his bills of fare.

This girl, Carole, is sort of one of Bernie's disciples, although she says she is starting to be somewhat skeptical of some of his high handed, and at times, downright mean tactics towards some of the students. Carole also says she is well aware of Bernie's scab-like behavior the previous spring during the student strike and was not at all pleased. It turns out, Carole is a working class girl from Garfield Heights, a suburb of Cleveland and is of Finnish descent, a junior just like I am supposed to be, and pretty intellectually oriented. A nice combination of politically and psychologically minded. We hit it off. I find her to be a good listener, empathetic, warm and sincere. It doesn't hurt that she is attractive. Dirty blonde hair, greenish eyes, petite, but zoftig, although that seems less essential in this instance. I can hear her streak of low self esteem which today I find endearing. Refreshing to be away from the arrogant personas of the east coast girls I am used to and the silly, rah rah patinas of some of the midwest girls I've met in Columbus up until this time, to generalize, possibly unfairly. Carole is refreshingly earnest, serious, but not humorless. The time flies by today at The Tavern, so much so that we stay through dinner and then she invites me back to her apartment. She has a roommate who lives there with her boyfriend and it is all very cozy. I spend the night and we make love. It feels really sweet, even natural.

This marks the beginning of nonstop togetherness that will last the next three months. Carole and I alternate spending nights together in each other's places, pretty much every night, up to and including the end of spring quarter. She is a palliative in the mourning of my mother's death and a true moving on from the actual and emotional ending of my relationship with Marla. Carole feels very in love with me and I with her and I'm not afraid to say so either. It just feels right. It feels true.

As a definite bonus, I seem to be developing some semblance of discipline toward my studies for the first time. Attending classes a

231

little more often. Starting to stay on top of the course requirements. Not a lot, because I find my mind still wants to go towards other intellectual interests and that it's difficult to consistently bring my mind back to courses that I find inherently dull, boring or difficult. Carole seems somewhat more adroit at this. She has a higher GPA, around 3.2 and is more able to hang in there with course work not to her liking.

I guess she's a good influence on me in this regard. Am I a good influence on her? That's a good and fair question. What do I bring to the table for her? I guess I am a caring, understanding presence and maybe she feels compatible with me in terms of values, outlook, and sensibility. And maybe my sense of humor. I really don't know. It's not something I have given a lot of thought to up until now. What do women like about me when they do? I'm not the best looking guy in the world. Maybe I'm funny, quick, outrageous, passionate with good timing. Who the fuck knows? Whatever it is, she feels it and seems to like being around me. Attracted and attractive. The next two or so months are blissful, actually. We spend all of our time together when not in class, mostly at her apartment. Occasionally she's at my flat where we co-cook spaghetti or Carole's specialty- burger meat, green peppers, onions and zucchini all mixed together. Recipes are basic and pretty good and in my cooking range. Carole teaches me some basics about cooking that I never learned from my mother who never made me learn about cooking or any other kitchen skills such as using oil or butter to keep food from sticking and keeping the flame at a reasonable height as to not incinerate the food. Of course, in my impulsive impatience and always in a rush to do things, I tend to do things in a way that I think will get things done the fastest without giving much thought to whether it is being done properly, or how it will turn out. I don't know if this is a genetic trait or a behavior

I developed in my childhood as a survival strategy to protect my "stuff" from my older brother, Dave, who resented my existence from jump street. I guess I must have internalized the admonition, "There are two types of people in the world, the quick and the dead." As a result, cooking wise, I could forget to keep the burners low and turn up the burners, rushing with impatience. It doesn't seem to matter what I know. Impatience often wins out..

April, May, June of '71

Carole and I fit together like a glove, sharing a similar political perspective, mutual interests in existential philosophy, humanistic psychology, Black Studies, anti-war protests, radical politics and a minimal interest in marijuana which we both shy away from. We seem to share the intuitive knowledge that our brain biochemistry does not handle the THC too well. So, during this time we get stoned maybe once or twice. Mostly, we read, listen to Carole King's *Tapestry* heavily, Cat Stevens' *Tea for the Tillerman*, Dave Mason's *Alone/Together* album and Elton John's first album, the one that featured "Your Song." It's a great time for music as the last 8 years or so have also been. It's been true since the British Invasion of '64, not to mention pockets of great music from the early sixties folk revival. There's always been a shit load of great music from the Black community whether R and B, soul, acapella or now the burgeoning funk. Carole and I inhale the music, the movies, the books, the times. We feel very alive, although frequently depressed. Grappling to understand our world, ourselves, each other, others. Passionately engaged, I guess you could say. Very in love and we share a similar family dynamic. A weaker, but beloved opposite sex parent. Carole has an alcoholic, sweet father. Me, a quiet, reserved and now dead mother. Alongside of that, we each have a problematic same sex parent. Carole describes her mom as a bitchy, controlling, critical, opinionated, and somewhat cold and embittered. I've got a narcissistic, blowhard father who sees me through the lens of his own unconscious fears, fantasies, needs and self expectations. We both feel unseen and disapproved of on a basic core level by our same sex parent when we allow ourselves to be vulnerable enough to admit our need for approval. But, really in some way, for the first time for each of us, we can talk to each other about the feelings we have toward our parents until the cows come home and we both feel comforted, understood in a way we never had before. It's nice. In fact, it feels like a haven. Alas, it doesn't last.

Spring quarter ends. Carole and I have different plans for the summer. Carole to stay in Columbus for summer school. Me to go on a cross country hitch hiking trip to California. But before we go our separate ways, I want Carole to meet my family and relatives because I want to show her off and because I think her meeting them will clarify for her something essential about why I am the way I am.

On the day after school ends, Carole and I take the "White Rabbit" hippie bus from Columbus to New Rochelle, arriving at Daisy Farms Drive on a Sunday around 2 in the afternoon. The entire bus load of hippie passengers gets off the bus, coming into the house to pee and get water. Dad has a look of consternation as if he's just been invaded by street people. Carole and I are in desperate need of baths. When Carole meets my dad, he is initially friendly to her but soon goes into his scrutinizing clinical investigator mode with her, which is predictably uncomfortable for her and me. It makes us both feel judged and disapproved of. Carole and I sustain, or I should say, tolerate a 5 day visit at the house during which time she meets the relatives, Aunt Janice, Aunt Mary, Uncle Bill, and the cousins Carla and Jerry up at the family summer home in Shenorock, New York, upper Westchester County.

There, on a typical hot, muggy summer Sunday, the whole kit and kaboodle of us go to the local Shenorock Lake to swim and then head back to the family home for barbequed burgers and dogs. Carole and I are at our most outrageous, spouting countercultural bromides and slogans, being provocative about free love, drugs and capitalism. All designed to provoke. Which we succeed in doing. Particularly, my Aunt Janice, a bitter person, who retorts a number of times to my provocations, "Your mother is turning over in her grave." Actually, I think my mother would not have been taken in by our bullshit and would have put me and Carole in our places, but in a nice way as was her wont. Like, "You really like to provoke, don't you Arnie?, Why don't you get off of that stuff?" Janis is more blunt than my mother ever was and reactively hurtful in return.

Carole and I both see my family as being stuck in the past. We think Janice, in particular, is preoccupied with the dead and the past. To ourselves, we refer to her as a "death tripper," in terms of her attitudes, beliefs and values. We see my relatives as frightened by us and what we represent. We like to believe we are very powerful in terms of the ideas and lifestyle we're living and I think we are pretty typical of a certain slice of our generation. A lot of people in their early 20's are having encounters with their parents' WWII generation about all this stuff. Sex, drugs, rock 'n' roll, Vietnam, Black culture, feminism, the environment. It's all bubbling up like lava and we are spewing it in their faces. And we're very arrogant. Very sure of our positions. We are the future. They are the past. We deliver our opinions like a cudgel. To put it mildly, we are tact and subtlety free.

After this onslaught in late June, Carole flies back to Columbus to begin summer school. After she leaves, Dad and I take a trip up to the Massachusetts coastline towns of Gloucester and Rockport. I think of it as a way to spend some time with Dad and offer support if I can. Dad, of course, is still heavily grieving Mom's death from just two months ago. Yet, in typical Milt fashion, he already has a new girlfriend, Lily, a woman about 15 years younger who is attractive, "theatrically" nice, and most likely a gold digger, given that Dad is a Jewish doctor, decent looking and recently widowed. Lily knows all the right things to say, but she doesn't seem sincere. I don't like her but do my best to hide it from her as it wouldn't be fair, even though diplomacy is not my strong suit. It's also true that I might not have liked anyone that wasn't my mother at that point but I am also actually glad my father isn't alone. Janice and Mary, my mother's sisters, feel differently about the matter. They have an unofficial, and up until now, unspoken rule about the length of time a mate should be mourned before dating is allowed and 6 weeks isn't it. My brothers and I don't give a shit. Gay gezunt er heit. Go in good health, for Christ's sake.

But on this trip to Gloucester, it is just Dad and me. No other brothers around to diffuse the tension. Dad is difficult and understandably moody, and I therefore find myself eager to be away from him… often. His interactions with me are prosecutorial which is how he rolls when stressed. It's off putting and I get very self protective, sarcastic and on guard with him. Despite the tension or maybe because of it, I agree to go on a fishing expedition with him.

I'm rewarded by catching a huge cod out at sea, exciting, until my empty stomach and the choppy waters get to me and I get the dry heaves. Triumph and tragedy almost simultaneously, which feels very familiar, meaning I have about five seconds to appreciate my successful catch before nausea, seasickness and vomiting kick in on my empty stomach. Which feels like the story of my life. Like, just when things are starting to get good ala Marla contacting me a few months ago, or back in my senior year when I started getting really good grades and things began taking shape, the shit hits the fan. Must be my fate. I think. Or should I say karma.

But all is not lost. My powers of resilience do not fail me and I pick up a waitress after my old man goes to sleep. Just for the record, in terms of my relationship with Carole, it feels legit. We have an open relationship. We don't even have any rules about talking about what kind of relationship we have. We are in love, but trying to live out some idealistic fantasy about free love. I don't even have the slightest inkling about how dumb, naïve, idealistic we may be. Tonight the hunt is more fun than the sex, although the sex isn't bad. After a few days up on the Massachusetts coast, I've had enough. Dad's in a tense place, we're not getting along, he has to go back to work and I need to start my trip out west. We drive back to New Rochelle where on the 3rd of July, I head out on foot to hitchhike to Columbus. My plan is to be with Carole for a week before continuing on the journey out west to California via Madison, Wisconsin.

CHAPTER 24

On the Road to Find Out

The Cat Stevens song reverberates in my head as I hitchhike on Route 70 to Columbus, alone. I'm picked up by hippies, truck drivers and more hippies. Going against my stereotype, I find the truckers to be very regular, non judgmental of this long haired, red bandana wearing, hole in the jeans guy. I feel an instant, mutual rapport with the hippies who pick me up with music, drugs, politics and sensibilities in common that astound me. It feels so great to be connected to others, strangers, in what feels like a deep way. The culture wars in America are writ large now. The war is still going on. Black, Hispanic, American Indian power movements are alive and well. Feminism and gay lib activism are picking up steam. The environmental and organic scene is also burgeoning and flowering. It's all so palpable. Up until now, it hasn't felt that this so-called "counterculture movement" is changing only a minority of people. It garners a lot of press, yes, as in publicity and attention from the cultural centers of New York, Los Angeles and San Francisco where it was born. But it's only when I travel to the center of the country that I get the sense of how much of a freak my fellow yippie-hippies are perceived. It's a little scary actually. But people are people, I tell myself on the road to calm myself down. A voice in my head says that "if you are friendly and nice, people will be nice to you." And I find it works out that way, at least on this hitchhiking expedition. It isn't what I had been geared up for, which was that I'd feel some animosity from the straight or redneck crowd. The fact that it doesn't happen, gives me momentary hope about the country.

I arrive in Columbus after a 14 hour hitching trek to find Carole in bed and I fall into her arms to sleep, exhausted. I plan to spend a week with her and with my politico friends Paul, John Flowers, and Tom and Curt, my old dorm mates, all of whom are in Columbus attending summer school. I see the week as an opportunity to get some emotional fueling for my trip ahead. Some needed comfort.

I spend the week mostly with Carole and get together with Paul, John on a couple of occasions for beers at Larry's Bar and for pizza with Curt and Tom on another night. Time with Carole is mostly cozy. We spend a lot of it talking about our respective fucked up families. Carole's bitch of a mother, her sweet but pussy-whipped, alcoholic father. And of course, my "all star team" of a family which Carole has just had a dose of just two weeks earlier. We are in agreement and a mutual support society for each other on this matter.

With Paul and John, conversations center on what is next for them. They've both just graduated from OSU and neither has the slightest idea what they will do next. It's a daunting thought and a lot of our time together is spent avoiding the topic. Talking about city politics and women instead. Tom is out the door. He's off to dental school in Atlanta, so some of our time is spent imagining what living in the south will be like for him. It's a mixed bag for Tom. He wants out of Columbus and Ohio, but hasn't necessarily bargained on going to school in the south. But it's where he got in so that's where he's going. Tom also tells me he's done with drugs. A veteran pot smoker and psychedelic warrior, he now proclaims, " It's time to get serious." Yes, I guess it is Tom. I ain't there yet. As for Curt, he's his usual sullen, depressed self. Now an english major, he articulates his love for the French poets, Rimbaud and Verlaine, who from the sound of it to my virgin ears, is a perfect fit for Curt's dark, pessimistic view of life. I see him just once. That's quite enough.

On one occasion during the week, in a randy furor, I go off looking for action, and stupidly announce it to Carole upon my return. Both of us believe my interest in other women is cool because we are so "enlightened" that we are beyond jealousy. Yeah right. Carole does a good job of repressing or suppressing her feelings, and not mentioning any concerns about this for fear of not looking cool. From knowing her, I know like me, she's trying to live up to some hippie ideal. Give me a break. Carole at least, has the good sense to not mention her erotic fantasies or behaviors to me, whatever her ideological position. So I never know of her goings on or if she even has goings on. We are young and foolish, yes. But very sweet and ardent, nonetheless. I can see some discomfort in her face when I talk of other women, but she and I are both caught up in this fantasy of non jealousy, so we keep it off the communication docket. Too uncool. Jealousy is uncool, but real nonetheless.

So after a week of this, I bid my friends and Carole adieu and head down the highway in Columbus, carrying a knapsack with a few days' worth of clothes on my back plus a sign that says "Madison." I'm not sleeping real well at this point. Excited, possibly overstim- ulated, but I'm still sleeping. Amped to be starting this adventure. First off to Madison and then on to California. As half baked as it is, with no plan other than to end up in San Francisco, nevertheless, I am unafraid. That's how I operate. It isn't all bad. A lot of times

I'm having fun and sometimes, I get into jams and I have to talk my way out of them. I discover that I'm fairly adroit at squirming out of tight situations and realize that I have a lot of confidence in my ability to do so. What I lack in good judgment maybe, I make up for in "big balls." I ain't afraid to take risks. And I ain't afraid now.

Columbus to Madison is another long, 12 hour day on the road. I have a few rocky moments hitchhiking on the outskirts of Chicago, where the city's "finest" bark at me with their rooftop electric bullhorn, "Get off the freeway or go to jail." The infamous Chicago pigs. I do as they say for a while, staying off the Chicago freeways, keeping my eyes peeled for "the man" while I continue my hitching. I arrive in Madison at brother Dave's, just in time to see Reggie Jackson's colossal all star game home run in Detroit.

Wired and excited. Looking forward to the adventure of hitchhiking. To the coast. Really, what was I thinking? A case of California dreaming: the east coast-midwest fantasy of California as the new "promised land," birthplace of peace and love. But just as likely, part of the fantasy is to fuck as many women as I can. Whatever, I am looking for something new, something different, something better. Maybe, not such a small thing. California, the experiment in living. That's what I have on my mind but I don't share it. Particularly, the sex part. It feels sort of unseemly in a way. The thought of fucking my brains out makes me sound not much different in substance from any garden variety frat boy, jock or macho dude. Yucko. Still and all, that's a big piece at the heart of my desire for adventure and witnessing the California dream first hand. The whole hippie thing, free love. But rebellion is in there too. Anger, rage, contempt for the "man." God, I get a glimpse of how typical I am of a certain type of character. There's nothing very unique or unusual about me. I just think so sometimes. It's kind of pathetic, if I give it a lot of thought, which I do sometimes. Immature, to be more accurate. I'm 21.

Madison is to be the opening salvo of my freedom. In my excitement and anticipation, I find the stimulation overwhelming. Though I try to sleep, I can't, and stay up all night two nights in a row. The energy inside me is like centrifugal force. And the next thing I know, I am all manicky, similar to '68 when my first breakdown hit me, but now I'm not delusional. I can't sleep and I can't slow down my thoughts. I can't stop speed rapping, even to strangers that I encounter. I'm hyper friendly as well. Fuck. I am fucked. Fear makes an unwanted appearance. A sign that I'm in trouble and starting to come apart.

Now three nights of no sleep and this incessant speed rapping. I am desperate. Not knowing what else to do, I wait for Dave and Cherise to come back to their house from the library. Dave and Cherise are hard at work on their respective dissertations, but hear me talking in tangents, not completing thoughts, see my rapid mood swings, speediness and fear. Telling me to try to relax, they serve me a cup of chamomile tea. Then, they summon one of their psychiatrist friends to come to the house to talk with me. This doctor guy, after talking with me briefly, is convinced I am manic and should probably get on medication. Inquiring about my psychiatric history, I inform him and Dave about Dr. Leuchter, the Columbus shrink I've been seeing for 14 months. With my begrudging permission, they get a hold of Leuchter on the phone after which time, Dave calls my dad. In two shakes of a lamb's tail it's agreed that I need to go back to the nut house. I can't go to New Rochelle as being around Dad would be bad juju for me. It's not a good idea to stay in Madison. Dave and Cherise are too busy and I really don't have any friends there. So, it's back to Columbus and this time to a different nut house, Harding Hospital.

I call Carole and tell her. She sounds alarmed, worried and upset. Angry and against it. She says she will take care of me but I am not in a state of mind to take her advice or even disagree with it. I'm too out of control to make a reasoned decision. I'm rendered scared and passive so I allow Dad and the shrink to have me hospitalized. "Goddamnit!" I think. "There goes another fucking six months of my life. There goes California. Fuck. God damn it. I hate everything and everybody." Blind rage at my biochemical imbalance or whatever. Off to the nut house I go. A fucking Mutate, once again. Dave takes it upon himself to call Carole, who is shocked to hear the final decision. So much so that she, as well, is unable to muster up any protest. Her opinion has gone unheeded and she relents, feeling overpowered by the shrink and my father.

Carole: Later that week

I hate myself. I should never have allowed them to talk me into thinking that going into Harding Hospital was the best thing for Arnie. I hate myself. Because I know they are wrong. He belongs with me. I could take care of him. I know him. He knows me. We understand each other. We belong together. I don't care how "out there" he is. How manicky? I could have handled it. So, why did I allow them to talk me into it? Because I'm weak, that's why. Maybe I secretly thought they were right. Maybe I thought he was too crazy for me to handle. I feel like shit for this. Arnie seemed so "out there," vulnerable, wild-eyed. I'd never really seen him like that. I wasn't really scared when I visited him at the hospital, just sad. You know, these last three months since we met at the Student Union in April have been the best three months of my life. Arnie's, too. We connect so strongly. We see things eye to eye so much. We both have fucked up parents. We understand each other so well. Particularly our fucked up families.

My dad, the sweet man that he is, he's kind of pathetic. Alcoholic, passive, depressed. Lets my mom push him around. I hate it. And she's such a fucking bitch. Hate that bitch. So fucking controlling and negative. Can't stand to be around her. And Arnie's dad. What an asshole, put down artist, know it all. I mean you can see he means well, but God, Arnie can't stand to be around him either, makes him feel bad about himself and then he gets super angry. Bad. So lucky we have each other. Plus, these people and that whole generation, if you must know, they're all fucked with their materialism, phony ways. I'm so glad we're not like that and aren't gonna be like that. They think a nice house, car, is all that matters. They don't have a clue about what's important. I know they survived The Depression and WWII, but Jesus Christ, there's more to life than comfort. The world is so fucked up. America is so fucked up. So racist, sexist, impe-rialistic. It so needs to change. And our generation is gonna change things, I swear. Arnie and I agree to the max about this stuff and what we're gonna do and how we're gonna live our lives.

Only now, Arnie's flipped out again and that puts a major damper on things. We were going to move in together this fall, get our own apart-ment together. Now this. Now I don't know what's gonna happen. Life sucks. I miss him already. I mean I was starting to miss him when he left for California, but now I miss him even more. One thing is for sure, I will be there all I can. Every day, if possible. Definitely phone every day. I'm sad for both of us. Feel so bad for Arnie. But we will get through this. We have to be together. We are supposed to be together. For life. I just hope Arnie doesn't get too zombieized like he told me he got the last time at that hospital in Hartford. That would be too much. Those fucking medications. They should just let him be. Let him recover on his own. Like we've been reading about in England with those experiments in treatment for psychotics that RD Laing has been doing. Sounds so much more humane and human. But that's not how it goes here in Columbus. Tomorrow, I will go see him. Can't let myself get too worried. It's not good for me or him. I need to be strong, for the both of us. I will. I'll try.

CHAPTER 25

We Can be Together/ Jefferson Airplane 7/22/71

Arnie:

Here we go again. Round four of nuthouse city. This one is feeling like it could be more like the first big, long hospitalization than the second and third shorter ones. The first, 9.5 months, a long siege, only ended by my deciding, with the help of my fellow inmates, that the only way out was to play the game. Pretend you are sane. Act appropriate. Keep all true feelings inside and all will be well. Just show your true feelings to your fellow inmates. Well, that wasn't so easy. Pretending and behaving "appropriately," but I did it. The second and third ones were briefer. Both of them were two week stints at OSU Upham Hall. The psych hospital. The first was the result of being high and agitated, a little crazy. The second time, very depressed. The fall out from the Marla breakup, not to mention another one by Jean later same day, two in one day. The old two on one fast break. Surely deserved but…….

Once again, the sleeplessness and euphoria get to me. I'm getting carried away. Getting too loose in my thinking. Can't keep my thoughts to myself. Have to to reduce everything in my life to a song. Not that I don't do that when I'm so called normal, but now, beyond. Flight of ideas or loose associations, I believe the shrinks call it. Not to mention my rapid mood swings. Well fuck it, I need a chance to mellow out and cool out. Not a looney bin. Carole agrees with me about this but both of us are too damn weak to resist the insistence of my old man and my Nazi shrink. Maybe secretly, I think they are right. But whatever it is, I am acquiescing. Carole is pissed but she is going along with it as well, not that she really has any say. Afterall, we aren't married.

As soon as I get to Harding, they whip a little Haldol on my head. Luckily, it doesn't work right away, so I can still think and feel. Not zombie city yet. So, in my semi-manic, semi-drugged state, I hang out on the unit. Try interacting with some of the other patients, two of whom I have something in common with. These two guys, Tom and Scott, are roughly my age, early twenties. One guy, Scott, is into this thing called "Dianetics" or Scientology. Kind of out of his mind. Keeps saying that I and everyone else here are using their "reactive minds." This apparently translates into meaning speaking or acting from an emotional place without thinking first before speaking or behaving. Makes some sense. But Scott is more than a "bit" obsessed with this concept. It's all he can talk about. I guess it IS all he thinks about. Then there is Tom, a brown-haired, hair-down-to-his-mid-back, mustachioed dude, a pot dealer, making a lot of money doing that, living in Jamaica, fucking alot of women. Living the life, when according to him, he just got too high and forgot to navigate that little thing the straight world calls "reality." So, welcome to Harding Hospital. Welcome Tom. Welcome Scott. Welcome Arnie. Once again, welcome to Harding Hospital, named after the family of one of our beloved presidents, Warren G, perhaps our most corrupt president ever. I'm hoping there's no correlation with the way the place runs. Well, we'll see about that. I vow to mellow out, but, to be honest, it's not easy. I feel agitated beneath the free associating rock lyrics and movie one liners. Tiring. Coming down is hard. Tomorrow, my Carole will pay me a visit. An island of love and care amidst all the bull shit of this place. This afternoon, I will see Leuchter, my private practice shrink with hospital privileges. I can't wait to see the fucking Nazi.....Yeah, right.

Leuchters perspective:

I just got back from seeing Arnie at the hospital for the first time in a year. Seeing Arnie again after all this time is a bit of a shock. Not that it's a complete surprise to me. When I saw him last, back in August of '70, he was a depressed mess. Sad and worried about his mother, carrying a torch for this Marla girl who had broken up with him twice in nine months. I wasn't sure what the best course of action was for Arnie, so I called his dad who was dealing with his wife's illness. I definitely knew that Arnie wasn't in shape to be a student, nor did I think it a good idea for Arnie to live back in New Rochelle given his tense relationship with his father, so Arnie, his father and I Arnie agreed that Arnie should go live in Madison near his older brother Dave and wife Cherise. From how it was told to me by Arnie and his dad, it sounded like it worked out ok. But then I heard that Arnie had come back to Columbus to work, and finally in the spring had returned to school. Again, it sounded like he was ok, mostly. But of course, not taking his meds, he got high and agitated again. Then he got involved with this young woman, Carole, who was nice enough, but from what I heard from Arnie's dad, she is an angry, sullen, depressed person in her own right, and particularly angry with us shrinks. Had bought into these half cocked ideas of the Scottish psychiatrist, RD Laing, about dealing with psychotic behavior without meds. Poppycock. Dangerous if you ask me. But she's another idealistic kid, who doesn't know shit from Shinola. I met with Carole, at Arnie's request, to brief her and I could tell she was doing her best to act normal. But I picked up the hostility. Look, not that we shrinks have all the answers, but treating psychotic people without medication, well, that is just a bridge too far. A recipe for disaster.

As for Arnie himself, when I met with him at Harding that first day, he was all over the map. Loose associating, hard to keep him on a coherent thought track, volatile. Clearly, he needs to be here. His dad agrees and Arnie himself is not really fighting it, at least not on the surface. But, I have given him a major dose of Haldol so his "fighting spirit" may be affected and making him feel more compliant. We'll see. I'll see him four times a week, briefly, for a half hour, and keep tabs on his progress from the nurses and rest of the hospital staff. This is Arnie's third relapse in 3 years. I'm not optimistic he's ever gonna get well and stay well. But hopefully the meds will get him back to some reasonable functional level, at least so he can be communicated with. The guy has to realize that he needs to stay on his meds, maybe for life if he is to have any chance of making it in the real world.

Dad's perspective:

We had to do something. Arnie was just out of control. We hate these goddamn hospitals. They're expensive and they don't really work. This is Arnie's fourth hospitalization in three years. Something is not working. Goddamn Columbus. Yet brother Dave can't keep an eye on him because he and Cherise are going to Paris to do research for their dissertations, so that's out. And I have my hands full with the grief over Barbara's death from lung cancer. I'm not in such good shape either. Just trying to hang on, myself. So, yes unfortunately, Harding Hospital is the best of a bunch of bad solutions. And Carole seems nice enough. Sure is devoted to Arnie, but I don't think she realizes what she's getting herself in for with Arnie. He may never get better. Most psychotics don't. But it's great she'll be there to buoy his spirits. We all need that. My Barbara was my person, and now I've lost her. Life sucks sometimes. But we must persevere. We must go on.

Carole's perspective:

Seeing Arnie in the hospital just a few days after he got there was so upsetting. I could tell he was starting to get doped up, but also battling it. His fight came out in lots of strange ways like lashing out at the nurses, some of the patients, crying, you know like when he would hear a song sometimes. All kinds of super intense stuff. This hospital is so depressing. I don't know how anyone gets better. I'm just not gonna put up with it. I know I have been putting on a happy face with the shrink and Arnie's dad and brother, but that is just for show. I haven't told anybody. Not even Arnie yet, but I've made up my mind. I'm getting him outta there. I'm gonna talk

251

with Arnie about it in a few days before they dope him up so much he can't think. I'm sure he will agree. He's coming to live with me, that's it. Fuck these people. They can't tell us how to live, or what is best. I just won't have it. Period. These fucking shrinks. These fucking fascists. Fuck them. No, it ain't happening. Arnie told me about his previous hospital experiences at the IOL in '68, and Upham in' 69. It sounded awful. These places don't do anything for people. They're just holding cells. It's bullshit. No, Arnie's coming with me. He's gonna come live with me and me and his mates, John Flowers, Paul Ricciardo, Jamie and Curt. We will know what to do. Love him. That's what we will do. It's not that goddamn complicated. Love and understanding. That's all Arnie needs and goddamnit, we can and will give it to him. You'll see.

The Next Bunch of Days: Back to Arnie

Carole came to visit me today and she told me what she's gonna do. Oh, yeah. I mean, after all, I signed in voluntarily. It's not like they can keep me here. I'm here of my own free will, so to speak. Carole and I talked in the day room today. You know what? She's right. This place sucks. Just today, a patient started screaming and then the fucking orderlies, excuse me, psych techs came in and they fucking put her in a goddamn straight jacket. Restraints. Great. Fuck these people. Fuck them. How can anybody get well here? Fuck this shit. Carole will be here in a few days after she comes back from visiting her folks in Cleveland, and the plan is to basically just walk out the door, without prior warning. August 6 is the date. So, for the next week or so, I will cooperate with these fuckers, pretend to go along with their rules, go to their required activities, you know, "volleyball and ping pong and a lot of dandy games" (leather shop, metal shop, art shop), you know, all that bull shit therapeutic stuff, and then when she comes to visit, I'll pack my bags in the morning and we will be OUTA HERE.

Meanwhile, after Carole's visit today, which included pizza from Mike's on High Street, my fave, I scarfed the slices down, and after that, we just looked at each other, into each other's eyes, I just felt this amazing surge of hope. Yes, things will be alright. For a change.

Carole just left and I'm out in the day room. It's hard for me to contain my excitement. And even though the plan is to tell no one, I just have to tell somebody. I'm frothing at the mouth. Certainly not telling Leuchter. Not gonna tell my old man. Not gonna tell Dave or Cherise. Those people mostly think I should be here, because they are out of options with me. Well, Carole and I aren't. But I can't contain myself. So when Scott and Tom and I are hanging out in the day room, Scott, a perceptive sort, despite his lunacy about "reactive mind" mutters, "What's going on here, Arnie. Something has changed. Your scowl is gone. You got this shit eating grin on your face. Something's going on but you ain't sayin'".

Tom too, less acutely out of his mind, mostly muttering angrily at himself for "blowing it," blowing his perfect life in Jamaica, when he had it all, in his self absorption, is momentarily distracted by Scott's emphatic, somewhat boisterous verbiage to Arnie. Tom interjects, "Leave him alone, Scott. Arnie's allowed to be happy. There's no law against smiling, you fucking douchebag."

I'm listening to this and can't contain myself. I have to talk. I can't keep it in. So, I take a chance that doesn't feel risky. I have a weird intuition that I can trust these guys and if they blow the whistle on me, accidentally or on purpose, I decide I'll just say it's bullshit. I'll deny that that's my plan. Afterall, these fuckers are supposed to be crazy, so why should they be believed. So I say, "Listen you fuckers. You gotta promise me. Mum's the word about what I'm gonna tell you. Promise. Scouts honor. That's right Tom, mother-fucking scout's honor. Ok. Raise your fucking right hand. You too, asshole," as I point to Scott. Scott temporarily awakens from his self flagellations as he sees Tom put up his hand to take his oath. He probably half hears what I just said about taking a vow of secrecy, and puts up his hand as well, Scout's honor style. "Good. Okay, you fuckers. Now that you've sworn to secrecy, here's the motherfucking deal. I'm out. My lady, Carole's coming to get me on August 6. I'm getting out of this fucking hell hole. And if you know what's good for you, you assholes, you'll leave, too. But, whatever. Stay. Leave. Regardless, I am outta here. If the shrinks, or orderlies, or nurses find out I will kill you suckers. Get it? I'm trusting you assholes. Don't let me down. Get it?"

It's like I'm "Little Caesar " in an Edward G. Robinson movie. My tone of voice, that is. All the while, I can feel the Haldol starting to work on me. In that exact instant I decide: no more meds. I'm gonna start cheeking, an old tried and true patient maneuver, meaning pretending to swallow medications while nurses are around and then as soon as they are gone, spit them into a tissue as if I'm coughing up a loogie. I'm not going into zombie land. Fuck them and the horse they rode in on. Strangely, I have a feeling I can trust Tom and Scott, especially Tom. I'm a little worried about Scott because he's so out of it, but I have a deep sense that he, too, is on the same basic page as I am about the inherent fuckedupness of the place. Social control mother fuckers are all using the pretense of trying to "help you." Bullshit. Anyway, now the ball is in play. Until August 6, I'll just do my theater routine. ACT.

August 6:

Nobody, not the shrinks, not the nurses, not the orderlies, nobody suspects nothing. Despite how crazy Scott is, he has been able to keep his word. Tom, too but I was never really worried about him. So, now after breakfast, the usual Kellogg's Corn Flakes, coffee and three cigarettes, I quietly go to my room. Luckily, I don't have that much stuff to take. A few shirts, maybe a week's worth of underwear, a couple of pairs of jeans, sneakers. That's it. I have a laundry bag. Stuff it all in with my toothbrush, deodorant, hairbrush and I'm ready to go. All quiet, incognito like. Carole will be here in an hour, around 11. Nothing much to do, but go to the outside area and sit and smoke. I give Tom the thumbs up sign. He knows what's happening. I don't know where Scott is, but both guys have come through big time. I'm not zombied out either. Feel pretty good. Excited and scared. It's not like I'm doing anything wrong, or illegal, it's just that it feels wrong and a little scary. Part of me is afraid of getting into trouble and another part of me is still wanting these people's approval. But fuck it. I'm doing it anyway. I love my Carole. She's so great. Fucking ballsy. Really loves me. These Viceroys taste good. The coffee sucks, but the V Roy's strangely satisfying today. So nervous, ten more minutes. Keeping my laundry bag hidden behind the bed. And then when she comes, gonna calmly get the bag, get permission to go out of the unit, while Carole, who will be wearing a loose fitting, almost sack dress, hides the laundry bag under her dress. Then, we will slowly, with permission, walk out onto the beautiful grassy grounds. Pretend we're just taking a leisurely stroll and just keep walking to the lot where Carole's Corvair is parked. Easy as pie.

Carole arrives. We follow our protocol to the T. I see Tom, give him the thumbs up as he sees Carole, and nods his assent. I open the hospital door leading to the parking lot as Carole and I exchange nervous yet determined glances. Not looking around as we walk, we both try to assume nonchalant poses. We arrive at Carole's Corvair. We get in. The ignition coughs and doesn't catch the first time, giving me a sudden jolt of fear, but the second time it starts. I'm relieved and duck my head down on the passenger side. Just in case. Carole backs out of the lot onto the street. Stops for oncoming traffic for an instant, puts on her turn signal and we are gone. Adios mother-fuckers!

8/6/71: Robert and Janie, Carole and Me

Oh yeah, oh fucking yeah. Home motherfucking free. Carole and I hug like it's the 7th game of the World Series and our team has just won. Tears of joy and gratitude leak down my cheeks. Carole, too, stifles a tear. But for her, it's a combination of gratitude that I'm with her and immense pride for the deed she has done. For me, it's "Fucking A! God, it's good to be home."

Janie and Robert, Carole's roommates, aren't home yet. They're at work. Robert works at the OSU Student Union waiting on tables and serving beer at The Tavern, the exact place where Carole and I met a mere four months earlier. Janie is working at the Trade Winds, an all purpose head shop and bookstore, where you can also purchase different types of incense, hand-tooled leather belts, Indian print bedspreads and dashikis. Your basic "generic hippie store." It smells really good there all the time. Mostly, of patchouli, which I person-ally love.

Carole and I have the apartment to ourselves and we use it wisely. Jumping into bed, we have wild passionate sex. The kind that smells of liberation. Loose and open. Most orifices available for insertion. What have you. Gee, it's so great to be back home. Carole and I, in between kissing and whatnot, can't not high five each other every other minute. Not so much speaking as yelping with glee. We are so happy and proud of ourselves. I'm relieved. But don't think I'm out of the woods yet. My boundaries suck, my impulses are in charge and I have a hard time not being tangential when we talk. And that's just with Carole and me. I'm just so overstimulated. But I'm determined not to take those fucking meds, no matter what. Even if it means some sleepless nights. I'm gonna "play out" this craziness inside me and see where it leads and what I can do with it. We've decided that that is how I'm gonna deal with this crazy shit. Carole is in all the way. Robert and Janie too, only they have their own shit to deal with, you know. Work, their relationship, keeping the apartment maintained, etc. So Carole is aware and has advised me that by and large, I'm gonna have to be a little saner, as much as I can around them. If I can. They're on my side, but like everybody else in this world, they've got their needs and responsibilities too.

A few hours later, Robert and Janie arrive together and immediately commence to lighting up a j. Carole and I take a pass on that activity as Carole knows that she and pot don't mix given her biochemistry. That's true too for me. Not pleasurable. Brings up too much obsessive shit, too much worrying. Not fun. And besides I don't like being paralyzed for hours on end, which sometimes happens. So Carole and I hang with Janie and Robert as we relay the events of the day and plans for tomorrow and future.

The phone call:

Long distance lines are working overtime. Leuchter gets wind of my AMA, AWOL almost immediately, like about an hour after Carole and I left the hospital and immediately calls my old man. They are both upset. Luckily for him, my old man has Carole's phone number as Carole was spotted on the grounds with me. There was no need to hide our visit on the grounds since I was a voluntary patient. So Dad gives Carole a call. He's pissed, but Carole wisely passes the phone over to me this night of the "spring." Dad wants to know what the hell I think I'm doing. Like what I think is going to happen.

"You're sick. You can't even speak a coherent sentence without veering into some off the topic, irrelevant verbiage. You're not sleeping. You think if you stop taking your medicine that's going to make you better. You goddamn irresponsible, inconsiderate fucking kid. As if I didn't have enough worries. You think Carole has the patience, the know-how, to be able to put up with your irrational crap. It's just beyond me."

In reply, I am bellowing, "You don't give a fuck. You don't understand. The fucking shrinks haven't got a clue, and you know what else Dad? I'm a fucking adult. I went into that fucking place voluntarily. You can't make me go back. The hospital can't. So too fucking bad. I'm out. I'm gone and there ain't a goddamn thing you can do about it. The best thing you can do about this situation, Dr. Brucher, is wish me luck. Because my days in the hospital are over. My days of medication that make me feel like the living dead are over. Even my days with the shrinks, fucking Nazi Leuchter, you know what, those days are over, too. I'm doing it my way for a change. So fuck you. If you don't approve, cut me off. Don't pay for my tuition. I'll take out loans. But either way, I'm going back to OSU. And I'm gonna fucking graduate even if it takes two years, that's what I'm gonna do. It's up to you Dad, but I ain't playing this 'Arnie sick, everyone else well' game any more. So, it's up to you, either support me, or get the fuck out of my life. I'm done."

And with that I slam down the phone, upset once again, but also feeling strangely relieved, released, happy. Yes, happy. I finally told the old Sherman tank where to get off and it feels good. Sure, I feel for my old man. I mean, he just lost his wife, my mother. But you know what, his days of controlling my life are over. Carole, who couldn't help but listen as the decibel level was so high, is initially alarmed. But when she hears me tell her what happened in the conversation, she is really happy for me. Happy, I finally told my father off. As far as she is concerned, my dad deserved it. She knew he could be a real, tyrannical, controlling prick. Carole is really proud of me, but at the same time, while pretty positive that she can help nurse me back to my "mental health," to be stable again, she also has the feeling that she's taken on an arduous task. But here again, Carole is no fool. While I was in the hospital and she was germinating the plan, she contacted my best mates, Paul Ricciardo, John Flowers, Jamie Olian and Curt Robinson, to notify them about her plan to spring me, but also to enlist their support to help her handle me and my "craziness," if it came to that. They all signed on to be available to stay over if I get too crazy, can't sleep or have some half baked idea to do something impulsive or stupid. They are all busy with school and their lives, but to a man, they all feel a loyalty to me, as if they are signing an oath, so I will not have to check back in the hospital once Carole sprung me. So, now those requests of my buddies would be needed. And the requests would start the very next day.

August 7, 1971: The Next Day

Despite all the anger I expressed towards Dad yesterday and the anger he expressed right back at me for my "stupidity, crappy judgment and my need to be in the safe confines" of the nut house, despite all of this and sensing that he was powerless to change my or Carole's mind, Dad must have decided that he couldn't or wouldn't leave me at 6's and 7's. Since he got that, I am hell bent on returning to OSU for fall quarter. He wants to be done with me and my "crap," so Dad decides to fully financially back me.

He notifies me in this phone call that he will keep paying for my school tuition and room and board. But there is one condition, that if I am not going to return to the hospital, that if I am not going to take my meds, that I agree to continue to see Leuchter twice a week at his office. Dad knows Leuchter isn't my favorite and if you want to know the truth, not his either, but at least Leuchter knows me after 2+ years. He thinks that will be my best bet and I agree. It is a compromise I can accept. Strangely, I feel relieved. I could hash out the med. situation with Leuchter, but Dad agrees that, in the final analysis, it will be up to me. In this conversation, I feel strangely calm because I'd gotten a good night's sleep for the first time in two weeks. I actually feel pretty good. It isn't that I just don't feel bad, but that I actually feel pretty good, like I said, for the first time in two weeks.

So here we are. We are gonna try this new experiment, with Dad and even Leuchter on board. I'm willing to try it. I call Leuchter's office after breakfast and book an appointment for this afternoon. Only this time, Carole will be joining us as she was the prime mover in all this and needs to be a part of the treatment plan to keep me out of the hospital, re-stabilize me, and get my life on an even keel and directed course, as much as possible.

But first I have other business to attend to so I can start to get my life in order. Before the appointment with Leuchter, Carole goes with me to the Registrar's Office to sign up for fall quarter courses. She's obviously concerned about my frustration tolerance and impatience, as am I. On a good day, my threshold for patience with bureaucratic bullshit was never very high, but now in my agitated state, I'm easily set off. The process of registering with all the paperwork details, long lines and rigid, grumpy and uncaring bureaucrats is just a set up for an outburst, and that is the last thing she or I want. We both know that I am still, in what Scott, my Scientology inmate, would have labeled "reactive mind," prone to easily flying off the handle and shooting my mouth off. So Carole is being careful. Advising, admonishing and prompting me to keep me in line. I don't like it, but I accept the temporary necessity for her "babysitting" me.

Luckily, the Registrar's Office is not busy, so registering is accomplished without incident. I barely make a peep, although I am quite edgy and pace a bit until they are able to see me and get me signed up. 16 units. Bio 100, Intro to Econ, the Sociology of Deviance and Ping Pong. Every course except the deviance class is designed to meet the OSU general ed requirements, which are vast and wide. Taking Deviance is designed to begin filling out my sociology major. My interest in deviance is pretty obvious to me. I'm drawn to deviant lifestyles, see myself as deviant, by society's standards which I mostly reject. You can have their idea of normality. Not for me. So I look forward to what the powers that be have to say in this course.

Having survived the registrar's office, next we hit Mike's, our favorite pizza place on High Street for relaxation, mellowing out. And then we will be off to Leuchter's office in North Columbus.

The meeting with Leuchter:

Arriving for our 3pm appointment, we are only in Leuchter's piney smelling waiting room a couple of minutes before he comes out to greet us. He has an all business look on his face, poorly masking some seething anger and dismay with Carole and me and the new circumstances. The session begins with Leuchter making a speech.

"To begin with Carole and Arnie, you should know that when your father called me Arnie, I was quite surprised. I thought that you were in agreement about your need for hospitalization and especially for your going back on medications, which I know you hadn't been taking for almost a year since we last saw each other, prior to your dropping out and going to live with your brother Dave in Madison. It's not a surprise that you don't like to take the meds. I don't know any patients who do. But in your case and in most cases of your kind, meds are a necessary evil. In my experience, it is a requirement for people if they want to get well. Those who don't take meds, never get well. And I mean never. So when your dad said no meds for Arnie on top of no hospital, my thought was you are being quite foolish and sabotaging any hopes for regaining your mental health. Your dad said you were adamant about both things. Is that true?"

"Quite."

"Would you be willing to tell me why?"

"Sure. The hospital, all it is is a holding pen. It doesn't help and just delays the inevitable, which is getting back to your life. That's not a hard one at all. I have better support with Carole and my friends than you or my dad could ever provide, so that's not even a debatable issue. Case closed on that one. And notice I didn't even curse you out, yet. Second, the fucking meds. Do you have any clue doc, how they make people, including me feel? Like a dead person. A piece of wood, an iceberg. No, that won't work. No thanks. I don't care how fucked up I am, the fucking meds are no substitute for the love I get from Carole, the understanding I get from Carole. That and the friendship of my buddies who care a whole lot more about me than you do. And you can throw in my old man on the understanding part. They get me, they care about me and they don't lay their judgment trip on me. Is that clear, Dr. Leuchter, of Munich, Germany?"

"Pretty clear but I couldn't disagree more. But a deal is a deal. I made a deal with your old man who is paying for this that I would try the new arrangement. So I'm willing to give it the old college try as long as you are willing to periodically assess how it's going. If you are, then we are in business."

"Not a problem. I'm certain everything will work out. I'm going back to school and I'm gonna try and finish my degree. Carole and I are living with her roommates, Janie and Robert, but by September 1, we will be living, just the two of us, together. Can't wait."

"That's okay, Arnie. Let's set up the times we're meeting. Tuesday and Thursday, I believe, is best because it won't interfere with your classes which are basically Monday, Wednesday and Friday with your bio class on Thursday mornings. Ok?"

"Great. 4pm, Tuesday and Thursday are just fine."

"Okay. We're in business. That's all I have for today. You're positive, no meds?"

"Yup."

"Ms. Carole, is Arnie sleeping ok? If not, what are you doing to make sure he does, because that's the most important element a person needs for good mental health."

"Got it covered. Chamomile, massage, bath and no drugs. Exercise as much as possible. Arnie has some tennis friends and they're gonna start playing again."

"Sounds good as far as it goes. Please be in touch, if Arnie doesn't mind, if you need help with Arnie's sleep habits."

"Ok, Arnie?"

"Absolutely."

"Okay."

"Good. I think we're in business. See you, Arnie, on Tuesday and nice seeing you again as well, Carole."

"Same."

"Okay, doc. Talk Tuesday."

And the meeting ends. I get into Carole's Corvair and we head back to OSU north campus for dinner with Janie and Robert.

8/7/71–8/20/71(Transition)

So back at the ranch… Janie, Carole's dark haired, sexy beauty, best friend. Sleek. Robert, tall, brawny, soft-eyed, sweet, muscular. They're on summer break. Neither working. Both stay up late at night playing bid wist, watching Creature Theatre and mostly fucking. The sounds at night emanating from their bedroom are thunderous grunts. Sometimes annoying. Often arousing. I'm attracted to Janie. I like Robert. I want to fuck Janie. She seems so into her sexuality. Unabashed about her love of sex. Robert is just more laid back. Passive, yet sweet. Their place just feels super homey and comfy.

But alas, for Carole and me, although we are welcome to stay indefinitely, as it's really Janie and Carole's place in the first place, they hold the lease, Carole and I are eager to go off on our own. Money is not really an issue for Janie. She comes from money, Cincinnati, blue blood. But she's super sweet and unpretentious. You wouldn't know that she came from a rich family by being around her, which only adds to her appeal. Robert comes from the Columbus ghetto. East Columbus. He's been around. When he tires of mooching off Janie, he sells pot to meet his share of the costs. After all, he's a good guy and has his pride, even though Janie couldn't care less. She's a generous sort and just likes having him around. Besides, he's a great fuck. Fit to order.

Getting back to Carole and me, our trip is not so simple. We've been through an ordeal, are really a relatively new couple, and need our space. So, the next day after the Leuchter meeting, we immediately check the local and school newspaper for places to rent. We want a two bedroom. They're not hard to find despite how quickly spaces are filling up ahead of fall quarter only about 7 weeks away. Carole does the leg work. I'm not really in shape for that kind of detail oriented activity. Still too impatient, impulsive and prone to flying off the handle for that kind of task. Besides, my sleep hasn't returned to normal. Still getting only 5 hours, at most, of straight or uninterrupted sleep. The lack of sleep contributes to my edginess and irritability.

Almost immediately, Carole has 2 flats for us to peruse, both on south campus, one on Chittenden, my old stomping ground, and one on 8th and High, a couple of blocks down. The Chittenden place is by far the least rundown. And Carole, almost as impatient as I am to get settled, with my eyeballing as well, commits to the Chittenden south campus flat. Two bedrooms, living room, small kitchen and a decent little backyard which needs mowing and flowers planted. A bit arid, but with potential. We book a 1 year lease at $180 a month, utilities paid except phone, gas and electric. Standard fare around campus. To move in Sept 1 or earlier, if we wish. We wish. So, despite the comfy digs at Robert and Janie's on north campus, we're eager to have our own place and be alone together. Any reference to the

Dave Mason album of the same title, *Alone Together,* is coincidental here although it's one of our favorite albums right about now.

This ends our little stay at the Janie house with all its sweet smelling toast, eggs, marmalade and a hint of pussy in the air. So relaxing. But alas, not ours anymore. In the words of Jesse Jackson, "We are movin' on up."

CHAPTER 26

Our House- Graham Nash, CSNY - *Deja Vu* 3/70

August 20,1971–June 15,1973
Whipping and driving to the finish line (BS,BA)

"**O**ur house is a very, very, very, fine house," except instead of two cats in the yard, we have one short haired beagle-looking mutt of a dog, named Doggy Dog because we are too lazy or busy to take the time to name him. Doggy Dog is quite a sweet, but energetic pup. Because he's a stray, we don't know much about him. But we do know enough, or should I say Carole knows enough, to find a vet and make sure he's got all his shots and that he's healthy. The vet estimates he's about 4. So not really a pup, but not an "alta cocker" like dog either. Somewhere in the middle. Just like Carole and me. We settle into our 2 bedroom. Start making meals and both of us immediately start looking for internships to meet our major requirements in our respective majors, Carole, education with an emphasis on special ed, and me, sociology with an emphasis on criminal justice. Carole has connections with the East Columbus School District, and it's incidentally the school district where my man, John Flowers attended. He is still connected with some of his former teachers and principal, so is helpful to Carole in securing work in the middle school, where she will be assisting the teachers instructing students with autism. Also helpful are some of her profs from the Ed Dept. Carole's commitment will be for the school year before she goes to work at the state hospital with the retarded kids who live there. This is the plan for her final year, her practicum, for the next fall.

My man John Alloway, my guerilla theater, red bandana brigade guy, works at CYA, the Columbus Juvie Hall and he, along with a professor Dinitz from the OSU Sociology Dept, facilitate my placement there as a guard/counselor. So now, with our internships in place and taking the classes we have resisted thus far, we are set for the year. The internships will start first of September, before school starts, so Carole and I will be busy.

House: check. School/ internships: check. Each other: check. Now, I'm thinking all I gotta do is come down and get my sleeping thing together, stabilize, see Leuchter and all should be cool. I'm psyched. Carole, also is excited. We decide to have a talk about the structure of our relationship, go to Goodwill to get kitchen stuff as well as the basic household rudiments, chairs, tables, and a couch. Bare bones but functional. On the 30th of August, two days before internships begin, we have the talk.

The Talk

The preexisting structure: Actually, more like a lived philosophy. Honesty, openness. Anything goes. In short, no structure. Just good will. Trust, a romanticized view of what we as humans need, want and can handle. We, who are liberated beings. People of the Aquarian Age. Free, without jealousy. Love conquers all. If we want to fuck other people, so be it. No strings. No chains. Free. Free love. This has been our governing ideology from day one until now. Carole discusses that maybe part of my craziness might have to do with the overly loose arrangement that we created and that maybe we are overestimating our capacity to operate as free agents and not have negative emotional reactions like suspicion, jealousy, betrayal, hurt, anger and resulting in guardedness with each other. Carole is doing her best and mostly succeeding in bringing up this delicate topic and not moralizing. Rather, she keeps the discussion focused on what she needs, what would be most comfortable, and finally what would provide the most safety, comfort and security for the two of us. She states, and I basically agree that for the time being, it makes the most sense to try to be exclusive, monogamous. Not because it is better or right on a moral level but because given my precarious psychology and her tendency to worry, it makes the most sense, at least for now, to go about our business in the simplest and least complicated fashion. Our agreement is verbal. No formal contract. Not that we don't discuss this as well. But we're trying to keep things loose. But practical. We both express a feeling out loud that it is the right way to accomplish all we want to accomplish with school, with a desire for a comfortable home life and just all around peace of mind, for Carole definitely, but especially for me, given my still precarious mental state. I decide that Carole is right beyond a shadow of a doubt. And so we go to monogamy, really for the first time. Protecting our love becomes the mandate and rallying cry. For the relationship, for our peace of mind and finally for our mutual self esteems.

CHAPTER 27

Long Time Comin' (Fall Quarter)

A comfy, relaxed, positive yet loving vibe pervades our apartment on Chittenden Street as fall quarter begins. Both of us are eager to get back to normal, whatever that means. Practically speaking, it means a regular and routine eating and sleeping schedule. Breakfast and dinners together, as well as meeting for lunch at the OSU Tavern where we first met nearly six months previously, but the lunch date is on a catch as catch can basis. We are studying at night and in the late afternoons, being diligent about staying on top of our classes. For me, this routine is really a first, maybe ever. For Carole, the routine is something she has practiced fairly consistently, except when caught up in some romantic relationship thing. But now that things with us are set, it feels relatively easy to follow through with our game plan. Actually, relatively easy for both of us.

Fall quarter flies by. Carole gets a 3.7, taking all courses in her education major by this time, because she has finally completed most of the onerous general ed requirements, but I also do very well. I ace econ, Sociology of Deviance and ping pong. I even do a bit better in my science requirement, Bio 100, despite it being a purely tv class in a huge auditorium with no live prof. In my determination, I muster enough motivation and discipline to make a C. No mean feat, for a guy like me who prior to this quarter had never gotten it together to study for a class I had no interest in or hated. But somehow the structure, the schedule, the routine, the comfort of having Carole around day in and day night make a big difference. I, too, do my best, a 3.375 with the C bringing down my GPA. But with the good grades and Carole as a model for how to exert discipline and study, it feels like it will be only the beginning of academic success.

Socially, too, things are pretty good. John and Paul come around a lot. They are both still unattached, so frequently on the hustings, looking for women. At times I go out with them, abstaining from being on the hunt but vicariously watching their "hustling" efforts with the women who are pretty much all White as at this point. Black women seem to be confining their interests to men of their own race, in keeping with the philosophy of the Black Power movement. John pretty much stays away from the Black women, saying there are too many hassles and he doesn't need the aggravation which he inevitably got when with them. Of course, if you asked a Black woman, she would say that John was nothing but a "trifling, irresponsible dude." But that's another story and a long one at that.

I resume playing tennis with Jamie and Curt and sometimes Carole's friend Janie joins in. A fairly decent tennis player in her own right. Carole and I team up against Jamie and Curt, more often than not, emerging victorious, playing 2 out of 3 sets doubles matches. Janie has lightning fast reflexes at the net. It is a pleasure to observe her sleek, sexy body in action. Jamie and Curt are also enamored, but are coupled up, too as is Janie. Still going hot and heavy with

Robert back on north campus. But it never hurts to look. And all of us do. Being human and all.

So overall, really a great quarter for me and Carole. Overall. But just because things are really good between us doesn't mean there aren't any problems. Carole has her own history of psychological problems: a hospitalization freshman year, which she told me about early on in our relationship at the point when we were confessing our deepest secrets. She had a bad experience in the same psych ward where I was in the summer of my freshman year. She felt like was treated like a dangerous person, even though she had not been suicidal, just severely depressed. And over medicated. It was there at Upham Hall that Carole experienced first hand the alienating and ineffective methods of inpatient psychiatry. It became clear to her that the major goal of these places was patient control, not patient care, and it left a bitter taste in her mouth about mainstream psychiatry but even worse, did nothing whatsoever to help Carole with her psychological problems. Being with me, taking care of me, I think is giving her temporary respite from her own stuff, but as soon as I begin to stabilize some, Carole's "shit" comes out. Carole has her own spells of depression that last a couple of days. She withdraws from socializing and wants to spend time alone. When we were together, she sometimes becomes very critical of me out of nowhere. It's like her resentment is building up inside her about my illness and her taking care of me, and instead of saying so, she becomes critical. It is uncomfortable for me, but feels like a small price to pay for how much love and care she showed me when I was down. Usually, after Carole goes off on me with her anger, she feels really guilty and down on herself which then requires me to have to comfort and reassure her. As bad as things can get for Carole at times, it still pales by comparison to my own difficulties and the problems I impose on her. I am almost relieved because it allows me the opportunity to be there for her and for it to be less of a one way situation, give and take wise. I am taking my turn helping her, being the strong one. Carole's outbreaks are much more short lived than mine, so we return to normal much more quickly. Her outbursts of anger, guilt and depression repeat pretty frequently, but given Carole's experience as a patient in the psych hospital, she is adamantly opposed to getting professional help. I am completely sympathetic to her feelings about going for therapy but because I cut a deal with my dad, as my way of getting money from him for school, I had no better choices really. So I went. In my mind, another small price to pay. Yet despite these "minor problems," it was still overall a great quarter. My bar isn't that high and the relative tranquility and success at school makes me pretty content. This time when the holidays roll around, I stay in Columbus. It's really a non issue now, as Dad plans to be in Switzerland skiing with Lew, and Dave and Cherise will be joining up with them both, via Paris. Zermat, I believe, is the meet up location. They'll be having their fun and Carole and I will be having ours.

With a medium sized Christmas tree, our funky place feels warm and festive for the holidays. We frequently have Janie and Robert over, sometimes with John and Paul, sometimes separately. We are a tight little group. Tight and getting tighter.

Winter - Summer '72

The next two quarters pass by without too much incident, unless you count Carole's depression and my mood swings as incidents. I don't. It's part of my new normal and the happiest time of my life up until now. In love, settled and focused on school. A sense of direction. Carole, too, seems happy, content, and comfortable when not dealing with my shit or going through her own. Actually, it seems a little unreal. Even though the bad times are pretty bad, the good times are better than ever. But I don't trust it and neither does Carole for that matter. Neither one of us is used to either being happy or things going that well.

She and I are even starting to talk about making some changes and leaving Columbus for Berkeley, so I feel like mentally preparing, as I often do, through picking up reading material. I purchase *The Family* by Ed Sanders, a former member of the rock band The Fugs. The book provides a detailed description of the Manson family and how they plotted to and succeeded in killing Sharon Tate and others. A grizzly story and a wake up call that California is not just the promised land that many of my east coast and mid western cohorts think the place is. Well, that is SoCal, I say to myself. I want to head to NorCal, so I pick up Kerouac's *Dharma Bums, The Subterraneans* and of course *On the Road* and gobble them up in no time. Kerouac's novels offers me a bird's eye view of hip San Francisco, and although not current, it takes place in the beat scene of the late '40s into the early '60s, laying in a backdrop for the counter cultural revolution, which of course I'm intensely interested in.

Carole is more hesitant about moving to California because she has deeper Ohio roots, but she, too, is growing tired of the flatness, the humidity and dullness of the populace in general. It isn't that she hadn't found a "hip" scene to her liking here as I have, but just that even with that you have to contend with the general "yahoo culture" and even worse, the pervasive jock mentality, and the football religiosity of Ohio State. It gets to be a bit much even if you are a football fan, which I am. The worst example of that was the jock, yahoo, frat celebration/melees on High Street after an OSU victory over

Michigan. The political consciousness of the average football fan was conservative at worst, but more typically nonexistent. High Street got totally trashed by these guys. It was awash in trash, beer cans, pieces of the stadium, broken glass, litter including the goal posts from the stadium. In the jocks' drunken celebration, fighting broke out, there was mayhem including smashed storefronts, looting and rape. There was more violence and destruction that one night than what occurred during the whole of the political riots. But in an article in the OSU Lantern, the president of the university, Novice Fawcett, glibly labeled that night's destruction as fans "letting off steam" in celebrating their beloved Buckeyes. Carole and I have grown sick of that shit. But California remains a long range plan. We still have to get through another year as we head into the summer months.

By fall, Carole and I both have internships as extensions of our majors. So from September to May, Carole puts in time as an assistant teacher at Columbus Unified. They place her in the ghetto, East Columbus, which is fine with her as she gets to spend time with some excellent teachers and some crappy teachers down there where she has the opportunity for learning what to do and what not to do.

I am also interning at the Franklin County Juvenile Hall as a counselor, mostly talking to incarcerated teens and being a gofer for the regular staff. I learn a lot about the families of these kids: a lot of alcoholism, drug abuse, absentee parenting and even worse, physical and sexual abuse. It's pretty gruesome. And the kids are, of course, quite angry a lot of the time, as one would expect. I mostly work on the boys side 2 days a week. But one afternoon a week, I get to work with the girls, many who are victims of early childhood sexual abuse. From really fucked up families. The experience, though tough, is salutary, in that it's giving me some perspective on my problems, really for the first time, getting a glimpse of how bad it can be for young people. I begin to feel some appreciation for some of the good stuff I'd been raised with. A nice roof over my head, economic security, basically responsible and reliable parents who provided at least the material basics, who basically cared and tried to help any way they could. In a way, my problems seem minuscule next to these kids'. Carole, too, feels the same way as a result of her inner city work and we would often compare notes on our experiences. Carole's folks, mother in particular, despite being a bitch, at least stayed in touch and showed some interest in her, albeit frequently critical.

In a way, interning in challenging environments make us strangely grateful, feeling almost normal, relatively speaking. This makes the winter and spring quarters not just successful, but meaningful. It really feels like Carole and I are on our way. Despite the flare ups of our psychological shit and how it affects our relationship at times, as a couple we are on our way. But like all things, it would not last.

August 1972

Even though we're both behind in finishing school due to mental health issues, neither of us can face taking academic courses this summer. We're burned out on school. Putting up with large classes, boring professors, takes a lot of energy. Exercising discipline is no joke. So our summer consists of working at our internships, hanging out with friends, and taking electives. Summer internships, both 20 hours per week, frees us up for leisure activities. Carole decides to take up tennis so she and I could play. She takes Intro to Tennis at OSU's stellar phys ed department to learn the fundamentals. Not willing to be outdone in the fun learning zone, I take a cooking fundamentals course in my spare time, to even the slate between us male/female wise. We're enjoying learning new skills and it makes us feel more egalitarian as a couple. It feels right and fair. We are hellbent on not repeating the fall out of our parents' unequal marriages. Even though Carole is a good and patient teacher and she is willing to teach me how to cook, I have trouble taking direction from anyone. Knowing this and not wanting to fuck up our relationship any more than necessary, it seems simpler to just take a formal class which works out well, reducing predictable and unneeded tension between us. Besides, in the name of fairness, Carole has done more than her share of caring and taking care of me. It is important for the relationship and my self esteem that I pick up some of the slack. In this regard, by the end of the summer, I can cook about 5 meals besides spaghetti. Fish, chicken, steak and their variations are now on my menu. Carole, in her tennis class, learns the rudiments of tennis: forehand, backhand, net play and serve, so much so that by August we're playing doubles against Janie and Robert, who are already intermediate level players, and starting to hold our own. In the kitchen, I take on cooking duties 2 nights a week, thereby relieving Carole of the burden of having the cooking completely on her shoulders. It's a nice arrangement, all around.

But all is not as perfect as I'm making it sound. There are other issues and distractions as you might expect with 22 year olds, healthy of mind and body: CARNAL LUST. Yes, carnal lust is once again rearing its ugly, yet intoxicating head. And it's not just me, but Carole as well. Only neither of us know of the other's hanky panky activities. Having taken an oath of exclusivity the previous fall, both of us are of course extremely embarrassed, guilt ridden and anxious at our mutual but undisclosed transgressions. The fact of the matter is that both transgressions take place within two days of each other in late August. But clearly, Carole feels the guiltier of the two of us. She can barely stand it and when around me feels so bad that she avoids eye contact. I, more experienced in the matter of sexual subterfuge while in high school with Marla, had been able to successfully date other women, including her friends without her seemingly knowing it, and was able to play it off with some aplomb. But alas, the proverbial shit hit the fan a couple of days after Carol's "sinning" was done. Confession Central. Absent a priest.

Of course, I was/am no angel. In my "rounds" at The Union on days when not at CYA, doing my juvie internship, one fine afternoon, while sitting at my usual perch at The Tavern, smoking my Viceroys, I saw this voluptuous redhead in a miniskirt sitting no more than five feet from me by herself, book in hand. She was furtively, but obviously, eye balling me while reading a paperback, the title of which I could read from a distance, *The Politics of Experience*. I, of course, was very familiar with the author, having read his famous tome a couple of years earlier, *The Divided Self*, which provided me with the rationale for my anti-psychiatry medical model disdain. I sized up the redhead as one of ours. A Jewess. A fairly rare commodity around these parts. I had to talk to her. I yelled over to her in earshot, "RD Laing. One of my main men." She looked up, smiled and said, "Wanna join me?" Leaping from my table instantaneously, I found her to be unabashedly vibing sex. And brazen about it in the conversation that ensued as well. She immediately reveals that she was in Columbus, studying Russian, soon to be leaving with her group from OSU- UC Santa Cruz to embark on a trip to the Soviet Union. Karen was her name, and as I had predicted, a Jewess from Berkeley, soon to be a Junior at U.C. Santa Cruz. And boy, was she knocking my socks off. I'd never met someone so progressive. So advanced. Both about politics, feminism and sex. Clearly, a feminist, clearly radical, and she was also very aggressive/assertive sexually. In only about five minutes, she was upfront about her attraction to me and was not in the least deterred at hearing I was in a relationship. In fact, she couldn't care less. Said she would like to ball me but needs one day until she is over her period before she can. Clearly, I am overwhelmed with anxiety but even more so with sexual desire and excitement. We exchange phone numbers and agree to meet at her dorm in two days.

Meanwhile, for Carole, things are heating up at her internship. Steve Johnson, who Carole is shadowing in his classroom this summer, informs Carole he is getting a divorce soon and one Thursday after class asks her out for drinks. Well one thing led to another and the next thing you know, they're getting a motel room, near the campus. Not only that, but they do so the next afternoon as well, until Carole, overwhelmed with guilt, puts an end to it which causes her to avoid eye contact with me for two straight evenings until she can no longer tolerate her guilt feelings and confesses.

Meanwhile, Karen and I, strangely on the same day as Carole's second matinee session, meet up in her dorm, a grad student dorm on south campus, designed just for the Russia program. A whole floor is freed up for the group and the rules are, while not looser, are less enforced, meaning that Karen and I can do the "nasty" unimpeded, which we do, but only once. I learn a lot about uninhibited sex from this woman, not to mention the exploration and utilization of various orifices, freely given without any hesitation or inhibition hassles. Just pure enjoyment and openness. Wow, what a joy. But alas, just like Carole suffers from guilt, I too, feel guilty in part for violating an agreement and of course, because I do not want to hurt Carole's feelings. I vow to keep it to myself. I tell Karen that despite the sexual ecstasy I felt with her, the guilt and potential risk to my relationship make it not worth the price of admission. She understands. And so we bid our adieus. Karen would be off to Leningrad the next week anyway, so the point becomes moot as to any future entanglements, literally and figuratively.

At home the next night, after I cook a spaghetti and meat sauce dinner with French bread and salad while drinking a Rolling Rock beer, Carole says, "I need to talk to you, Arnie." Of course, Carole's solemn air kind of scares me. I don't know what to think. My mind immediately goes to the most catastrophic: she has leukemia or some fatal disease. I am taken aback when she goes into a confession of her sexual dalliance. I, of course, am equally guilty. But at first, I attempt to bury it, start acting a bit upset, but then think better of it. I mean, what is there to be gained? Some momentary power in the relationship as the aggrieved party? That seems both silly and dishonest. But I kind of enjoy the momentary feeling of moral superiority as I hang back watching Carole feeling intense remorse and regret. This lasts only for a moment. Yes, I like the power, don't get me wrong, but my desire for openness wins over the momentary "hit" I get from feeling superior. So while Carole is squirming, literally, I can't stand the subterfuge and confess my "sin" as well about Karen. Upon hearing about Karen, Carole is dumbfounded, shaking her head with a quizzical look, while I, of course, am secretly relieved not to be the only one.

After a few moments of strange and unusual silence, Carole manages to say something, "Are we all right?" in an unusually loud voice.

"I think so. I hope so," I hear myself say rather rapidly. And proceed to go into a "rap" about how hard it is to be monogamous. Carole agrees and then wonders aloud what we should do about it.

I say, "Let's try to be monogamous. It seems to work better for us both. It eliminates the need to feel like we're sneaking around. Eliminating the jealousy we both claim to be able to do is ridiculous, and when push comes to shove, we both feel. As in we're both human."

Carole mostly listens and nods in agreement. But the events of the previous few days takes a toll on her. It makes her exhausted. She uncharacteristically goes to bed early and although she feels relieved to know that there won't be any lasting consequences, still hasn't forgiven herself for her so-called misdeed. She walks around, vacillating between avoiding physical contact with me or excessively wanting hugs, both weirdly uncharacteristic for her with me. I, on the other hand, am mostly relieved that I'm not the only one, but don't really feel guilty about having had my brief encounter. I see it as a mistake, yes, but not one to excessively beat myself up about. Of course, I don't want Carole's feelings to be hurt. The fact that Carole is dealing with a whole different kettle of fish, guilt feelings wise, makes that a non issue. I'm not angry with Carole. I don't really feel like I have a right to be. And neither does she. In the end, we both vow to try to be more upfront about our desires instead of acting on them. That makes sense. At least in theory. We then both try to return to the status quo of prior monogamy which we are able to, with one exception. The two incidents surprisingly makes things better. Less taking each other for granted. Our sex life gets hot again, probably because the threat of others on the scene has strangely re-aroused the ardor we felt for each other when we first met. We humans are sure strange, complicated beasts.

September '72–June '73

We both commit to behaving ourselves for the next 9 months, putting the bulk of our focus on school, internships, friends and each other.

And it seems to be working really well. I continue to succeed at school as does Carole. We have a lot of fun together. Carole likes to imitate my New York accent. No "r's", and lots of "aw's", as in New Yawk. Whereas I go after her heavy emphasis on "r's", Cleveland style, like "charrrges." Lots of good natured teasing. We seem to be getting along really well with both of us trying hard not to be bossy or bitchy. We have a great time with our friends as well. My mood, I can say, has been really even. I'm sleeping well, and I feel really stable. And really loved. We fit together like a glove. And in some ways, for the first time really, I am feeling free to love someone, Carole. But I wonder if part of it comes from a place of fear. Like from a protective place. We'd both been burned before in relationships. So neither of us want to lose the other and we're both open about how fragile the relationship is, so the conservative, traditional route is making the most sense. I find that not being on the hunt for other women or letting myself be distracted by other women is allowing me to give of myself emotionally. If anything, the infidelities that happened almost simultaneously remind us both about how precious love, our love is, and how important it is to try to protect that love and even more important than to try to live up to some "hippie-counterculture" ideal about jealousy and freedom. We both decide after that experience that it is just too risky and complicated to be fucking around. The experience of mutual dicking around seemed to sober both of us up and we are both grateful it didn't destroy the something wonderful we created.

Those 9 months are the best 9 months ever for me, in a way. We focus on each other, but a lot of the feelings the two of us walk around with are from a place of fear. We do so well together that by June 15 of the next year, 1973, we both decide we need a change of scenery. In the literal sense. For me, it has been a foregone conclusion for a long time. California. Since my abortive hitch hiking fiasco and resulting hospitalization back in '71, California remains on my docket as a place to move to. Not just to check out. I talk it up a lot with Carole, in my enthusiasm for the San Francisco bands like the Jefferson Airplane or in my begogglement at the redwood trees that I saw in pictures. For me, moving to California has been just a matter of time. Carole seems to pick up on my enthusiasm, and over time she grows more and more critical of Columbus and its "Neanderthal-like sports culture." So much so, that in June of '73, we decide to say goodbye to Columbus and hello to the west coast and Berkeley. We feel really ready and up for it.

CHAPTER 28

On my Way to Sunny California...
"On my way to spend another sunny day"...

Graduation day at the football stadium and Carole decides to skip it. It takes her five years, a lot of stops and starts, emotional turmoil, a reduced academic schedule at times, so that by the end, Carole is really fatigued by the process and less inclined to celebrate than pack up her stuff and hit the road. Our rent is paid up until July 1, so that isn't an issue. I am 16 units shy of graduating, but I'd already decided to arrange for the last 16 units to be done at UC-Berkeley, in sociology. I arranged it and it was approved by the OSU Sociology Department. Carole, for her part, has also done some prep work for our move to Berkeley. She was in contact with the Berkeley Unified School District, and managed to get a job as a teacher's assistant for the special ed resource classrooms at Martin

Luther King, Jr. Middle School. She found a position, so that she would be paid, and earn the requisite hours California mandated to be able to sit for her teaching credential. The school was renamed MLK in 1970. Change was already in force there, part of what I was looking forward to about the Bay Area. It's progressive, anti-racist attitude, light years ahead of the rest of the country.

Not to be outdone by Carole, I cash in some chits, use some connections and find work in the Bay Area with the help of my old time OSU Oval friend Hal, now living in Berkeley. After he graduated from OSU in social work, he moved to the east coast and got a job with Vista, the domestic peace corps program, worked on Rikers Island in NYC and jails outside Boston. But he too got sick of the east coast scene and was California dreaming. Hal and I keep in touch by phone and I know he is working as a psych counselor at a halfway house outside of Berkeley in a town called Concord. He and I are of one mind in our philosophical outlook about mental health. Basically anti-medical model. He suggests to me that it might be fruitful for all concerned if he and I work together there. Because the program works with psychotic adults, he's able to convince the executive director that my experience in nut houses as a patient will provide a unique and special perspective to the agency. The executive director, Stu McCullough, and I talk over the phone. He likes what he hears, mostly my recitation about what was helpful and unhelpful in my psychiatric care as a mental patient and hires me on the spot as a part time night watchman and relief counselor. Both Carole and I are ecstatic at our good luck and we decide to set up our current work commitments to allow us a good two months to travel and settle in before our respective work begins. So it is that on June 15, after bidding a wistful goodbye to my pals Jamie, Curt, John and Paul that we start our prep to leave for the west. Carole says goodbye to her friends which is very tearful and sad for her, having never left Ohio. There's relief to her that her close buddies, Robert and Janie are planning to head out soon to Berkeley as well. Carole and I are really feeling good but more than that, proud of ourselves. Kind of grown up. Organized. On top of shit. Ready to have an adventure, looking forward to the beauty and vastness of the west. Excited to be traveling together on our first big trip.

But all is not right. A kink in the armor. The night before we plan to leave, Carole has an intense panic attack. It's scaring the shit out of her and me. It seems to come out of nowhere. Super anxious, Carole struggles to catch her breath, worries that she's dying. It lasts almost ten minutes. But ten minutes of hell. Coming down from it, by slowing down her breath, drinking some water and with my reassurance, she gets somewhat calm again, and we talk. It becomes obvious that Carole has overestimated her readiness for leaving Columbus. In fact, the more she speaks, the more she begins to realize that the reason she was leaving Columbus and moving to California was for me. She doesn't want to disappoint me and ruin my dream by not coming, just like how she did to please her mother, please everyone actually. It's painful for her and me. I'm disappointed but try to be supportive. The more Carol vents, the more adamant she gets. Leaving is wrong for her. She needs more time. She isn't ready. She says she's scared, feels too attached to her friends, even the place. Whatever else, Columbus feels like home. I should go. And she will catch up with me later.

I am bummed. Dumbfounded actually. Sort of numb. Pushing back feelings. Finally, I gather myself together to say, "Didn't you have any inkling that you felt this way before? I feel a little ambushed," trying to control a feeling of irritation.

"I see how you could feel like this. But I really didn't know I felt this way before that stupid panic attack. It took me by surprise, too but now I know the timing of this just isn't right for me. I'm sorry Arnie. But if I went with you now, it would be wrong. I know now that I'm just not ready yet."

"Well, I obviously don't want to force you to do something that doesn't feel right. That wouldn't work for either of us." I am clearly trying to be as understanding as I can be, but I am really disappointed. I don't want to go to California without her. Carole is my rock, my foundation. But I just can't stand it in Ohio anymore. Too stultifying. But I'm not sure what to do.

We agree I will go alone and in a year or less she will meet me out west. I wonder if she is placating me or really means it but I keep that to myself. I'm suddenly too disappointed and exhausted to continue the conversation. And so don't.

I delay my departure until that Friday morning, June 22, and hit the road. I have already purchased my dad's Toyota Corona and he is glad to sell it to me because he is thrilled with my progress. He sells me his '72 red Corona, practically brand new. He gives me an insider's deal on it, only 1500 bucks. Carole's mom, Martha, although more begrudgingly, expresses her approval of how the two of us have progressed in the past 21 months, but is now not so secretly glad that Carole will be staying. She was never that thrilled with me anyway and only thinks of her needs first and foremost. But, she is an embittered person, so I don't think she would be happy with any man Carole picks. So I don't really take Carole's mom's opinions very seriously. My dad, when he hears the news, is disappointed. He has even gone so far as to tell me he hopes that the two of us will marry. But for Carole and me, that is a long way away. And now even longer. We are only 23. Way too young both of us believe. Money wise, between the two of us, we have about $3,000 saved up from our internships, plus the $1,200, my old man chipped in to help us get started. He can really be generous when he wants to, my old man, particularly when he approves of the direction things are going. And now, after all the turmoil of the previous years, he is truly delighted and happy to help with money.

So flush with $2700 in cash, I bid adieu to Columbus, Ohio forever. My heart is heavy but I can't stay. And Carole, for all her reasons, can't go. So after a long, tearful goodbye, I get in my car and go. I'm tearful, crushed, but hopeful. My first stop will be Madison, Wisconsin where my younger and older brothers are living and attending school.

As I hit the road, I notice I am having a delayed reaction. Not just sad but pissed. How could she do this to me after two years of being together? What the fuck? The more I drive, the angrier I get and about 30 miles out of town, I can't stand feeling this way any more and get off the road to find a payphone to call Carole. She answers on the second ring. Her voice has a welcoming tinge but soon changes when I give her a piece of my mind. Whereas, the previous day, I was all accepting and understanding and shit, today is an entirely different story. "How could you do this to me? To us?" I want to call her a bitch and even worse, but even in all my fury, it's just not my style to be abusive or that disrespectful. Besides, I learned something in all my years in therapy. Just say how I feel. Don't go accusing. It isn't fair and it surely isn't productive. It just leads to bigger blowups. And that's not at all what I want from Carole at this moment. I just want her to hear how hurt and pissed I am, even rejected by this sudden turn of events. Turning my world upside down. I do manage a couple of "fuck yous" in my mostly appropriate tirade. I finally just can't help myself. She deserves it. And in my anger, I can't contain it any longer. Carole really has nothing to say in her defense. The best she comes up with is she is scared. And not ready to leave Ohio but she really didn't want to leave me. I'm not buying that bullshit and tell her so. "You are rejecting me," I yell. "And if you're not gonna come with me, I'm gonna feel free to see whoever I want. Fuck it, fuck you and the horse you rode in on."

"I understand Arnie. But please let's not break up. Just take a little break and then we'll see where we are after a while."

"You're damn right I'm gonna take a break. And no guarantees. I'm gonna do my thing. And I'm gonna assume you are, too. It's a fucking shame. But that's just gonna have to be how it is. Adios." And with that. I slam down the phone. Enraged.

Getting back in my car, now driving and still fuming, I notice that I am going a lot faster than usual. A bad sign that usually means I am in an angry mood. Doing 80, 85 in a 65. Luckily, I cool off before I get a ticket. But it is a good half hour before I do. I'm still angry and hurt and despite all of Carole's protestations to the contrary, I feel rejected, even betrayed. I now vow to try to screw as many women as I can for revenge and because it's the "go to" salve for my pain. But now I am heading for Madison, Wisconsin to see my two brothers and my sister in law. But the excitement of starting a new life and a new life as a couple that I had felt is obviously gone. Crestfallen, I do the almost 8 hour drive practically without stopping.

I arrive around dinner time at Dave and Cherise's place, where I instantly register the concerned looks on their faces. They can see immediately that things have changed. No Carole and a disgruntled Arnie. They ask and I go through the whole story with them. They are sympathetic and encourage me to try not to let my letdown fuck up my trip out west. Easier said than done, they acknowledge, but I agree that it is good advice.

The visit with Cherise and my brothers is pretty downbeat so I stay for only two days. I'm not in the mood to review the whole fiasco, and I feel a depression coming on and don't want to expose them or anybody to that. My visit with Lew, living in a freshman dorm, isn't any better. We hit some of the local bars around campus where Lew and I do some heavy drinking the night before I leave Madison. Heavy drinking for me, 4 beers. It doesn't help. I'm bad company and I know it. Lew tries to buck me up, but unsuccessfully. Mostly, I want to be alone so I take off early the next morning, leaving

Dave and Cherise's apartment at 5:30am. Avoiding their concerned looks is my primary motivation for the early departure.

On the road and headed for the Badlands, apropos of my emotional state, I'm in a funk, but desperate to get out of it and follow brother Dave's advice to not let my disappointment fuck up my trip. I pick up a couple of hippie-looking guys on the highway, a Black guy with a large afro and a White guy with hair down to his ass. Both guys are from Chicago. Somehow, strangely and unexpectedly, the three of us hit it off, and for the time being, my dark mood lifts. These two guys, Earl and Steve, are fun loving characters also heading for California, but in no hurry. They hang with me on my way to South Dakota, about an 8 hour drive, where we find a campsite, eat some hot dogs and beans that we picked up at a roadside 7/11. With marijuana for dessert, we commence to speak in cowboy lingo. Every other word out of our mouths is "dry gulch," "bushwhack," or "I reckon." We barely know what these words mean but like the sound and feel of the words coming out of our mouths in a western drawl, which the three of us are pretty good at imitating. It's ridiculous, stupid, but hilarious. Just what the doctor ordered.

The next morning, which is a Sunday, Steve, Earl and I find a greasy spoon diner in Mitchell, South Dakota, the town George

McGovern is from. We saunter in with our ripped jeans, bandanas and scraggly long hair, and probably pretty stinky from camping and driving all day. The diner is deserted except for the waitress. Adele, from central casting, is a 50ish, no nonsense but warm lady, who takes our order and doesn't bat an eye at the three hippies she is serving. So far so good. The radio has some country and western music on. But the next thing that happens is central casting on steroids. A bonafide cowboy comes barreling in with cowboy hat, chaps and spurs making that clicking sound that spurs do, dusty as all get out, asking for a cup of joe. Steve and Earl, sitting next to each other, both look at me at the same time, then each other and then back at me. The next thing you know, 3 hippies trying to control themselves are exploding in paroxysms of hilarity, coffee spurting out of the sides of our mouths. At the same time, the looks on our faces confirm that we collectively fear that the cowboy will catch on to what we're laughing about and shoot us with his six gun loosley parked in his holster. A tense 10 seconds or so elapses, and alas, we are safe from being shot. Steve, Earl and I escape with our lives, surviving our first taste of the wild west.

This only whetted our appetites for cowboyese. The rest of the day is spent mimicking all the westerns we've seen on tv as we frolic through the Badlands, Black Hills and Mt. Rushmore, pretending we are lawmen and outlaws, playing hide and go seek in the badlands, dry gulching and bushwhacking each other to our heart's content.

Things feel so good that for two days I completely forget about Carole until I drop Steve and Earl off in Denver on the third day where they plan to continue their hitchhiking adventure to California. I'm planning a hang with OSU friends living in Denver. As soon as I arrive and meet up with George and Jenny from Third World Solidarity days, my dark mood returns. Seeing them paired up, just reminds me of my aloneness but I feign sociability as George and Jenny show me the sites. It's Denver and

the mountain towns, especially Nederland, which according to George and Jenny, is a haven for political radicals and drug dealers on the run. The place has that feel. It feels safe from the law. Somehow the canyons of Nederland give it that secluded, protected feel. Again, because my mood is not the best, and still feel quite uncomfortable pretending to be social, I cut short my visit with George and Jenny without trekking up to Utah and Yellowstone and then into Canada, which was the original plan with Carole. I decide to head straight for Northern California and Berkeley. A two day schlep. I spend the first night camping in West Wendover, Nevada on the Utah border. It's an arid desert and stark. Alone again and not in the best of moods. I wake up with the sun, dirty, grimey and needing coffee. Finding another 7/11, I purchase a large coffee and two snickers bars and drive straight into Berkeley, the place I've wanted to live since I was 16. Now I am here. But somehow it doesn't feel the way I'd hoped. My mood is dictating what I see and even the beautiful Berkeley hills and delicious smell of eucalyptus doesn't put a dent into my grumpy negativity.

I ring up Hal, one of my first OSU friends and the guy who got me the job working in a halfway house. He is glad to see me but surprised, of course, about what happened between me and Carole. I relay the sad tale and Hal expresses his sympathy for my plight. He's unusually emotionally tuned in for a male and he gladly invites me to stay with him until I find a place. He'd been expecting to put both Carole and me up until we got settled. It's comforting to know that he and I will be working together at the halfway house, where, thanks to him, I have a job. Hal is a comfort. The more we talk, the more I realize how much I miss Carole.

I decide to call her one evening in a state of longing. Carole picks up the phone and says she is really glad to hear from me. Really misses me and has been doing some thinking since I left. She feels that she made a mistake not coming with me, but, in the meantime has gotten a student teaching job where she interned in East Columbus and feels she needs to commit until January. Then she will be coming to Berkeley to be with me. She misses me too much, she realizes and begins to offer her thoughts.

"Soon after you left, I realized that I fucked up. I should have been paying closer attention to my feelings so that you and I could have talked about our plans before we made any decisions. I'm sorry for this."

I speak with some distance in my tone of voice, "Yeah. It would have been better."

As we talk I feel vestiges of the anger from having been jerked around and am somewhat mistrustful. But I also sense a sincerity and determination in her voice that feels different this time. I tell her I will find us a place to stay, probably in a "collective living" situation but that when January comes around we would find a place, just the two of us.

For the first time in a few weeks, my heart feels lighter. Getting off the phone, while a smidgeon of anger and mistrust lingers, I feel hopeful, optimistic and once again full of love. We agree to speak weekly. But after getting off the phone two things occur to me. One is that I have gotten better at taking a punch (Carole's sudden flake out) and two,

my surprising resilience and determination to live my own life. Feelings of pride bubble up. I have this good feeling about myself. It's kind of new. I like it.

I begin my job, which I love, working with psychotic adults, either who've been hospitalized or who are trying to avoid hospitalization. And this is the kicker, with as few meds as possible. It feels like my place. I feel at home. I have a natural understanding and compassion having been where they are "hanging," as it were. It's great. I connect with the residents and staff including Hal, both groups who respect and admire me. It's great to be working at a place where the staff share my perspective about "the medical model," but even more than that, they are in agreement about the vital therapeutic role of healing relationships.

Only a few days after starting the job, I find a house to rent for myself that is available in South Berkeley, near campus, and so I become the lessor. I quickly find tenants, all Cal Berkeley students, either current, newly graduated, or as with one guy, in law school. Three guys, two women. We share food, cooking responsibilities and cleaning. As I am the organizer, all of my new roommates agree to these somewhat communal arrangements as prior conditions to moving in. We agree to meet weekly for house meetings to discuss issues and problems. Carole and I have our weekly phone conversations on Sunday night, similar to the way Marla and I talked when we planned to get back together. Only with Carole, there are significant differences which feel reassuring and right. Carole and I have already lived together and made love unlike Marla and me. Our calls are cozy, warm and close. This goes on for about a month. I have this feeling that things are coming together on both the work and relationship front. Not that there aren't hassles. Bay Area traffic can be impossible. I still have a hard time getting to work on time. I tend to sleep too late and put unnecessary pressure on myself dealing with the incessant traffic, especially when I'm rushed. Plus working with residents in severe and acute emotional pain has its own stresses.

But at least up till now, I seem good at being able to make positive emotional connections without getting overly burdened by residents' problems. Clearly an occupational hazard to pay attention to. But so far so good.

It is late September. A Friday evening. I'm home after work on a Friday evening after a traffic-filled half hour from Rose Lane House in Concord. It's been a somewhat harrowing day with a suicidal resident and I'm feeling somewhat distraught and worried about him. Wondering whether he would be better off in the hospital or whether he could ride out his suicidal thoughts with staff support at the house. For some uncharacteristic reason, upon arriving home, I pour myself a Scotch. I'm usually a beer man, but Otha, the law school student roommate, is home and is a scotch guy. He gladly pours me a jigger and is happy for a drinking partner. I take a sip and feel the warm liquid reaching my cockles as I breathe a sigh of relief, letting out some stress.

The phone rings. Otha picks it up and quickly passes the phone to me saying it is a girl named Janie wanting to talk to me from Columbus. Before I can think about what it might be, I can tell it isn't good. Janie is crying. Barely able to get her words out, she chokes out,........." Carole's dead. She was driving home from work this afternoon in her Corvair and a car jumped a red light and t-boned Carole."

I can barely register what Janie is saying.

"I'm sorry, Arnie. I'm beside myself."

"Jesus fucking Christ," I hear myself shriek. Stunned. All I can do is hold myself, as I rock back and forth in disbelief and anguish. Just rocking back and forth. The phone on the floor, I suddenly remember I was talking to Janie and grope around looking for the phone as Otha hands it to me, putting a hand on my shoulder as he does. I tell her I will fly back tomorrow to help with the funeral arrangements. I make a half hearted attempt to comfort Janie but I'm in too much anguish to comfort anyone. I quickly get off the phone. Otha tries to comfort me but I'm beyond that. I'm gone. She's gone. I'm gone. Just nothing. This is a knockdown that might require more than a mandatory 8 count. I don't know. On the canvas again. Maybe this time for a count of 10. Maybe I'll never get off the canvas. Maybe for good. Maybe forever. Oblivion. Just gone. All I can think, if you can call it thinking, is I'm cursed. Thoughts of '68 appear, when I had my first psychotic break. Then too, things were starting to go my way and then next thing I know I'm in a nut house. On the canvas. Hope for the future, what a scam. Only this is by far the worst. True love. Now she's gone. Why bother getting up off the canvas this time. Stay down, it's not worth it. Don't bother. Be gone. OUT. 1,2,3,4,5,6,7,8,9.........

Lover, there will be another one
Who'll hover over you beneath the sun
Tomorrow, see the things that never come today

When you see me fly away without you
Shadow on the things you know
Feathers fall around you
And show you the way to go
It's over, it's over

"Birds" – Neil Young

www.ingramcontent.com/pod-product-compliance
Lightning Source LLC
Chambersburg PA
CBHW070909120626
46546CB00001B/188